National
College of
Ireland

The Changing World of Work Series

The world of business management is centrally focused on strategy creation and decision-making. An organised approach to problem-solving and decision-making is therefore an essential part of the management toolkit in the rapidly changing world of work.

Through its involvement with adult learners over more than five decades, the National College of Ireland has been at the forefront in understanding and mapping changing developments in the workplace. Its reputation for providing relevant learning experiences and disseminating 'best practice' has attracted large numbers of business professionals, providing an understanding of the underlying concepts and the acquisition of new skills.

In the *Changing World of Work Series*, we seek to capture the latest developments in Irish and international business management. The series includes an exploration of up-to-date themes around coaching and personal development, organisation leadership, challenges facing the trade union movement and managing change in both the private and public sectors. The goal for this book on problem-solving and decision making is to significantly add to the current understanding of how this critically important skill is deployed in practice.

The *Changing World of Work Series* addresses these issues at a time when productivity, cost reduction and improved business processes are critical requirements for Ireland Inc. if we are to seriously compete on the world stage. The series examines the underpinning concepts within each area addressed and outlines the challenges which lie ahead for those tasked with managing them. We hope that you enjoy this book and thank you for your support for the National College of Ireland.

About the Author

Dr. Eugene O'Loughlin is a Lecturer in Computing at the National College of Ireland (NCI). He received his PhD in 1988 from the University of Dublin, Trinity College. He then worked as a Production Manager and later as Director of Global Service+s for over 13 years with the e-Learning company SmartForce (now SkillSoft). Since 2002 he has been teaching in the School of Computing at NCI where the subjects he teaches include Learning Technologies, Project Management and Business Systems Analysis at undergraduate and postgraduate levels. He is a keen enthusiast for using technology in the classroom. Dr O'Loughlin lives in Dublin and relaxes by riding his Harley-Davidson motorcycle.

AN INTRODUCTION TO BUSINESS SYSTEMS ANALYSIS

Problem Solving Techniques and Strategies

Dr. Eugene O'Loughlin

An Introduction to Business Systems Analysis

ISBN 9781731557872

CONTENTS

LIST OF TABLES AND FIGURES

List of Tables

List of Figures

PREFACE

Since I first started as a Lecturer for the Business Systems Analysis module on the Certificate in Business Analysis and Consultancy in 2005 at the National College of Ireland, I have entertained the idea of writing a textbook to provide a resource for students to match the needs of this module. Somehow, I never quite got around to doing this even though I have built up detailed notes and resources for module delivery over the years. The first inspiration to take the plunge and write this book came from Dr. Paul Mooney, President of the National College of Ireland. I remember well his assertion that my book "will be published" when we first discussed the idea. To Dr. Mooney, I owe my sincere thanks for motivating me from writing regular course notes to finally writing a book. There are many other friends and colleagues from whom I have drawn inspiration. I would first like to acknowledge the academic support, guidance, and time given to me by Dr. David Keane, Dr. Declan Kelly, and Dr. Pramod Pathak during my days as a Lecturer in Computing at the National College of Ireland. Philip Chambers of the Business Analysts Association of Ireland has been an inspiration and an unflinching support not only in my efforts towards this book, but as someone who inspires belief in the education of Business Analysts at the highest level. For the many students who have "suffered" at my hands during many of my classes, I thank you all for your hard work, challenges, inspiration, fun, enthusiasm, and participation. To you all I remind that the purpose of our class is to learn to think differently when problem-solving, not simply to learn how to use analysis tools.

This book would not have been possible without the help of the many individuals who have assisted in both large and small ways in providing me with ideas, guidance, material, examples, exercises, and reviews. Thanks to Margaret Brennan, Mary Buckley, Rosa Callery, Dr. Leo Casey, Des Gargan, Brian Hayden, Chris Hyland, Dr. Tim Hastings, Paul Hederman, Richard Hogan, Dr. Orla Lahart, Tim Lawless, Dominic Martin, Gráinne McIlroy, Mike Neary, Neil Newman, Julia Reynolds, Anna Rowan, Paul Stynes, and Dr. Stephan Weibelzahl – I will be forever grateful to you all for your expertise, help, and support. To my publisher, David Givens of The Liffey Press, my heartfelt thanks for putting up with the many questions that this first time author has asked over the past year. My thanks also to Professor Nigel Slack of Warwick University, and Prentice Hall publishers, for permission to reproduce his Importance-Performance Matrix diagram (Figure 12.9), and to Michael Cullen of the Beacon Medical Group for permission to use his stakeholder diagram (Figure 4.1). I would also like to acknowledge the support of the National College of Ireland Foundation, which has supported the publication of this book. All profits from sales of this book will be donated to the Foundation.

I would like to thank my family without whose support I could not have kept going. To my Dad Joe, thank you for all your love and guidance since I was a boy – you are the one person who has helped me solve more problems than any other. For my Mum Phil, my heartfelt thanks for your unwavering dedication to my education for the past 50 years – you have taught me that life is about getting things done, not just thinking about things. To my three beautiful daughters: Claire, Kate, and Vicki – my thanks and love for making fatherhood a joy. Finally to my darling wife Roma, who has always stood by me and helped me to follow my dreams – still mad about you.

Dr Eugene O'Loughlin
October, 2009

Dedicated with all my love to
Roma, Claire, Kate, and Vicki

INTRODUCTION TO BUSINESS SYSTEMS ANALYSIS

"If you don't know where you're going, any road will take you there." – George Harrison

Introduction

Business systems play an essential and vital role in the growth and survival of organisations in today's ever more competitive business environment. Without them, many organisations will fail or lose competitiveness – hence the huge emphasis placed on developing the right systems that add value to an organisation's business goals and objectives. Business systems are therefore often the key mechanism used by organisations to convert their business strategy and vision into reality. Business Systems Analysis is about aligning Information and Communication Technology (ICT) systems, and sometimes non-ICT systems, with business objectives – business analysis is now an essential skill that must be part of all Business Systems Analysis projects whether they are small, medium, or large. However, many organisations lack this essential skill which is often not part of the systems development curriculum provided by educational institutions.

An Introduction to Business Systems Analysis is a book aimed at describing problem-solving techniques and strategies for the Business Analyst. Many of these techniques and strategies will also be useful for other professionals such as Project Managers, Systems Analysts and Consultants. This book will serve as a general text for Business Analysts who are engaged in eliciting and analysing requirements, identifying priorities, improving processes, making decisions, and measuring and benchmarking performance. Many analysis tools and techniques are described in detail in this book, and feature easy to understand examples and exercises to explain the concepts involved. By using these analysis tools you will build up a very useful toolset that will improve your ability to solve problems whether you are planning new business systems, or looking to improve existing systems.

What is Business Systems Analysis?

Before looking at what Business Systems Analysis is, let's take a look at a formal description of business analysis. The Business Analysis Body of Knowledge (BABOK®) Guide Version 2.0 describes business analysis as:

> ... the set of tasks and techniques used to work as a liaison among stakeholders in order to understand the structure, policies, and operations of an organisation, and to recommend solutions that enable the organisation to achieve its goals.

At its simplest, business analysis is about solving problems and proposing solutions. Sometimes this involves analysing an existing process or system that is not working well and needs to be improved. At other times, business analysis involves analysing what needs to be done when planning and designing new processes or systems. Business analysis can be applied to almost any project – easy or complex, small or large, and long or short. At all times, the Business Analyst should use standard and accepted analysis tools and techniques to provide for solutions to problems that must be aligned with the overall business goals and objectives of an organisation.

Business Systems Analysis makes use of many of the tasks and techniques associated with business analysis. It is most often concerned with identifying the requirements and solutions for ICT needs such as creating a web site, expanding a network, or developing a new software system. However, Business Systems Analysis is not exclusively related to ICT – it can also be effective in planning and designing non-ICT needs such as a queuing system in a bank, the recruitment system in a human resources department, or a marketing campaign for a new product. Both ICT and non-ICT needs should be expressed as requirements, processes, and rules that all stakeholders involved in a project interpret the same way. Business Systems Analysis involves understanding how organisations work and how to solve structural, technical, operational, and logistical problems. By analysing and asking questions about an organisation's systems, you can identify and analyse problems that organisations face. Ask questions such as:

- What system or part of a system is not working well?

- What processes are in need of improvement?

- Which improvements should be prioritised over others?

In many ways, the work of a Business Analyst is about asking the right questions. The answers to these and many other questions can be used to redesign an organisation's functions, improve processes, increase efficiency, and enhance effectiveness.

Throughout this book you will learn how to use several tools and techniques that are essential for Business Systems Analysis. Many of these tools will only be suitable in certain circumstances, while others may be useful on almost any occasion. However, knowledge of how to use analysis tools and problem solving techniques alone will not lead you to success as a Business Analyst. It is not enough to first choose an analysis tool and then to see how it can be used to solve a problem. It is much better to first look at the problem, and then to decide which analysis tools and techniques are best suited to help you solve that problem. Choosing the right analysis tool can sometimes be difficult – often the Business Analyst is faced with serious problems that cannot be solved by simply using a particular tool and hoping for a solution to emerge. It is also possible to over-analyse a problem – striking a balance between examining a problem and using only appropriate analysis tools will be a key to success in Business Systems Analysis.

Structure of Book

The first part of this book is about providing a background in Business Systems Analysis before discussing the analysis tools and techniques that make up the bulk of this book. In Chapters 1 and 2, the concept of Business Systems Analysis, the role, responsibilities, and the skill set of the Business Analyst are introduced. In Chapter 3, you will examine the importance of data and information so that you will understand the value of having accurate foundations for any of your Business Systems Analysis and problem solving efforts. This chapter will also describe the role of business systems in an organisation. The remaining nine chapters describe in detail the tools and techniques required to conduct a detailed analysis of almost any business system. These chapters are categorised into three main sections that emphasise the three main aspects of Business Systems Analysis. Each section is further broken down into subsections which make up the separate chapters – see Figure 1.1.

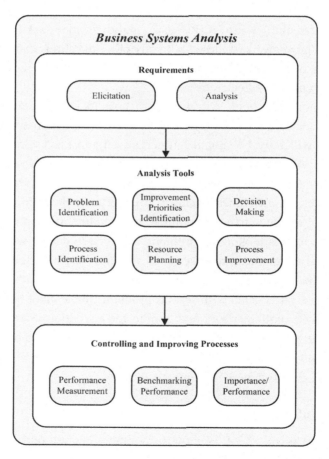

Figure 1.1: Business Systems Analysis Structure

The first category is concerned with requirements. Eliciting and analysing requirements (Chapters 4 and 5 respectively) are the key aspects of Business Systems Analysis, and form the central ingredients for the role of a Business Analyst. The second category is made up of Chapters 6, 7, 8, 9, 10, and 11 and describes in detail 17 techniques and tools used to support requirements elicitation and analysis, general problem-solving and decision-making efforts. The third category relates to techniques for controlling and improving processes, and describes how to measure, compare (benchmark), and determine the important factors when measuring performance.

Learning Journal

At the end of each chapter, you will be asked to reflect on your learning experiences and to contribute to a Learning Journal based on what you've read. Reflection is a proven process that when applied to learning, challenges learners to think critically in order to analyse and embed what they have learned, challenge its validity, and come to conclusions based on the results of their experience in learning. Learning is about meaning and making connections with the content – the more connections you think about and reflect upon, the more embedded the learning will be. By reflecting on the analysis tools and techniques presented here you should ask yourself to think about what you did, and even see what you liked and disliked about a subject. In general, by reflecting on what you have learned you will improve your learning and you can achieve a better understanding of concepts – in the case of this book, these are Business Systems Analysis tools and techniques.

A series of questions at the end of each chapter will help you to start reflecting on the things you will have learned throughout the chapter. This will range from simple questions like "What have I learned in this chapter?" to more specific questions about how you would use a particular analysis tool to solve problems in your own organisation. You should also critically analyse your learning by asking yourself questions like "What sections in the chapter am I surprised with?" and "What sections am I most comfortable (or uncomfortable) with?" As a Business Analyst you will be encouraged to stop and think about each situation before you proceed with analysis. You will also be encouraged to look back at your efforts to examine if you can learn from mistakes and constantly look to improve your own skills in order to do a better job next time.

A Learning Journal is a personal journal – therefore it will be different for everybody. Figure 1.2 outlines some typical elements of what a Learning Journal might look like, though each learner may adapt this sample Journal to their own learning needs. In creating your own Learning Journal be sure to keep it up-to-date by making regular entries about what you have learned about each of the analysis tools and techniques covered in this book. In this way you will reinforce what you have learned and be in a better position to use the analysis tools and techniques for all your Business Systems Analysis efforts.

Learning Journal	
Reflective Question:	*Your Answer:*
What have you learned in this chapter?	
What did you find difficult in this chapter?	
What did you find easy in this chapter?	
What sections in the chapter surprised you most?	
Can you think of situations where you can apply the analysis tools and techniques described in this chapter?	
Are there tools described in this chapter that you do not see any immediate use for?	
Try to think critically about what you have learned – what are the positives and negatives about each of the tools you have learned about?	
What are the advantages and disadvantages of the tools and techniques in this chapter?	

Figure 1.2: Sample Learning Journal

2

THE ROLE OF THE BUSINESS ANALYST

*"Every block of stone has a statue inside it and it is the task of
the sculptor to discover it."* – Michelangelo

Introduction

Business Analysts have an important role to play in business systems
development. However, sometime the role of the Business Analyst is not
clearly defined – especially in small to medium sized projects where
there may not be a separate Business Analyst role. Business analysis can
also sometimes be a very difficult task to carry out – especially when a
difficult problem to solve has limited resources and must be fixed quickly. Often, as a Business Analyst, you will be working with vague requirements from customers, inaccurate information, vast quantities of
information, and have to deal with diverging opinions from stakeholders
that conflict with each other. In small and medium sized projects, quite
often the Business Analyst fulfils multiple roles such as project manager,
systems analyst, and subject matter expert.

In this chapter you will examine the typical roles and responsibilities
of the Business Analyst. You will also look at the skill set required to do
your job effectively, and examine the position of business analysis in the
overall business systems development life cycle. This chapter will examine some of the common problems that a Business Analyst is likely to
encounter. Finally, you will consider the value of business analysis certification in a career as a Business Analyst.

Business Analyst Role and Responsibilities

The Business Analyst often fulfils multi-disciplinary roles within an organisation – this is especially true in small and medium sized organisations where resources are limited and business systems may be smaller. The opposite of this is also true – many other people involved in roles such as that of a project manager or ICT specialist will also carry out the tasks normally associated with a Business Analyst. Therefore many people, regardless of job title, are involved in business analysis activities. According to the BABOK® Guide, the Business Analyst:

> ... must analyze and synthesize information provided by a large number of people who interact with the business, such as customers, staff, IT professionals, and executives.

The key role of the Business Analyst is to do this analysis and synthesis as part of the definition and validation of solutions that meet business goals and objectives. As a Business Analyst your main role will be to elicit and analyse requirements for a solution from all stakeholders involved in a project. This means establishing the actual needs of stakeholder and not just their preferences or desired needs. The Business Analysts Association of Ireland (see www.businessanalyst.ie) defines the role of the Business Analyst as follows:

> The role of the Business Analyst is to identify the Core Business Objectives of an organisation and its constituent parts and to ensure that the Processes, Procedures, Systems, and Structures that are in place are the most effective and efficient to enable it to achieve its Core Objectives.

This definition emphasises core business objectives as playing a central part of what a Business Analyst does. Anything that does not add value to the business core objectives should not be considered by the Business Analyst, though it may become important at another time. Figure 2.1 summarises the role of the Business Analyst – the identification of core business objectives is the starting point for all business analysis. After this, the Business Analyst's role involves eliciting, analysing, documenting, and communicating requirements before finally identifying possible solutions that meet the core objectives.

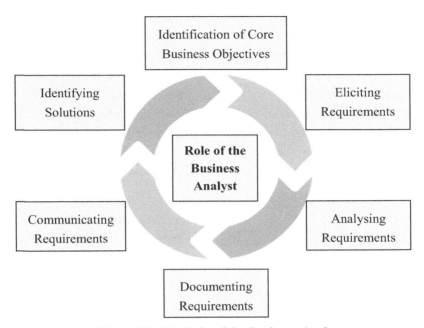

Figure 2.1: The Role of the Business Analyst

The role of the Business Analyst is to stay on the path outlined in Figure 2.1. In general, most projects that fail do so because of poor planning and lack of management support, but they also fail because requirements have not been correctly elicited and analysed. Poor communication can be detrimental to a project - the Business Analyst is often involved in facilitating communication between the stakeholders and their separate business units. Good communication ensures that everyone knows and understands what is important and what is relevant as well as what is not important and is not relevant. This means that all the information that is needed to help identify solutions to a problem has been presented by the Business Analyst. Maintaining alignment with the core business objectives will ensure that both the Business Analyst and the organisation will achieve success by ultimately identifying solutions that satisfy all requirements and add value to the core business objectives.

Business Analyst Skill Set

Due to the nature of the role, as a Business Analyst you will have to possess a wide variety of skills to cover the ever widening range of business analysis tasks and functions. There are four broad main categories that make up the ideal skill set for a Business Analyst: Analysis, Communication, Technical, and Business skills. To be successful in this role, you will have to acquire a mastery of skills in all of these areas. Figure 2.2 summarises the key skills in each of the four main categories. This may mean that you will need to undergo a lot of training in each area in order to build up the skill set – constant learning is a hallmark of the successful Business Analyst. You will now take a brief look at each of the four skill set categories.

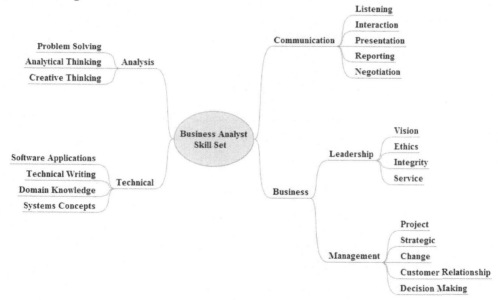

Figure 2.2: The Business Analyst Skill Set

Analysis Skills

The ability to analyse a given problem or situation is a fundamental competency requirement for the Business Analyst. Both qualitative (opinions from experts) and quantitative (measured data) analytical skills are vital to be able to get at the real root of a complex problem and to propose intricate solutions. First and foremost, a Business Analyst must have good problem solving skills. The best way to develop these skills is to build up a portfolio of problem-solving techniques. In this book, several problem solving techniques are outlined for the Business Analyst (see Table 2.1). You will find these techniques very useful in your problem-solving efforts.

Brainstorming	Flow Charting
Interviews	SIPOC Diagrams
5W2H	Project Network Diagrams
Requirements Workshop	Use Cases
Surveys/Questionnaires	Capacity Planning
MoSCoW Analysis	Simple Estimation
Weighted Scoring Model	Work Volume Measurement
Cause and Effect Diagrams	Observation
Check Sheets	Activity Sampling
Pareto Analysis	SREDIM Process Improvement
Value Analysis	Radar Charts
SWOT Analysis	Benchmarking
PEST Analysis	Importance-Performance Matrix
Cost-Benefit Analysis	

Table 2.1: Problem-solving Techniques for the Business Analyst

Analytical thinking uses a step-by-step scientific approach to problem-solving. With this approach you will be able to assess and define a problem, break the problem down into its components, understand the situation as completely as possible, and make judgements about solutions that you propose based on your analysis. Each of the tools listed in Table 2.1 will help you to think analytically about most problems. Good attention to detail will also help in improving your analytical thinking skills.

Creative thinking allows you to look at a problem in different ways and to consider the possibility of coming up with a new solution to a problem that did not exist before. To do this you will need to cultivate the ability to generate new ideas by bringing together, altering, or reusing existing ideas. Some creative ideas may lead to brilliant solutions that add enormous value to a business. However, it is often the easy and practical ideas, which no one thought of before, that work best. Analysis tools, particularly brainstorming which can pool creativity from several people, should be used in an effort to look at a problem in different ways than before. For example, you may normally consider a Cause and Effect Diagram to determine the root cause of a problem in a process, but how about combining it with a Flow Chart to map out how the process works, or a SIPOC Diagram to examine the inputs and outputs of the process? You should constantly be looking for creative ways to examine a problem from different angles. You may not always come up with new ideas, but you will have a better understanding of a problem if you look at it in different ways.

Communication Skills

Much of the work of a Business Analyst involves regular communication with the stakeholders of a project. Excellent written and verbal skills are vital – for example, you may have to communicate technical information to a non-technical audience, which can be equally as difficult as communicating business concepts to a technical audience. Business Analysts must therefore be comfortable presenting information and preparing written reports to customers and stakeholders. This may also mean being expert in the use of virtual communication tools such as video conferencing and on-line meetings.

Eliciting requirements often means interviewing stakeholders and hosting requirements workshops. Interviewing skills and the ability to facilitate and control meetings are therefore important skills to learn. Good Business Analysts are able to interact well with the people they elicit requirements from. For example, you may often be eliciting requirements from people who are unsure of what they really need, or who don't understand fully the problem at issue. You should learn the importance of building good relationships with all team members and stakeholders. Establish ground rules for communication, and stick to them.

Listening is a key foundation skill for good communication. Active listening gets the Business Analyst to focus on who they are listening to, either in a one-to-one interview or in a group meeting such as a workshop, in order to understand what they are saying. As a listener, you should be able to repeat what has been said in an interview in your own words so that the interviewee is satisfied with what you have said. You need to be careful here – while you are eliciting requirements it is important to listen to and understand what the interviewee is saying. This does not mean that you agree or disagree with them, only that you understand what they are saying.

Finally, negotiation skills can be important for the Business Analyst as quite often you will be involved in negotiations throughout a project. At the beginning of a project, you might be involved in negotiations with a customer or stakeholder as to what should be included or excluded in a project. Later, you may be negotiating to determine which needs or requests become real requirements, and again when prioritising the requirements. While it is important to remember that as a Business Analyst you should rely on trusted tools and techniques, you will find many things are negotiable, for example – when you are competing for limited resources within your organisation. As a Business Analyst you should make sure to add negotiation skills to your skill set.

Technical Skills

In Business Systems Analysis it is important for the Business Analyst to at least have some knowledge of the domain – especially systems engineering principles and concepts. It is not essential to the success of a project that the Business Analyst has detailed technical knowledge of the system being analysed – other experts can provide this knowledge when it is needed. It is important that when eliciting requirements that the Business Analyst remain neutral in discussions and not introduce any bias based on their own understanding of how a system works. Remember, it is the customer or stakeholder's requirements that you are eliciting, not your own.

A key technical skill is the ability to write technical documents for a non-technical audience. While some of the people who will be reading your documentation will have strong technical abilities, many others – such as the project manager, customers, testers, administration, and support people, will not. In ICT projects that involve business systems, it is easy to get wrapped up in technical jargon – this must be avoided where possible. Other technical skills that are necessary for the Business Analyst are the ability to use common office applications such as word processors, spreadsheets, presentation software, and database tools. When you have vast quantities of data to analyse, using tools like spreadsheets and databases to sort, organise, calculate, present, model, and carry out statistical analysis on, will help to speed up and increase the efficiency and accuracy of your efforts. Other software tools to consider are project management, charting, and user modelling tools. Whatever tools you use, you should always be aware of the advantages and disadvantages of each tool, and know what the right tool is for the job at hand.

Business Skills

The Business Analyst must be process-focused and be able to understand the environment in which a business system operates. This does not mean that you should have detailed knowledge of the business domain, but a good understanding of general business principles will certainly make your job easier. Knowing what solutions are already available for business systems may make it easier to solve a problem. Get familiar with the ICT industry, especially in the domain of the business systems that you are analysing. There are a vast number of business skills that can be useful for the Business Analyst. Here, you will examine just a few skills that should be considered essential for you to be able to carry out your job effectively. The two main types of business skills examined here are leadership and management skills.

Most Business Analysts will work as part of a team, but may not be the team leader. Nevertheless, some leadership business skills should be part of your repertoire. Leaders are people with ability to communicate a vision – a good sense of direction can be achieved by expressing a strong vision of what a future situation will be, for example, the solution to a problem. As the Business Analyst plays a critical cross-functional role in a project – communicating a sense of vision will also be critical to the success of the project. People have to believe in what you are saying and doing, other leadership skills such as a having a strong sense of integrity and adherence to a code of ethics will gain you their respect. The basis of good leadership skills combines this sense of integrity and ethics with dedication to honest service to your organisation.

Good management skills play an important part in your everyday work as a Business Analyst. Even though the project manager has overall responsibility for a project, the tools and techniques used by the project manager are also very effective for the Business Analyst too. In fact, many of the tools and techniques described in this book, such as Project Network Diagrams, SREDIM process improvement, and Weighted Scoring Models, originated as project management tools. In most cases, you and the project manager will work very closely together on a project – it therefore makes sense that both are familiar with each others skills. Other types of management have an impact on the job of the Business Analyst. Strategic management is about planning long-term objectives and specifying the organisation's mission and vision to achieve these objectives. If you are involved in a long term project, or in planning for future projects, it is imperative that you know and understand what your organisation's mission and vision are. Many business systems will change the way people work. Change management involves thoughtful planning about a change and the sensitive implementation of this change. The most important thing to do when managing change is to consult with the people affected by the change. If you do not consult with people and force change upon them, problems will inevitably arise. It is also important to manage the relationships with your customers. Customer Relationship Management (CRM) tools can help you to manage and organise contact with your customers. Remember that without customers, your organisation will fail – customers are assets, and should be managed carefully. Finally, much of management is about making decisions. To make decisions you should first analyse the choices available and then choose the one with the best probability of success that is also aligned with your organisation's mission and vision. A good knowledge of techniques such as SWOT Analysis, PEST Analysis, and Cost-Benefit Analysis (see Chapter 8) will help you to make better, more informed decisions.

The Business Systems Development Life Cycle

The business systems development life cycle can be a long and complex combination of many tasks and phases that involves many participants in different roles. The Business Analyst should certainly be aware of and have a clear understanding of every phase in the cycle, though will only be directly involved on a day-to-day basis with some of the stages. In proposing possible business systems that will solve a particular problem for an organisation, it is important to understand how the system is developed from start to finish. Figure 2.3 outlines at a high level the six main phases of the business systems development life cycle.

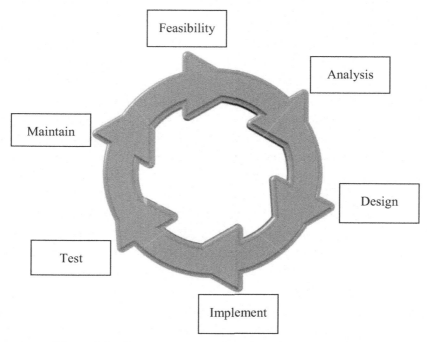

Figure 2.3: The Business Systems Development Life Cycle

As a Business Analyst you will spend most of your time in the Analysis phase. You will also be involved in the Feasibility phase as the project sponsor and other stakeholders who are planning a project will need input about how requirements are to be elicited and how best to deliver the solution. All the requirements elicitation and analysis takes place in the Analysis phase – at the end of which you will have a complete set of validated requirements that will now be passed on to the design and development teams. For the most part, the job of the Business Analyst is done at the end of this phase, but the remaining phases may require further input and consultation. Regularly throughout the Design and Implementation phase, requirements may need to be clarified or even modified as a result of changes that may occur. Finally, the Business Analyst will have a keen interest in how the developed system is tested and maintained. In particular, the new or improved system must demonstrate that it meets the original needs and that it adds value to the overall organisation's mission and vision by meeting the goals and objectives originally set out.

Common Problems Faced by the Business Analyst

The role of the Business Analyst is sometimes a difficult one to carry out effectively and successfully. As you have seen, there is a wide ranging skill set required. Combine this with the many analysis tools and techniques that you should be able to use – there is a lot to learn before you even start. It is therefore important that since this is a crucial role within an organisation that there is adequate investment in training and development of Business Analysts.

Many common problems will be faced by you as a Business Analyst, and it is very worthwhile to be aware and take heed of these problems. The first is that very often you will not have specific domain knowledge about the business systems and processes that you will have to analyse. In many cases you will have to get "up to speed" quickly so that you can have some understanding of how everything works. In most cases you will not need expert knowledge, but it does help your analysis efforts if you have at least some knowledge. Use Flow Charts and SIPOC Diagrams (see chapter 9) to help you understand how processes work. Keeping up with the latest business and technology trends can also be difficult. You can overcome this problem by staying up to date with the latest business and technology news, networking with other Business Analyst professionals, attending conferences, and joining professional bodies such as The International Institute of Business Analysis (IIBA®).

Another problem faced by Business Analysts is that they sometimes have too much influence on a project, or that project team members look to you to solve every problem. There can also be conflict between different groups involved in a project and it is easy for the Business Analyst to get caught in the middle. The project manager has overall responsibility for the project, therefore if you are facing problems in this area you should communicate with the project manager to resolve issues as they arise. The roles of project manager and Business Analyst are separate and distinct – however, any conflict between the two roles will have a detrimental effect on a project.

Finally, there is a danger that the Business Analyst may fall into the "paralysis-by-analysis" trap. This can occur easily when too many tools or techniques are applied to try and analyse a situation – particularly when a difficult problem relating to a business system needs to be resolved. Seek expert help when it is needed to help you overcome problems you face. Remember also that your customers will expect value for money when you report to them – long detailed reports containing large amounts of over-analysed information may lose you credibility with your customer.

Business Analysis Certification

Anyone working as a Business Analyst, or is considering a career in business analysis, should consider gaining formal qualifications that recognise and certify their skills as a practitioner. The International Institute of Business Analysis (IIBA®) has created the Certified Business Analysis Professional™ (CBAP®) which is awarded to learners who have demonstrated successfully their expertise in the business analysis field. To achieve this award, learners have to pass an examination as well as complete 7,500 hours of business analysis work experience. This certification programme is based on the principles covered in the BABOK® Guide, and is highly recommended for people wishing to pursue a career in business analysis. Many training and educational institutions provide courses towards the CBAP® certification, but be sure to check that they are members of the IIBA's Endorsed Education Provider (EEP™) Program.

Many educational institutions offer courses in business analysis related subject areas – these can range from short certificate and diploma courses, to undergraduate degrees and postgraduate awards. Other courses that learners should consider are courses on subjects such as business systems analysis, user modelling, business communication, and general management skills. There will also be occasions when user training for existing business systems will be required in order to get a good understanding as to how they work.

Finally, as the work of the Business Analyst requires a lot of project management skills, it makes sense to consider some formal education in this field. The Project Management Institute (PMI) offers several certifications, including Project Management Professional (PMP®), that may be useful for the Business Analyst to consider. While PMP® certification is aimed at project managers, it will cover several useful skills that the Business Analyst will make use of. If you do not want or need to attain PMI certifications, you should definitely consider taking courses in project management that are commonly offered by educational institutions.

3

BUSINESS SYSTEMS

*"The goal is to transform data into information, and
information into insight."* – Carly Fiorina

Introduction

Much of the work of a Business Analyst will involve using information
to help make decisions, identify problems, and prioritise improvements.
Business systems are the computer hardware and software that will provide much of the information needed to do this – for example; financial
figures, schedule times, customer records, employee details, resources
usage, web site hits, and number of defects. The information that we all
use is only as good as the data that it is based on. For a Business Analyst,
gathering top class information about systems or processes is totally reliant on the accuracy of the data upon which the information is based.

In this chapter, you will examine the value of good data that will lead
to accurate information. As a Business Analyst you will need the best
information you can get. It is therefore important to understand the difference between data and information, and how this understanding relates to business systems.

Making Sense of Data and Information

The Sights – Hindsight, Insight, and Foresight

We have all looked back on events in the past and wished we could have
done things differently; for example, measured something more accurately, collected better data, or spent our money more wisely. Equally, we
would also like to be able to look into the future; for example, will a solu-

tion work, will a project be finished on time, or will our customers be satisfied? While we are doing this, we are actually living in the present. It is
useful here to examine the three Sights – Hindsight, Insight, and Foresight.
First, a formal definition of these words taken from the Webster's Encyclopedic Unabridged Dictionary of the English Language (Figure 3.1).

Sight	Definition
Hindsight	*"Recognition of the realities, possibilities, or requirements of a situation, event, decision, etc, after its occurrence."*
Insight	*"An instance of apprehending the true nature of a thing, esp. through intuitive understanding."*
Foresight	*"An act of looking forward."*

Figure 3.1: Definitions of the Three Sights

Business Analysts should use hindsight to look back and learn from what
has happened before. This means learning from what you did well, as well
as learning from your mistakes by asking "What has happened?". You can
learn from your own experience, but it is also an opportunity to learn from
the experience of others. By looking back in hindsight, you will have a
better insight to give you a deeper understanding of where you are now by
asking "Why did it happen?". This insight will inform you better when
you start to look forward and ask "What will happen?" Hindsight therefore
leads to insight, which in turn leads to foresight (Figure 3.2).

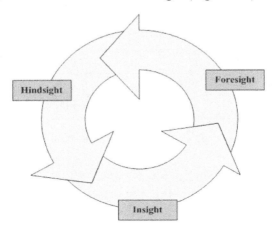

Figure 3.2: The Three Sights

Predicting what will happen in the future is obviously something that you can't totally rely on in business, but you can look at ways to build your confidence in looking to the future. If you can develop the discipline of looking back at past experiences to see what has happened (hindsight), then to look at the present to understand what you are doing (insight), and finally to anticipate possible outcomes of what may happen (foresight), you will be in a much stronger and more secure position to make important decisions.

Data and Information

As will be shown later in this book, much of a Business Analyst's work involves using information to identify problems, improve processes, set priorities, and make decisions. Business systems play a key role by capturing, processing, storing, and distributing information throughout an organisation and its environment. Information is based on data, and it is important to first distinguish between data and information as they are often confused or considered to be the same thing.

Data are streams of raw facts, for example, business transactions. For the most part they are practically useless on their own. Table 3.1 shows some raw data that it is very difficult to establish what they actually mean without guessing. Examples of data include dates, supermarket checkout data, sales figures, and number of web site hits. Information makes use of data by transforming and processing the data into useful information for people to use. Table 3.2 takes the data from Table 3.1 and makes it meaningful.

1.189	1.055
1.199	1.079
1.179	1.060

Table 3.1: Sample Raw Data

Here you see that the figures representing raw facts are actually the prices in euro of a litre of petrol and diesel at three separate service stations. By transforming these data into information you are now in a better position to make a decision about where the best value in petrol (Station C) or diesel (Station A) is before you buy. Other examples of information are things like phone bills, share price trends, a customer list, and best performing sales region.

	Price per Litre (euro)	
Service Station	Petrol	Diesel
Station A	1.189	1.055
Station B	1.199	1.079
Station C	1.179	1.060

Table 3.2: Sample Data and Information

A business system is a set of connected ICT components that manages data and information. A business system can range from a single stand-alone computer to a global network of thousands of connected computers. It will transform raw data into information by making calculations, sorting, arranging, and classifying the data. At its simplest, the system will take data as input, process it, and make information available

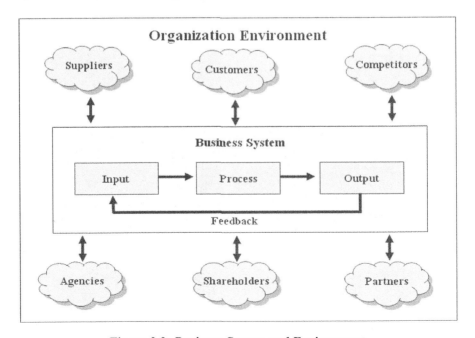

Figure 3.3: Business System and Environment

as output. Every system operates in an environment which will contain other systems as well as other organisations such as competitors, suppliers, and regulatory agencies (see Figure 3.3). The business system therefore contains data and information about the organisation and the environment in which it is situated. The availability of accurate raw data and information is vital to the Business Analyst who must be able to analyse each of these using tools such as spreadsheets, databases, query languages, and reporting software.

Business Systems in the Organisation

In the twenty-first century, almost every organisation, whether it is a small start-up company or an international conglomerate, uses business systems for many business processes. Organisations will typically have systems to manage diverse business processes such as payroll, sales, accounts, human resources (HR), email, and marketing. These types of systems can be regarded as support systems. This means that they provide information and support for functions within an organisation, but are not related directly to the core business of the organisation. Figure

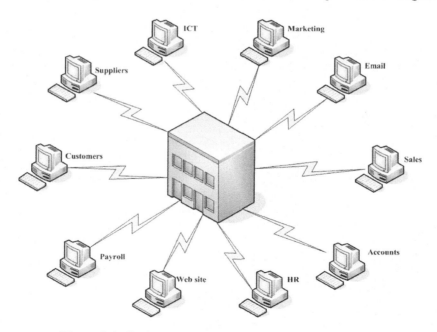

Figure 3.4: Typical Business Systems and Their Functions

3.4 outlines some of these systems and the functions they are used to manage which are typically found in most organisations. Each of these systems can in turn be made up of several sub-systems. For example, an accounting business system would typically be made up of sub-systems such as accounts payable, purchasing, and order entry systems. Figure 3.5 outlines the components of a typical accounting business system. The accounting system and its sub-systems are part of a hierarchy of systems that provide the support functions in an organisation.

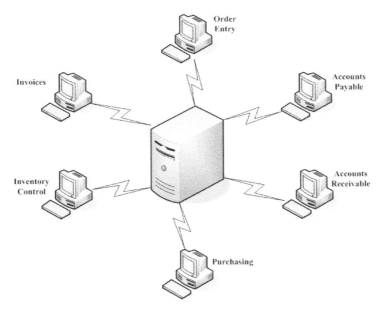

Order Entry

Invoices

Accounts Payable

Inventory Control

Accounts Receivable

Purchasing

Figure 3.5: An Accounting Business System

While support systems such as those outlined in Figures 3.4 and 3.5 are found in most organisations, other separate business specific systems are also to be found. These are the core systems in which the core business of an organisation is managed. For example, these could be systems to manage an automated production line in a manufacturing facility, an on-line store to sell products and services, or a system to manage deliveries in a transport company. These by their nature will be different from organisation to organisation. Figure 3.6 shows a high-level outline of the architecture of a core business system for a financial institution such as a bank. The bank's core business functions such lending, borrowing, interest payments, investments, Internet banking, ATM management, and managing customer accounts, are all managed by a central suite of application servers linked to a central highly secure database. These systems are in turn connected to other business systems such as those in the Central Bank, the Revenue Commissioners, clearing banks, and international offices. The core system is at all times connected to the bank's general ledger so that management can monitor the overall bank's performance. Managers can also get reports, while other users such as internal employees and external customers can access relevant parts of the core system through an on-line secure web interface. Finally, the core system architecture may be connected to the bank's support systems – in many financial institutions these are often kept separate for security reasons.

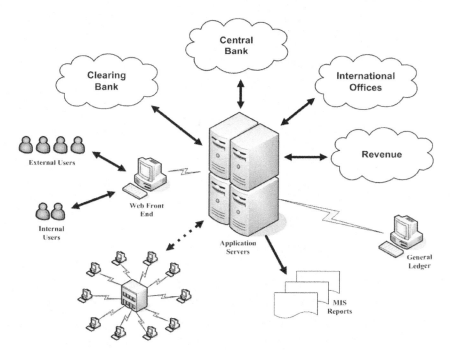

Figure 3.6: Core Business Systems in a Financial Institution

By bringing the core business systems, support systems, and support sub-systems together (Figure 3.7), you will have some understanding of the complexity of a combined business systems architecture in an organisation. This has major implications for the Business Analyst. Supposing that a process improvement or change is necessary for the Order Entry sub-system (see Figure 3.7). This is one of many support systems, so a change could have implications for how processes work in other sub-systems. This in turn could affect the functioning of the core business system and how it processes information throughout the organisation. Therefore, you should at all times be mindful that any business system, no matter how small, is part of a larger system into which it may send and receive data for other systems to use. With this in mind, any change will have to be checked thoroughly to ensure that no difficulties are caused elsewhere in the system. Many organisations will have sophisticated development and test environments that run parallel to the "real" environment to ensure that all changes are fully tested before being released to the "real" working environment. An awareness and understanding of the position of a business system within the overall architecture is therefore vitally important for a Business Analyst to grasp.

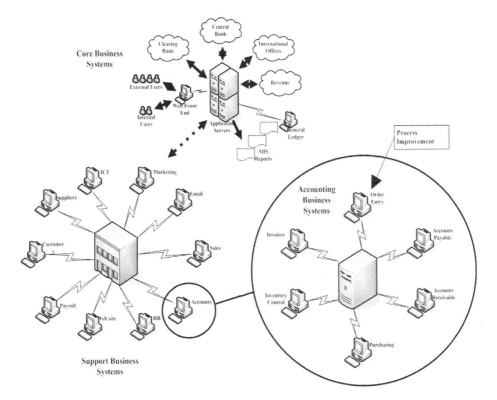

Figure 3.7: Combined Business Systems Architecture

Role of Business Systems

The environment in which a business system operates in can range from simple to complex. At this stage you will be aware that these systems are often interlinked and provide data and information to other systems as well as to the system's users and managers. However, it must be remembered that most systems are in fact made up of computer hardware and software. The computer (system) on the desk of a top executive may in fact be very similar to one used by a new recruit in an entry-level position in the organisation. From a hardware point of view, there may be very little difference between these systems. Most systems will also have similar software used throughout the organisation – for example, common office applications such as word processing, spreadsheets, and web browsers. The new recruit may in fact be using the exact same version of a word processor, and the exact same model of computer as the top executive. However, as we will see – this is where the similarity ends.

Most business systems will be used by different people, in different roles, for different purposes, at different times. The new recruit may be using a system for basic tasks such as logging a business transaction, while the top executive may be using a similar system for creating a long-term strategic marketing plan. In this section you will look at the role of business systems in the organisation, and how they are used to manage business processes and applications.

Types of Business Systems

As we have seen, business systems are common across many functions within an organisation. While the hardware and software may in many cases be similar or identical, the purpose for which each system is used will vary dramatically. Business systems provide information – the people that make use of this information will have different roles to fulfil and be at different levels within an organisation. These people will range from chief executives, senior managers, middle managers, junior managers, to front-line staff. In general, the people who use business systems can be broken down into four levels. The business systems triangle in Figure 3.8 shows these four levels – transaction processing, operational, tactical, and strategic levels. As the diagram illustrates, you can normally expect that there are fewer people operating at the top of the triangle compared to the number at the bottom, there will also be fewer business systems at the top. Most transactions take place in the bottom half of the triangle.

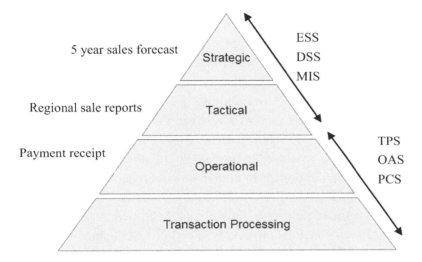

Figure 3.8: Applications and Usage of Business Systems at Different Levels in the Organisation

Source: Adapted from *Business Information Systems: Technology, Development and Management for the E-Business* 4th Edition (Bocij, Greasley, and Hickie, 2008).

At the operational and transaction processing levels, large volumes of data are usually generated on a daily basis by the organisation. These data need to be processed – this is most commonly done by different types of business system. Transaction Processing Systems (TPS) are used to monitor the everyday transactions and activities in the organisation. Examples of a TPS are machine control, order entry, purchasing, and inventory control systems. Process Control Systems (PCS) are usually used to handle the large amounts of data that are generated in production processes. Examples of a PCS are order processing, material requirements planning, and computer-aided manufacture. Finally, Office Automation Systems (OAS) are used to increase office productivity and efficiency. Examples of an OAS include word processing, media storage, and document imaging systems.

At the strategic and tactical levels, less volume of data are generated than at the lower levels. There will also be fewer systems and users at these levels. Business systems at the strategic and tactical levels rely heavily on data generated from the lower-level systems. Management Information Systems (MIS) and Decision Support Systems (DSS) are used at the tactical level, in the main by middle managers in the organisation. Managers need these systems to analyse information and to make decisions. Examples of an MIS are inventory control, sales figures analysis, budgeting, and reporting systems. Examples of a DSS are relocation cost control, contract comparison analysis, cost-benefit analysis, resource allocation systems. As the tactical level is in the middle of the business system triangle, quite often information is taken from the lower operational level, and then processed to provide information for the upper strategic level. It is also important to note that many roles overlap the tactical and operational levels. For example, an administrator working at the operational level may find information on an MIS, while a middle manager may need to extract data from a PCS or TPS. At the top of the business systems triangle you will find Executive Support Systems (ESS). This type of business system provides senior managers with systems to help them make strategic decisions that will affect the organisation in the long-term – this is often also called business intelligence. These systems are used to compare, analyse, highlight, and predict trends that will inform strategic decision making. They rely on all the data and information that can be fed up the business systems triangle within the organisation, and will also be connected to external systems that can provide information such as interest rates, stock prices, and market prices of goods. Examples of a DSS are a five year operating plan, pension planning, and health care planning.

You have now seen that different business systems are used at different levels within an organisation, by people in different roles, and for different purposes. The data that are input into the systems, processed into information, and then made available as output, will also vary according to where the system is located on the business system triangle. But what does all this mean for the Business Analyst? When a business system needs to be modified, improved, replaced, or developed from new – as a Business Analyst, you will always need to be alert as to what type of system it is, which level in the organisation it is used, what it is used for, who uses it, what other systems communicate with it, what data are fed in to it, and what information is extracted from it. Making even a simple change in one system can have serious "knock on" effects for other systems if not planned and monitored carefully.

Business Processes

The business systems described above support flows of activities and work which are called business processes. A business process is a collection of tasks and activities that is designed to produce a certain output for a particular customer or another process. Each business process has input and output (as seen earlier in Figure 3.3), but also has an overall goal, uses resources, and has a number of activities. Later, in Chapter 9, you will examine in detail two analysis techniques for identifying how processes work – Flow Charts, and SIPOC Diagrams. A business process implies that there is a strong emphasis on how work is organised, coordinated, and focused. This means that each process has a defined beginning (usually triggered by an event), a specific order of tasks and activities, and an end. Figure 3.9 outlines a business process model that summarises the components of a business process for dealing with a customer order. This process is triggered by the event of a customer making an order. One or more inputs, such as a customer or inventory database, are required. The order handling process is broken down into several steps. The final output is the completed order.

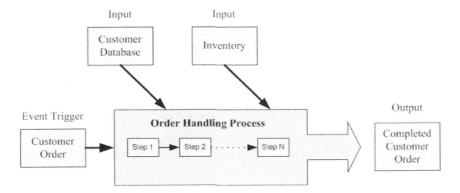

Figure 3.9: A Sample Business Process Model

There are many other examples of business processes in organisations, such as production of bills of material, identifying your best customers, creating invoices, and recruiting new employees. Many organisations will have documentation for each process so that they are executed by the correct method. This ensures that there is a clear workflow of material, information, and knowledge in each process. Looking for existing documentation is a good starting point for you to examine how business processes work in the areas that you will examine as a Business Analyst.

Enterprise Business Systems

Many business systems provide support for business processes that coordinate activities across many different systems, levels, and roles, within an organisation. Enterprise business systems provide support for these types of processes that may cross over the boundaries of different functions. Today, many of these systems use the Internet or Virtual Private Networks (VPNs) to integrate the data and information that are generated by internal business processes with external stakeholders such as business partners, suppliers, and customers. There are three main business applications that make up the centre-piece of an enterprise business system: Enterprise Resource Planning (ERP), Supply Chain Management (SCM), and Customer Relationship Management (CRM) systems. Figure 3.10 represents a high-level view of a typical enterprise business system architecture. ERP, SCM, and CRM are placed at the centre of the diagram, and as you can see they do not operate in isolation. In addition to communicating with each other, they also communicate with other systems, such as a Knowledge Management System (KMS) and a Partner Relationship System (PRS). Let's take a look at each system in turn.

ERP provides a single business system for coordinating and integrating the key internal business processes in the organisation, such as financial, production, and distribution processes. With ERP you can deal efficiently with business challenges and increase productivity in the organisation. A typical ERP uses a central database to provide all the data necessary for areas such as financials, human resources, analytics, procurement, service delivery, operations, and corporate services (Figure 3.11). This information is central to the operations of the other components of the enterprise business system architecture.

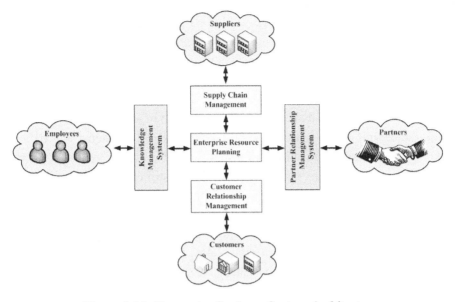

Figure 3.10: Enterprise Business System Architecture

Source: Adapted from *Seven Steps to Nirvana: Strategic Insights into e-Business Transformation* (Sawhney and Zabin, 2001).

Figure 3.11: Components of a Typical Enterprise Resource Planning System

ERP software is typically used to provide an organisation with real-time information based on data from areas such as production, inventory, order processing, and invoicing. With ERP systems you can track your organisation's resources such as availability of raw material, manufacturing or production capacity, and cash-flow. They can also be used to monitor the status of the fulfilment of commitments made by the organisation such as purchase orders, customer orders, delivery schedules, and payroll. This monitoring can take place as all components of the ERP have fed data into the central database from their own systems. ERP systems will therefore provide the organisation with significant business benefits. Quality and efficiency in areas such as production, distribution, and services to customers and partners, will improve. ERP can also lead to reduced costs, easier decision-making, and can result in a more flexible organisation.

CRM focuses on customers – how to acquire, manage, and retain profitable customers with marketing, sales, lead generations, orders, and customer support information (Figure 3.12). A good example of a benefit that CRM provides is sales force automation where sales leads are managed, for example during a marketing campaign. Here, sales leads are generated, assigned, categorised, qualified, and followed up, while all the time being tracked by the CRM system. Good CRM account management involves acquiring new customers by doing a good job in managing prospects, contacts, selling, marketing, fulfilment, and delivery. The CRM system also manages how the relationship with the customer

Figure 3.12: A Typical Customer Relationship Management System

is enhanced by providing excellent customer service and support. Finally, a CRM system can also help to retain customers by providing information such as who the most loyal and best customers are in order to provide a better, more customised service.

SCM focuses on suppliers – how to develop the best and most efficient way to source and procure products and services from suppliers. An SCM system links the organisation's key processes with those not just of its suppliers, but also customers and business partners. In effect, the organisation has a chain of suppliers that provides it with the goods and services it needs to generate its own products and services. Figure 3.13 shows the components of a typical supply chain – this shows a supplier to a manufacturing process having a series of suppliers who in turn have a further series of suppliers.

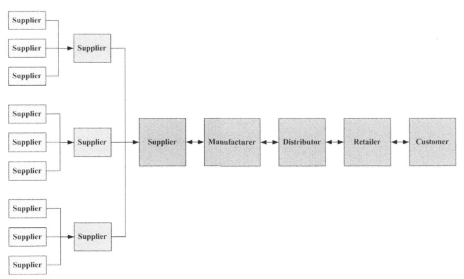

Figure 3.13: Components of a Typical Supply Chain

Managing the supply chain through an SCM system facilitates an organisation's ability to create an efficient, fast, and reduced-cost network of business relationships with its suppliers. To create its own goods and services, an organisation must source materials from external suppliers. Many organisations need to have several suppliers for similar services that they may need to switch to in the event of another supplier being unable to meet its commitments. If a part of (or a link in) the supply chain fails or a supplier cannot deliver on time, then the whole chain may be compromised unless another supplier is found. With SCM you can rapidly communicate orders and track their status, decide what to produce, move, or store, and track shipments. The ultimate goal of SCM is to provide for a better, more efficient and reliable system of suppliers.

The final two components of an enterprise business system are Knowledge Management Systems (KMS) and a Partner Relationship Systems (PRS). A KMS is used to collect and manage relevant knowledge and experience in an organisation that can be used to support decision-making. The primary purpose of a KMS is to acquire, store, and distribute knowledge in an easy to use way so that it can be applied by employees of the organisation. Figure 3.14 outlines the role of a typical KMS. A KMS will typically store information in the form of documents, databases, reports, recordings, and videos.

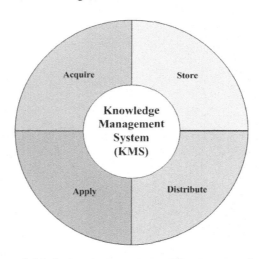

Figure 3.14: Role of a Knowledge Management System

A PRM system can help an organisation to improve communication between itself and its partners, such as dealers, distributors, and channel partners. This can enable organisations to better manage, customise and streamline administrative tasks by making real-time information available to their partners. A typical PRM system will manage communication with partners in areas such as service level agreements (SLAs), contracts, reporting, business rules, price plans, and product catalogs (Figure 3.15).

Figure 3.15: Role of a Partner Relationship Management System

Organisations can benefit enormously from a PRM system. A well-managed partner network can help to streamline operations, reduce costs, extend the organisation's enterprise reach, and ultimately increase revenue. You can also improve links with your partners in an efficient and positive way – especially for your most important partners. Ultimately, you will develop mutually trusting and beneficial relationships with your partners.

Planning New Business Systems

The Business Analyst has a key role to play when organisations are planning new business systems. New systems are often introduced in response to a specific business problem, such as a system to track faults in a manufacturing facility, or to a new opportunity that has arisen, such as selling products or services on-line. Quite often they are also introduced by an organisation in an effort to sustain or gain competitive advantage over its competitors, as well as to enhance decision-making. In this section you will look at some of the factors that should be considered when planning new business systems.

Competitive Advantage

The goal of many organisations is to achieve a sustainable competitive advantage over its competitors by being a market leader or by achieving profits that exceed the average for the industry in which the organisation operates. An organisation can achieve competitive advantage in two ways: cost, and differentiation. A cost advantage occurs when an organisation can produce the same benefits as its competitors, but at a lower cost. A differentiation advantage occurs when an organisation produces benefits that are superior or exceed those of its competitors. When an organisation achieves a competitive advantage position it should provide better value for its customers while at the same time improve profitability.

In order to understand how organisations can work towards achieving competitive advantage, it is important to first look at the influences on an organisation's ability to serve its customers and to maintain profitability. In 1979, Michael Porter first developed the Five Forces model to measure the power of the five most important forces that determine competitiveness in a given situation – Figure 3.16 summarises these forces. The centre of the model represents competitive rivalry that exists between an organisation and its competitors. You will need to know both the number and capability of your competitors, as well as having a good general knowledge of the industry. Outside of this force are four other forces that impact on your competitiveness. The first of these is the bargaining power of your organisation's suppliers. Suppliers provide the resources (goods, services, raw materials, and labour) that you need to create your own products and services. This gives the supplier power over your organisation – for example, a supplier could charge high prices for a unique resource. Here you will need to be aware of the number of suppliers, their size, the uniqueness of their service, and how much it would cost to change supplier. The fewer suppliers you have, the more you will have to rely upon them. Customers also have bargaining power – the simplest of which is their ability to go to another supplier if your organisation is not giving them a good deal. With customers you will need to be aware of their number and size, sensitivity to prices, and how much it would cost for them to change another supplier. Put simply, your customers will want the best product and service for the lowest price, while suppliers will want the highest price they can get from you – your organisation is stuck in the middle of this.

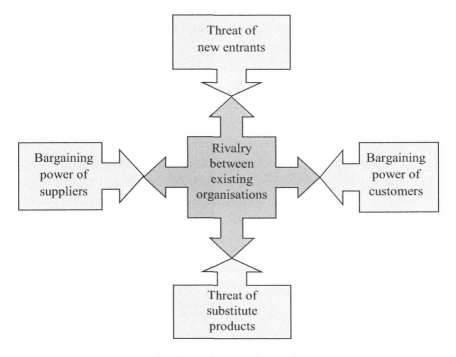

Figure 3.16: Porter's Five Competitive Forces

Source: Adapted from *Competitive Advantage: Creating and Sustaining Superior Performance* (Porter, 1985).

The threat of new entrants comes from the ability of others to enter into your market space. If it is easy and cheap to do, new competitors can enter the market quickly and possibly weaken your organisation's position by decreasing profitability. While there is often very little that you can do to stop others entering the market, you can take steps to make it more difficult for anyone to do so. For example, by building a brand name, protecting your products with patents, and keeping your own costs low. The final force is the threat of substitute products that provides the same service, but in a different way – for example, a new software system to replace a previously manual process. If a substitute product or service is available to customers at a lower price, then this affects your competitiveness as they are more likely to switch to the substitute. To maintain competitive advantage you will need to ensure that the performance of your organisation's products and services stays ahead of that of any substitutes, that it costs less to run, and that the cost of changing to the substitute makes it unviable to do so.

While there are many forces to keep in mind when you are considering your organisation's competitive advantage, there are several strategies that you can consider to sustain this advantage. Following on from the Five Forces model, Porter suggests three generic strategies that can be adopted in order to gain and sustain competitive advantage – these are summarised in Figure 3.17. The two main strategies are to become either a low-cost producer, or to differentiate your products and services. You can do this by either targeting a narrow target market, or a broad market. Let's take a look at each of the three competitive strategies.

	Lower Cost	**Differentiation**
Broad Target	1. Cost Leadership	2. Differentiation
Narrow Target	3. Focus (cost, differentiation)	

Figure 3.17: Porter's Three Generic Competitive Strategies

Source: Adapted from *Competitive Advantage: Creating and Sustaining Superior Performance* (Porter, 1985).

The first strategy is differentiation – this involves selecting one or more criteria used by customers in the marketplace and then putting the organisation in a position to uniquely to meet those criteria. This strategy often means charging a premium price for the product or service that reflects high production costs associated with high value. A good example of this type of strategy is pursued by organisations that develop high-end products such as executive cars, or specialist audio equipment. In this case, the organisation is providing products at a high cost to a wide market. The opposite of this is the second strategy – to become a low-cost producer for a wide market. With this strategy, an organisation aims to be the lowest cost provider in the marketplace. This strategy is mostly associated with large-scale organisations providing basic or standard products and services with little differentiation that are acceptable to most customers. Examples include low-cost supermarkets and low-cost airlines.

The third competitive strategy is a focus on a narrow target market. There are two types of focus: differentiation and cost focus. In each case an organisation is looking to provide products and services for a specific target market segment. This is also referred to as a niche market. For a differentiation focus, an organisation seeks differentiation in its target market. If there are specialist customer needs, then there are opportunities to provide products and services that are clearly differentiated from competitors. A cost focus strategy in a narrow market aims to be a low cost producer, but in a narrow marketplace. In effect, an organisation looking to focus on either a differentiation or cost basis is looking to tailor its business to achieve competitive advantage in its target markets only.

The advent of the Internet has greatly influenced competitive advantage. Barriers to entry are reduced, and new substitute products and services are easier to get. This often means that the bargaining power of customers is increased, though at the same time it will raise your organisation's bargaining power over your suppliers. With the Internet, the whole world is a potential marketplace, however – this will also increase the number of competitors and reduce the differentiation between competitors.

Making Decisions

Business systems of all types can provide valuable information that is used in the decision-making process. They also help people like managers to communicate and distribute this information. Herbert Simon in 1960 developed a three stage model for decision-making which consists of intelligence, design, and choice. This was later expanded by George Huber in 1980 to incorporate implementation and monitoring by linking decision making with problem solving (see Figure 3.18). As decision-making is part of problem solving, it is therefore important for the Business Analyst to be able to understand how decision making relates to the problem solving process. Later in this book you will examine in detail three techniques that will equip you to make better decisions: SWOT Analysis, PEST Analysis, and Cost-Benefit Analysis.

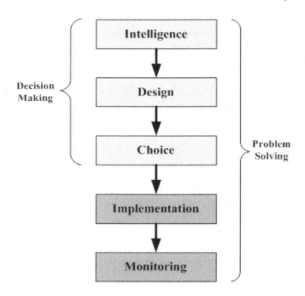

Figure 3.18: How Decision-making Relates to Problem-solving

In decision-making, the first phase is the intelligence phase. In this phase the potential problems or opportunities are identified and defined. During the second phase, design, alternative solutions to the problem are developed. In this stage you will also examine the feasibility of each alternative solution. In the third phase of decision-making, choice, a course of action is selected. Problem-solving incorporates the decision-making process and adds two more phases. In the implementation phase, the solution selected by the decision-making process is put into effect. Finally, in the monitoring phase the decision makers evaluate the implemented solution to ensure that the original requirements were achieved.

The different types of business systems described earlier in this chapter can be used support the decision-making process. However, this will depend upon which level on the business systems triangle (see Figure 3.8) – transaction processing, operational, tactical, or strategic, that the business system operates. It also depends on whether the decisions are classified as structured or unstructured. Structured decisions are those that are routine and repetitive and they usually involve a definite step-by-step process. Unstructured decisions rely on judgement, insight, and the ability to evaluate the problem. A business system such as an Executive Support System (ESS) can be useful to support unstructured decisions at the strategic and tactical levels. While a Transaction Processing System (TPS) is more suited to structured decisions at the operational and transaction processing levels (see Figure 3.19). Some systems, such as Decision Support Systems (DSS) and Management Information Systems (MIS) can support both structured and unstructured decision-making.

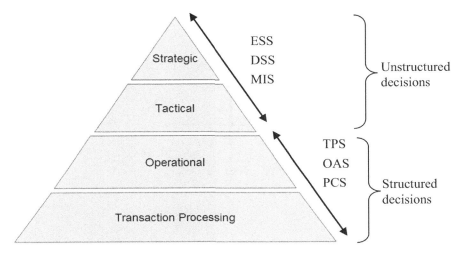

Figure 3.19: The Role of Business Systems in Structured and Unstructured Decision-making

Organisational Factors

Implementing business systems in an organisation has consequences for the people that will use the new system, the tasks they do, and the structure of the organisation. As far back as 1965, Harold Leavitt proposed a model to show organisations as interdependent multivariate systems (see Figure 3.20). This means that there is in-built organisational resistance to change brought about by technology. According to Leavitt's model, business systems (described as technology in the model) are strongly linked with tasks, people, and structure – in order to change any one of these four components, all four must change simultaneously. In the model, tasks are the organisation's purpose – for example, to provide a service or manufacture a product. People represent those who carry out the task. Structure represents the work-flow, decision-making authority, and communications. Business Analysts should be conscious of organisational resistance to the introduction of a new or improved system. Most organisations will have clear guidelines for managing different types of change – you should ensure that any change resulting from the implementation of a new business system is carefully managed, and that it is aligned with the overall organisational goals.

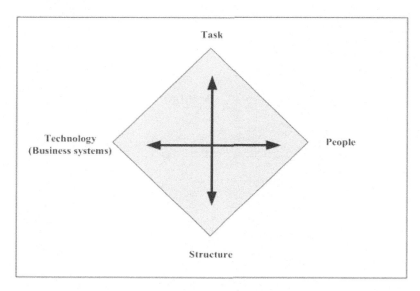

Figure 3.20: Leavitt's Model for Organisational Resistance

For a business system to be successful, it must be designed and developed with a clear understanding of how and where it will work in the organisation. The organisation's environment, which includes its tasks, people, and structure, is one of many factors to consider when planning any new system. Other factors include the organisation's culture, politics, and style of its leadership. The key stakeholders affected by the system will need to be consulted, and a thorough understanding of all the decisions, processes, and tasks that the system is designed to assist with needs to be acquired.

Exercise – DIY Store Performance

It is important to be able to use raw data provided by a business system to extract information to enhance the process of decision making. Table 3.3 shows some data that represent sales figures on four products for a chain of DIY stores. The four products are pliers, vice-grips, tape measures, and hammers. For accounting purposes, the DIY chain of stores is divided into two regions – northside and southside. Each region has three stores. Unit costs and annual sales figures for each product are also provided. Using these raw data, answer the following questions:

- Which is the best performing sales region, northside or southside?

- Which is the best performing store in each region?

- Which is the best performing store overall?

- Which is the best performing product overall?

Prepare a short report summarising the sales performance of each product by store and by region. Suggest ways in which you can use this information to improve performance in the weakest selling products. Finally, suggest ways in which the sales performance of each product could be tracked by store and region over time.

Store #	Region	Part Number	Description	Unit Cost	Annual sales
1	Southside	PWU792	Pliers	€14.99	2,150
1	Southside	LKW331	Vice-Grip	€15.99	1,750
1	Southside	WEJ778	Tape Measure	€9.99	2,250
1	Southside	ERM835	Hammer	€9.99	1,980
2	Southside	PWU792	Pliers	€14.99	995
2	Southside	LKW331	Vice-Grip	€15.99	630
2	Southside	WEJ778	Tape Measure	€9.99	715
2	Southside	ERM835	Hammer	€9.99	875
3	Southside	PWU792	Pliers	€14.99	2,450
3	Southside	LKW331	Vice-Grip	€15.99	2,210
3	Southside	WEJ778	Tape Measure	€9.99	2,650
3	Southside	ERM835	Hammer	€9.99	1,755
4	Northside	PWU792	Pliers	€14.99	850
4	Northside	LKW331	Vice-Grip	€15.99	1,120

4	Northside	WEJ778	Tape Measure	€9.99	1,350
4	Northside	ERM835	Hammer	€9.99	875
5	Northside	PWU792	Pliers	€14.99	1,050
5	Northside	LKW331	Vice-Grip	€15.99	650
5	Northside	WEJ778	Tape Measure	€9.99	2,150
5	Northside	ERM835	Hammer	€9.99	1,750
6	Northside	PWU792	Pliers	€14.99	950
6	Northside	LKW331	Vice-Grip	€15.99	750
6	Northside	WEJ778	Tape Measure	€9.99	1,250
6	Northside	ERM835	Hammer	€9.99	975

Table 3.3: DIY Store Sales Data by Region

Reflection

At the beginning of this chapter you set out to understand what a business system is, what role it plays in an organisation, and how important data and information are to the decision making process. The key to making good use of information that is produced by a business system is to understand where the data on which it is based originated, how it is processed, who will use it, and how you can use this information to make better decisions.

In your Learning Journal, answer the following reflective questions:

- What have you learned in this chapter?

- Can you think of any everyday examples of where you use raw data to provide the information that you need to make a decision?

- What business systems do you use in your own organisations?

- Where on the business systems triangle would you place the business system that you use?

- Can you identify different business systems used by other employees in your organisation?

- What are the support and core business systems in your organisation? Are they separated from one another?

Building an understanding of how business systems are used, who uses them, what they are used for, and what information they provide, will give you a solid foundation for using these systems in business analysis. Whatever analysis task you are doing that involves business systems; keep in mind that you will be reliant upon accurate sources of data and information. You should always check the accuracy of your sources and consult with any subject matter experts when you need extra help understanding information. Finally, as you may often be dealing with huge quantities of data you should consider enhancing your data management skills by improving your knowledge of spreadsheets, databases, querying and reporting tools.

4

REQUIREMENTS ELICITATION

"The greatest challenge to any thinker is stating the problem in a way that will allow a solution." – Bertrand Russell

Introduction

Requirements elicitation, also commonly known as requirements gathering, is perhaps the most important task that a Business Analyst will do. Requirements are the foundation for the solutions to the problems that you will face – therefore it is essential that they be elicited in an accurate, clear, concise, and consistent way. However, many Business Analysts and their teams spend very little time in developing the skills necessary to elicit requirements. Using proven methods to elicit requirements will not only improve your own skills, but will also ensure that the solutions you propose will be founded on a solid basis.

In this chapter you will examine the process of eliciting requirements in detail. First, you will define what a requirement is, and then what requirements elicitation is. You will also look at some critical success factors for requirements elicitation. Finally, you will examine five of the most effective requirements elicitation techniques. As a Business Analyst you should be able to select and use the most appropriate technique, or combination of techniques for a given situation, and acquire the knowledge necessary to be able to plan, execute, and deliver solutions based on these techniques.

What is Requirements Elicitation?

Requirement Definition

Before examining what Requirements Elicitation is, we need first of all to have a clear understanding of what a requirement is. The IEEE Standard Glossary of Software Engineering Terminology defines a requirement in two parts as follows:

- A requirement is a condition or capability needed by a stakeholder to solve a problem or achieve an objective.

- A requirement is a condition or capability that must be met or possessed by a solution or solution component to satisfy a contract, standard, specification, or other formally imposed documents.

In practice, a requirement is a short and concise statement about a proposed solution that all stakeholders have agreed must be made true in order for a problem to be satisfactorily resolved. It usually says something about a procedure, process or system that is intended to solve a problem. Most importantly, a requirement will help solve a customer's problem – a collection of requirements is often referred to as a requirements document, which is prepared for the customer. The Business Analysis Body of Knowledge (BABOK®) uses the following classification to describe requirements:

Business requirements	These are high-level statements of the goals, objectives, or needs of an organisation as a whole. They describe the reasons why a project has been initiated, what the objectives are, and how success will be measured.
Stakeholder requirements	These are statements of the needs of stakeholders, and how the stakeholder will interact with the solution.
Solution requirements	These describe the characteristics of a solution that meets both the business and stakeholder requirements. There are two main types: functional and non-functional requirements. Functional requirements describe what a system will do. Non-functional requirements describe the environmental conditions in which a system will work.
Transition requirements	These are temporary requirements that describe what is required by a solution to transition from the current state to a desired future state.

Requirements Elicitation Definition

Before defining Requirements Elicitation, let's take a look at what the word "elicit" means. According to Webster's Encyclopedic Unabridged Dictionary of the English Language, "elicit" is defined as "to draw or bring out or forth; educe; evoke". This means that the Business Analyst must be able to draw out the requirements from the stakeholders – often in cases where a stakeholder may be unsure exactly what the condition or capability is when they need to solve a problem. This requires good communications skills, e.g. one of the key skills is being able to interview stakeholders as part of the Requirements Elicitation process.

There are many different Requirements Elicitation techniques – typically a combination or two or more techniques will be used by the Business Analyst. The BABOK® Guide lists nine generally accepted elicitation techniques:

- Brainstorming

- Document Analysis

- Focus Group

- Interface Analysis

- Interviews

- Observation

- Prototyping

- Requirements Workshops

- Surveys/Questionnaires

Each of these techniques will be used in different situations in different ways – many Business Analysts rely on four or five techniques that they have most experience in. In this chapter, you will examine four of the nine techniques above: Brainstorming, Interviews, Requirements Workshops and Surveys/Questionnaires. In addition to these four, you will also examine another very useful technique called 5W2H.

Requirements Elicitation Stakeholders

During Requirements Elicitation you will be communicating in many different ways with several stakeholders. These are the individuals and groups of people affected by and capable of influencing the development and implementation of your problem-solving efforts. Therefore, identifying the key stakeholders and their issues is a vital part of the Requirements Elicitation process that you should conduct early on in the project. The first thing to remember is that as the Business Analyst, you yourself are a key stakeholder in a project. Normally, there will also be a project manager who is responsible for managing communication with all stakeholders. Other types of stakeholder will vary depending on the project. However, in general, the types of stakeholder that you are likely to be

Stakeholder type	Description
Business Analyst	The person responsible for eliciting requirements from other stakeholders.
Project Manager	The person with overall responsibility for a project and the communication management with all stakeholders.
Project Sponsor	Usually the person responsible for a project's budget, and who gives overall project direction and final approval.
Customers	The person or persons who have a business need for a problem to be resolved. Sometimes they are also the project sponsors.
Users	The people who will actually use the product or service when it is delivered.
Subject Matter Expert	The Subject Matter Expert (SME) is a person with in-depth knowledge of the area under investigation.
Suppliers	Any organisation who will be supplying goods and services for the project.
Lenders	Lenders, such as banks, are key stakeholders and they may be providers of finance for a project.
Employees	People in your organisation who will be affected by your project. They may also be people who contribute and provide support to the project.

Table 4.1: General Types of Stakeholder

dealing with are described in Table 4.1. Identifying all the key stakeholders will increase the prospects of the success of your project. The
interests and expectations of stakeholders must be considered otherwise
they may not participate fully in the project.

To illustrate how important it is to identify stakeholders, let's take a
look at an example of a large construction project for the Beacon Medical Group (BMG). BMG develops and operates co-located hospital facilities in Ireland. Key to the success of a large project such as building a
hospital was that BMG identified stakeholders and implemented a process for construction stakeholder management. Figure 4.1 summarises
the key stakeholders in a BMG hospital building project.

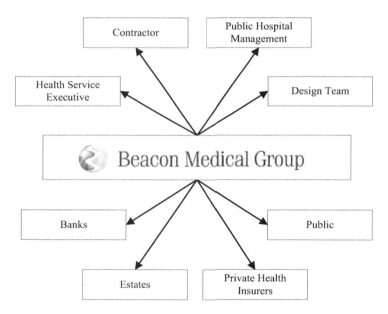

Figure 4.1: Constructor Stakeholder Management

Source: Diagram courtesy of Beacon Medical Group.

In this project, BMG identified eight key stakeholder groups and appointed a dedicated stakeholder coordinator in each co-located hospital
to oversee all aspects of the project. Regular meetings were held with
each group – weekly meetings in the case of the design team, and monthly meetings with the remaining groups. A risk analysis was completed

with each stakeholder; this analysis was updated and acted on regularly. As a result, stakeholder issues were identified promptly. With this approach, BMG built the Beacon Hospital in Sandyford, Co. Dublin, which is a full service hospital that comprises over 22,000 square meters with a capacity for 183 beds.

Critical Success Factors

Each Requirements Elicitation technique will have its own set of critical success factors (CSF), but there are some general factors that you should consider that apply to all elicitation techniques. For general business activities, a CSF is a factor or activity that is required to ensure that your business is successful, in other words the factors or activities that you must concentrate on. Good examples of CSFs are managing cash flow, new product development, and effective distribution. For Requirements Elicitation, we need to be more specific in determining CSFs. P. G. Daly, writing in the Intranet Journal (see www.intranetjournal.com) in 2003, identified seven CSFs for gathering (eliciting) requirements as follows:

- Choose the right member of your team

- Meet with the customer early and often

- Ask questions

- Clarify what the system will not do

- No technical jargon allowed

- Document and reconfirm

- Revisit the requirements often

Let's now examine in turn each of these CSFs for Requirements Elicitation.

Choose the Right Member of Your Team. The best person to elicit requirements is not necessarily the strongest technical person on your team. People and communication skills are of the utmost importance here – remember you will have to draw out the requirements from your customer or stakeholder. Quite often, too much technical detail at this early stage of the process may intimidate or confuse a customer. Whoever is going to do this job, they will need to meet with the customer and establish effective communication right from the start. Good written and verbal communications skills are essential. This is because you will have to communicate the requirements to a more technically knowledgeable audience once your requirements elicitation is complete. A detailed training course in communications and consultancy is strongly advised for you, or a member of your team, if these skills are lacking – without these skills, your requirements elicitation efforts may be destined to fail. Commitment is also vital here – you and your team should commit to the process of eliciting customer needs and expectations into a verifiable requirements document.

Meet with the Customer Early and Often. In any business environment, a major challenge for organisations is to stay focused on their most valuable asset – customers. All organisations want to keep their best customers and get the most out of every customer interaction – this goes for Requirements Elicitation too. Your customer must be kept involved right from the beginning of any project – after all, not only do they pay the bills, but they are also best placed to tell you what they need.

One of the most demanding tasks that you as a Business Analyst will have to do is to deal with customers. No matter how demanding or difficult customers are, you should try to meet them as early as possible in person. You should establish the ground rules for both the method and frequency of communication. While modern tools like video conferencing can be effective, you should not underestimate the importance of meeting your customer in person – human contact is very important. Whatever ground rules you establish, for example – weekly conference calls to update and clarify issues that arise, or progress reports via email, you should ensure that you adhere to these rules and keep your customer involved in the project.

Ask Questions. The ability to ask questions is an important communication skill for the Business Analyst. Even more important is the ability to ask the right questions – these are the ones that will elicit requirements. Failing to ask the right questions may be the difference between the failure and success of your efforts. This is not an easy skill to learn, but experience will count as you attempt to get your customer to think deeply by asking powerful questions about what they really need. An interview is the best way to do this – in an interview you will have an opportunity to ask clarifying questions or follow up on an aspect of a problem that needs further analysis. You must establish what functionality is required in a new or improved system, and agree these requirements with your customer. Finally, even after the most successful interview, follow up questions are almost inevitable. Be sure to follow up quickly – never assume that you can anticipate what a customer would answer. Use email and telephone contact if you cannot meet your customer in person.

Clarify What the System Will Not Do. In project management, scope creep is one of the major causes of project failure – this is where the scope changes or new features are requested after the initial scope has been decided. Project managers usually put detailed plans in place to prevent and manage scope creep. It is equally important for the Business Analyst to understand scope creep. When you draw up a list of requirements for a new system and get agreement from your customer as to what they are – this requirements list will later form the basis of a scope statement. An important rule to remember about scope statements is that "if it's not on the scope statement, don't do it". Therefore, while it is vitally important to clarify what a system will do, it can sometimes equally be important to clarify what a system will not do. This is also important in software development where several versions of a solution are often produced – in this case clarify what each version will do or not do as appropriate.

In addition to clarifying what a system will and will not do, it is also important to specify how people (or other systems) will interact with the new system. It is good practice to work with Flow Charts (see chapter 9) and Use Cases (see chapter 10), to illustrate and document systems and how people interact with them. When your documentation is complete, share it with your customer, elicit their feedback, agree any changes, and get them to sign off and approve the document.

No Technical Jargon Allowed. When you are eliciting requirements, using technical terms and abbreviations can be a major obstacle when communicating with your customer. Jargon of any kind should be avoided when eliciting requirements – customers and stakeholders who are not familiar with any jargon in use may feel intimidated by your use of jargon. As this stage in eliciting requirements, you should focus your efforts solely on the business processes involved, what the problem is, and what needs to be done to resolve the problem. Technology of course is an important factor in many problem solving efforts. Whether the solution eventually involves an automated process, an electrical device, specialised computer hardware, or a software application – remain focused on the business requirements. At the later design stage in a project, where more technical people will be involved, technical details will eventually become important.

Document and Reconfirm. Once you have elicited all requirements from your customer and got their agreement on what should be on the list of requirements, you will need to document everything onto a formal requirements document. A key to success here is to be clear, concise, and thorough – this document will be a vital piece of information for all stakeholders and team members involved in a project. Many organisations will have templates and guidelines for producing requirements documentation, so be sure to check what is in place. You should also check out previously used requirements documentation to give you an idea of standards used. Even when your documentation has been completed to your customer's satisfaction, you will need to revisit and reconfirm requirements documentation at regular intervals throughout a project.

Revisit the Requirements Often. In a systems development life cycle, the Requirements Elicitation phase occurs at a very early stage in the overall cycle. It is therefore imperative that the requirements are elicited as accurately as possible and documented in a professional way. The rest of the development life cycle will run smoother if this is the case. An error discovered at the early stage will cost a lot less and be easier to fix, than if discovered later (see Figure 4.2). For each requirement that is incorrectly elicited or specified, businesses can sometimes pay 50 to 200 times as much to correct it at a later stage in a project. Requirements can also be used as a measure of project success or failure – therefore it is important to revisit them on a regular basis to see if you and your project are on target to meet the requirements. It is easy to lose track of what the initial requirements are, especially in long projects, or of what your customer is expecting.

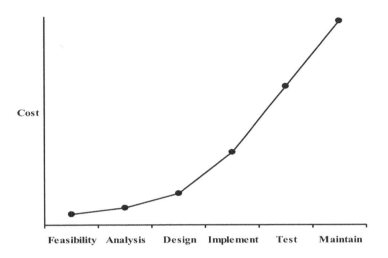

Figure 4.2: Cost of Errors Over the Systems Development Life Cycle

The Requirements Elicitation Process

The Business Analysis Body of Knowledge (BABOK®) outlines the process of Requirements Elicitation in four main tasks: prepare, conduct activity, document, and confirm the requirements. These tasks have a series of inputs and outputs which are summarised in Figure 4.3. This elicitation process will vary depending on what technique is used. For example, if you use an interview to elicit requirements the output results will be set of interview notes, while the output of survey will be a different set of results. Each task will also be different depending on the technique used. Let's now take a look at each of the four main tasks in more detail.

Prepare for Elicitation

As with any project, preparation is vital for success. For Requirements Elicitation you will need to ensure that any resource that you will need is ready – the most important part of this is to ensure that you have a detailed schedule in place. Of the six inputs on Figure 4.3, you will need four in place as part of preparing for elicitation: case, need, scope, and roles and responsibilities. With these four inputs you will need to understand exactly what information should be elicited from the stakeholders. The business case and need reminds you that the requirements must be aligned with the goals and objectives of the project stated at the outset. The project scope is necessary to ensure that you adhere to the agreed solution scope. The list of roles and responsibilities helps you to determine which stakeholders will take part in, or should be consulted, as part of eliciting the requirements.

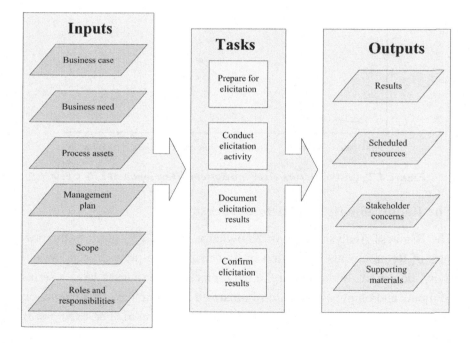

Figure 4.3: Requirements Elicitation Input and Output

Source: Adapted from the Business Analysis Body of Knowledge (BABOK®).

The main elements when preparing elicitation to watch out for are that you should specify the scope for the selected technique that you will use, and that you have the necessary resources in place. All resources such as people, equipment, and facilities, need to be scheduled. Each of the stakeholders needs to be notified of your plans so that all can agree to proceed with your plan. Of the four outputs on Figure 4.3, two will result from this stage – a schedule of resources, and a list of supporting materials. These outputs now become inputs to the next task.

Conduct Elicitation Activity

This task involves meeting or contacting all the stakeholders to elicit the requirements based on their needs. For example, you may interview individual stakeholders, gather the stakeholders together in a workshop, host a brainstorming session with relevant stakeholders, or distribute a survey to the stakeholders. Of the six inputs on Figure 4.3, you will need five in place as part of conducting the elicitation activity: case, need, process assets, scope, and a management plan. These five inputs are combined with the outputs from the preparing for elicitation task and are now all used as part of the conducting the elicitation activity task.

Regardless of which technique you use, there are several elements that you need to keep in mind when conducting the elicitation activity. Make sure that you adhere to the scope of the project as outlined in the preparing for elicitation task. If you are in any doubt as to whether a requirement should be included, refer back to the original goals and objectives of your Requirements Elicitation project. As you are conducting the elicitation activity task you should document details on each requirement such as its source, value, and priority. This will help you to manage each requirement throughout the entire Requirements Elicitation process, and will also help in any future projects that you will be involved in. The output from the conducting the elicitation activity task is a set of elicitation results, which will be used as the input for the next Requirements Elicitation task. The format of these results will depend on the elicitation techniques used.

Document Elicitation Results

The document elicitation results task is a straight forward recording of all the information elicited from the stakeholders. The input into this task is the elicitation results from the previous task. While other tasks may involve several stakeholders, documenting the elicitation results is the job of the Business Analyst. Documenting the elicitation results will depend on the technique used; these results could vary from written documents, notes, meeting minutes, recordings, and survey results. Whatever technique is used, the results should be documented into a report that collates and summarises the requirements.

There are two outputs to the document elicitation results task. The first is obvious: a list of requirements. These should be stated from the perspective of the stakeholders – the requirements must be stated to reflect the needs of the stakeholders. The second output relates to stakeholder concerns. Throughout the Requirements Elicitation process, stakeholders may express concerns such as constraints, threats, risks, and assumptions. These too should be documented and referred to throughout the process. The outputs of stated requirements and the stakeholder concerns are now used as inputs into the next task.

Confirm Elicitation Results

Once you have documented the elicitation results you will need to validate and confirm them. Even though you may have been careful in eliciting and documenting the requirements using proven techniques up to now, you should still regard your list of requirements as unconfirmed. Hence the need for a separate confirm elicitation results task. In this task you will take the outputs from the previous document elicitation results task and confirm that your understanding of what the requirements are matched with the stakeholders' understanding and needs. This is best done by meeting with the stakeholders again so that the requirements can be reviewed. It is also an opportunity to confirm the stakeholder's concerns.

Any stakeholder that has participated in any of the other requirements elicitation tasks should be contacted so that you can review, alter (if necessary), restate, and confirm each requirement with them. In large projects, some time may have passed between when you first met a stakeholder and when you have documented the requirements – so it is a good idea to recheck your results and discuss the concerns raised. The output from this task is a restated list of confirmed requirements, and a confirmed list of stakeholder concerns. These documents now form the basis for Requirements Analysis (see Chapter 5).

Effective Requirements Elicitation Techniques

Brainstorming

The first of the Requirements Elicitation techniques that you will examine is brainstorming. This is an easy to use tool that is often used to develop highly innovative and creative solutions to a problem. The main aim of a brainstorming session in business systems analysis is to produce several new ideas based on the problem to be solved. While it can be done by an individual, it is far more effective when carried out in groups.

Brainstorming was first introduced by Alex F. Osborn who is the author of several books on creative thinking. In his book *Your Creative Power* (1948), Osborn describes one brainstorming session with a client where 150 people were organised into 15 groups to brainstorm one subject. This resulted in over 800 ideas, 177 of which were chosen for submission in the form of concrete suggestions.

Brainstorming can significantly increase creative problem-solving output. It can be applied to almost any problem, or any situation. There are no set rules for conducting a brainstorming session, but you should have some structure to ensure that you get the maximum benefit from such a session. In general, the following guidelines are effective when taken into account for a group brainstorming session:

- Ensure that you carefully prepare for elicitation before each session. Make sure that you have resources such as flipcharts and whiteboards available, and that the session is being held in comfortable surroundings

- Appoint an experienced facilitator to manage the session

- Conduct the elicitation activity and start by identifying what the problem to be solved is. Focus on one problem at a time and make sure that everyone in the group understands clearly what the problem is

- Start with an "anything goes" approach – allow everyone in the groups to say what they want about the problem. Document the elicitation results by recording all suggestions

- No criticism should be allowed. Even if you think that someone else's suggestion is the stupidest thing that you have ever heard, it may prompt another person in the group to come up with another idea

- When idea generation starts to slow down, use some tricks to encourage more ideas. Some suggestions are to get the group to describe in detail the opposite of what is needed, physically move people, introduce roadblocks (for example, a limited budget), and remove roadblocks (for example, allow unlimited funds)

- Encourage everyone in the group to contribute to the session.

***Tip*:**

To get creativity going in a brainstorming session, start out by brainstorming something simple, like things you can do with a coat hanger or new ideas for an advertisement campaign for chocolate.

Once the brainstorming session is complete you should have a long list of ideas and suggestions relating to the problem under investigation. Before you can confirm the elicitation results, you may need to find a way to refine and narrow down the items on your list, especially if the list is very long. Deciding on an evaluation criteria for reducing the list will not be easy – however, if you focus on the business needs of your customer you should have something to work on. You could for example come up with reduced list of possible low cost solutions that could be implemented quickly, or in a software project decide that only a certain number of features can be implemented in the first version of the product.

When you have refined and shortened your list of ideas, it is a good idea to use these as the basis for a second brainstorming session where further ideas may be generated. If this, or the earlier session fails, to provide any useful suggestions or ideas, it may be that the problem statement was not clear and concise enough for everyone to understand. In this case you may need to refine the problem statement and try again.

Brainstorming has great advantages in that it can be easy to set up and can be used to elicit requirements in a relatively short period of time.

Creative thinking is very much enabled by the "no criticism" environment. It can also be fun to do and can relax participants – especially where there are new members of your team present. However, there are disadvantages too. For example, a successful brainstorming session relies on people's willingness to participate fully – it can be difficult for people to share ideas in a group, especially when informed that "anything goes" and even silly ideas are welcome.

Interviews

An interview is a highly structured approach to eliciting requirements that allows the Business Analyst to gather experiential, technical, nontechnical, and specialised information by asking relevant questions and documenting the answers. This is an excellent way to provide quality data in a face-to-face interview when you can question directly stakeholders on location. One-on-one interviews are the most common type of face-to-face interview, and are also considered to be the most valuable type of interview on the basis that you can easily clarify questions on the spot. Less common are group interviews, but they can also be a valuable method of eliciting requirements. Telephone interviews could also be used, but you are more likely to get a poorer response rate.

Interviews are most often used to elicit data from a small target sample of an identified population. For example, interviews can be used to elicit employee perceptions, reactions, and attitudes to issues such as an organisation's leadership, and how change is introduced and managed. A common use of interviews is to validate requirements elicited by other means such as surveys – this can help to define customer expectations more clearly. There are two basic types of interviews: structured, and unstructured. In structured interviews, a Business Analyst will have a predefined set of questions (such as those outlined in the 5W2H Requirements Elicitation technique described later in this chapter). For an unstructured interview, the Business Analyst and the stakeholder will discuss topics of interest in a free and open-ended way.

Almost anyone can perform an interview, but only experienced interviewers who follow a structured process are most likely to be successful in eliciting requirements from stakeholders. Making a success of interviews is not easy. The key factors to successful interviewing are planning, preparing, initiating, conducting, closing, and following up the interview. Planning for an interview involves coming up with an interview plan – for example, you might plan to interview top management before middle and lower levels of management. Preparing for an interview means doing some background research in order to reach a level of understanding of the subject matter that you are investigating. You will also need to identify potential interviewees, design the interview with both open-ended and closed-ended questions, and finally contact the interviewees to set up the actual interview. When initiating the interview you should first state the purpose of the interview and address any concerns that the interviewee may have. Provide a description of the interview format and try to make sure that your interviewee is at ease throughout. If you are recording or taking notes during the interview, you should agree with the interviewee that it is OK to do so. When conducting the interview you should focus on the established goals and objectives. In general, open-ended questions will generate more information and are useful in establishing the scope of the problem by placing fewer constraints on your interviewee's responses. Most importantly, you should pay attention and listen carefully to your interviewee's responses. You must ensure that their responses are understood and that they are appreciated. When closing the interview check first with your interviewee if there have been any areas that have been overlooked in the interview. This is also a good time to summarise the interview and go over your notes. Remind the interviewee that at this stage the requirements are unconfirmed and that you will be following up at a later stage to confirm the requirements.

Interviews have several advantages and disadvantages as a technique for eliciting requirements. The main advantages are that an interview is a two-way communication where it is easy to clarify and explain misunderstood questions and answers. You can also observe non-verbal behavior and glean useful information that an interviewee might express in private, but not in public. Interviews are flexible and relatively easy to organise (though scheduling difficulties may arise), and of course the response rate will be very high. The main disadvantages of interviews are lack of anonymity and that there may be possible interviewer bias (leading the interviewee). To avoid bias, an interviewer should use neutral language, ask open-ended questions, adhere to the planned question sequence, and record all responses exactly as given by the interviewee. Finally, interviews will only yield data from a small sample size, and may therefore have to be used in conjunction with another requirements eliciting technique, such as surveying.

Tip:
Avoid leading questions that may hint at an answer you're expecting. Try something like, "What aspect of the current process do you find the most difficult?" rather than, "The current process is hard to use, isn't it?"

Business Analysts may take some time to acquire good interviewing skills to be able to conduct effective interviews. Training will be required to learn the special skills needed to facilitate an interview such as, knowing what questions to ask, following up effectively, and listening. As a Business Analyst you will also have to gain knowledge in the subject area which can often itself take up a lot of time. You should also be aware that recording, taking notes, documenting, and analysing interview data takes up a lot of resources – it can be a very time-consuming activity.

5W2H

The Requirements Elicitation technique known as 5W2H is a structured method for asking specific types of questions that can be used to try and solve most problems. 5W2H is so called because five of the questions begin with the letter "W" and the remaining two being with the letter "H". The questions are: What? Why? Where? When? Who? How? and How much? The technique is thought to have originated from Rudyard Kipling's poem "I Keep Six Honest ...":

> *I keep six honest serving-men*
> *(They taught me all I knew);*
> *Their names are What and Why and When*
> *And How and Where and Who.*

When used as a Requirements Elicitation technique, 5W2H should result in answers to seven questions. The main purpose of the 5W2H technique is to examine and question a problem or process so that you can determine some improvement ideas. As it is a highly structured approach to asking a specific set of questions, it will engage your team in discovering forgotten or overlooked issues. It is therefore useful in helping to identify potential problems or opportunity for improvement. Table 4.2 outlines some examples of the types of questions that can be asked about almost any problem. By asking these specific set of questions, you and your team can consider and question every aspect of the problem or opportunity being examined.

Issue	5W2H	Description
Purpose	What?	What is being done? Can this task be eliminated?
Activity	Why?	Why is this task necessary? Clarify the purpose
Location	Where?	Where is it being done? Does it have to be done there?
Time	When?	When is the best time to do it? Does it have to be done then?
People	Who?	Who is doing it? Should someone else do it?
Method	How?	How is it being done? Is this the best method? Is there some other way?
Cost	How much?	How much does it cost now? What will the cost be after improvement?

Table 4.2: 5W2H Issues, Questions and Descriptions

Tip:
When planning interviews, use the 5W2H method to generate your initial list of questions.

The main advantage of the 5W2H technique is that it encourages open questioning. A team member can use the technique with prompts from the rest of the team, for example in a brainstorming session as a way of generating ideas. It can also be very useful if you are having difficulty identifying or understanding what the issue or problem is. It is a good starting point when you are faced with a problem. Finally, if you are using interviews for Requirements Elicitation, you can plan for your interview using 5W2H and even design your interview questions based the general questions described in Table 4.2.

Requirements Workshop

A requirements workshop is a facilitated working session that involves the key stakeholders and is designed to achieve consensus on what the requirements are in a structured way. By using a requirements workshop to focus on requirements, you are ensuring that the key stakeholders are involved at the beginning of a process improvement project. Particularly important are the critical requirements as these are usually the most influential and are vulnerable to project risk and uncertainty. Getting these issues settled early in the requirements workshop will get your project off to a good start.

A requirements workshop is considered one of the most effective ways of eliciting requirements. They are particularly effective in promoting trust and understanding among team members and stakeholders. They are usually short sessions – one to two days is normal. For best results, an experienced facilitator should be appointed as well as a person to document all the proceedings in detail. As a Business Analyst you may carry out one or both of these roles, but you need to be careful to be neutral and to avoid introducing any bias. A requirements workshop can be divided into three parts: planning, conducting, and reviewing the workshop.

In planning a requirements workshop you will need to determine what resources are required for the workshop. First, you will need to determine which stakeholders should participate in the workshop. Make sure that you provide any resources, such as reading material, in advance of the workshop. If necessary, meet with the stakeholders before the workshop to clarify their needs and to ensure that they understand the purpose of the workshop. Be careful here to avoid having a full Requirements Elicitation interview when you do this, otherwise you will cause replication of work, and confusion. Finally, make sure to plan the workshop so that it is formally scheduled and that you have a set agenda to follow. At the end of the planning stage you should have a clear set of objectives for the workshop.

The primary purpose of conducting a workshop is to elicit, analyse, and document the requirements. It is important that you maintain focus on the set objectives of the workshop and that where there are conflicting views that you should get agreement from the stakeholders. The facilitator has a crucial role here in keeping the workshop on track. Use techniques such as questioning, paraphrasing, listening, and brainstorming to help achieve session objectives. The facilitator should remember to engage non-participants and control the group. It may from time to time be necessary to be able to handle difficult participants, mediate conflicts that arise, and force the group to stay on topic. Ensure that all stakeholders have a say in the workshop, for example you should allow participants to evaluate what is working well in an existing process and gain consensus on this. It is important that the right questions are asked – use the 5W2H technique to help you probe deeply into problems. Finally, ensure that your documentation is complete and that it includes any stakeholder concerns discussed in the workshop. Remind the stakeholders that the requirements are as yet unconfirmed and that you may need to re-visit the requirements with them before finally confirming them.

Tip:
To get the workshop going, use ice-breaking activities or warmup activities to help participants get acquainted with each other.

After the requirements workshop is complete, you should review the documentation and act on any action items that arose during the workshop. Your output should be a clear set of documented requirements and stakeholder concerns. It is a good idea to distribute all documentation to the stakeholders as soon as possible after the workshop. This will allow them to check the documentation to ensure that they agree with the requirements listed, and that their concerns (if any) are properly documented.

There are several advantages to using a workshop as a Requirements Elicitation technique. Workshops can provide a wide view of an organisation if there are representatives from all or most departments. Problems are easier to solve if all interested parties are present, this can also promote ownership of results. Workshops can be arranged and conducted in a relatively short period of time. They are more likely to promote cooperation among participants and stakeholders than other Requirements Elicitation techniques. Everyone can have their say in a group setting and hear the point of view of others. If you use brainstorming within the workshop, you will encourage creativity and get the most out of the participants. A requirements workshop can also save money for your organisation, especially if they are used to replace more expensive one-to-one interviews. Problems can be resolved much quicker by reaching a consensus on what the requirements are. Finally, in a requirements workshop feedback is immediate – participants can review and confirm the requirements on the spot.

Requirements workshops also have some disadvantages. If the workshop facilitator is inexperienced or does not have good communication skills, you may not have a successful workshop. They require a lot of commitment from participants, some of whom may be uncomfortable in a group setting. It may be difficult to fit everything that you want to cover into a single workshop, and you are highly dependent on the experience of the facilitator and the expertise of the participants to ensure success. It is also difficult to get the balance right for the number of participants. Too many and the whole process may be too cumbersome or time consuming. Too few and you risk overlooking some important requirements, or getting an unrepresentative viewpoint. Each workshop will be different – hence the importance of the role of the facilitator and the identification of the most appropriate stakeholders to attend.

Surveys/Questionnaires

Surveys (or questionnaires) are a useful Requirements Elicitation technique when you are seeking to acquire a large amount of data from a lot of people that makes a requirements workshop or a series of interviews impractical and too costly. With a survey you can reach hundreds of people, while interviews or workshops are aimed at much smaller numbers. A survey is easy to administer and is a cost-effective and flexible technique for eliciting requirements. You will not be limited to a geographical area, and results can be elicited anonymously in a relatively short period of time. Surveys should be designed carefully to provide reliable, valid, and unbiased data in response to a series of structured and repeatable questions. Many organisations will survey their customers, or potential customers about their expectations of new or existing products and services.

Surveys are used to administer a set of carefully designed questions to a specified target audience. You can use lots of different types of closed questions such as true/false, multiple choice, and numerical questions. You can also ask your target group to rate items, for example on a scale of 1 to 5. The most common type of scale is the Likert scale – when responding to this type of survey question, respondents specify their level of agreement to a statement. The format of a typical five-level Likert scale question is:

1. Strongly disagree

2. Disagree

3. Neither agree nor disagree

4. Agree

5. Strongly agree.

Tip:
Keep your survey short and to the point – five to ten minutes is ideal. Also set a deadline to complete the survey – this is proven to increase response rates.

You may also use open-ended questions in a survey. This type of question allows respondents to openly express a view by responding as they wish, rather than having to select an option from a list. While this type of response can yield valuable information, it is often not practical in very large surveys – these types of question are often limited to just a few or avoided completely as they are more difficult to analyse. While a survey can be used to elicit requirements from a lot of people, they do require a lot more up-front work in preparing and distributing the survey. Preparation is key to a successful survey – the more attention you pay to detail the better.

The first thing to do when designing a survey is to decide what it is that you want to know, and how you will analyse the results – this is done before you develop any survey questions. Next, identify the target group for your survey – these could be customers, employees, or members of the public. Once you have established who your target group is you should determine the best way to distribute the survey and to collect the results. You can make use of a wide variety of survey methods such as on-line surveys, direct mail, email, or telephone. Many organisations will also use independent third-parties to carry out surveys on their behalf – this is especially useful when anonymous surveys are required. The last step before developing the survey questions is to project the desired levels of response. A high response rate is the key to validating survey results resulting in more accurate findings. Low response rates can damage the legitimacy of survey results, because the sample may be unrepresentative of the target group. You may need to indicate a margin of error with your results, see chapter 10 to find out how to determine sample sizes for different levels of confidence.

Now it is time to write the survey questions. Writing questions for any type of survey is not as easy as it may initially look. With careful writing, reviewing, editing, and rewriting you can create a good survey. You need to be able to ask the right questions in the knowledge that you do not have an opportunity to clarify or explain questions within the survey. Here are some important guidelines for writing survey questions that can be applied to any type of survey – including Requirements Elicitation:

- Start the survey by explaining on an introductory page what the objectives of the survey are about with a rough guideline as to how long the survey should typically take – this should help to make the respondents comfortable about taking the survey

- All questions should be focused on the requirements that you are eliciting

- If possible, start out with easy or interesting questions. Some surveys will require demographic information such as sex, age, and educational background – you should start with these

- Use simple language and grammar, and avoid difficult questions – especially those with lots of options

- Write questions in a logical order so that they tell a story. Group questions of a particular format together for easier completion and analysis

- Each question should address one item only

- Avoid double negatives as they can lead to confusion.

Once you have written all the questions, it is strongly recommended that you try out your survey on a small sample group first in order to ensure that there are no ambiguous questions and that the survey makes sense to the respondents. Use a panel of experts to review the draft to ensure that your questions will be effective in eliciting requirements. Conduct a "dry run" to test that the survey is working properly (particularly if an on-line tool is being used), and that the results can easily be analysed. Finally, you will need to distribute the survey, collect all the results, and document the findings.

Surveys can provide several advantages as a technique for eliciting requirements. The biggest advantage is that you can reach a much wider audience than you can with any other technique. Surveys can provide excellent results when used to confirm assumptions and results after a series of interviews. They can also be used as a lead in to interviews or requirements workshops where the outputs of the survey can be discussed and analysed in more detail. Surveys require little scheduling effort or much commitment of time and effort on the part of stakeholders.

There are disadvantages to using surveys as a Requirements Elicitation technique. Often the response level will be low, especially in large surveys – sometimes incentives (which can add to the overall cost) may need to be used to increase the response rate. Creating successful surveys requires trained and experienced developers – for example, use of statistical methods to analyse results requires quite a high level of expertise. The time taken to create a survey can be significant, while analysis time will also increase if you use a lot of open-ended questions.

Exercise – Online Banking Services

ABC Bank is looking to introduce some new on-line services for its business customers. One of the proposed new services will allow business customers to scan cheques and to send an electronic version of the scan over the Internet to their bank branch for processing. Business customers will no longer have to go to their bank branch in person to lodge cheques into their accounts. The new service is intended to speed up transactions, introduce new efficiencies for ABC Bank, and to save time and money for business customers. ABC Bank has up to now not used on-line banking for this type of activity. On-line transactions are limited for business customers, and ABC Bank is aware that its competitors are increasing the number of on-line services for their clients – ABC Bank have recently lost two significant business accounts due to lack of online services.

You have been hired as a Business Analyst to investigate the possibility of ABC Bank introducing the new service that will allow business clients to scan and lodge cheques remotely. This involves eliciting requirements from not just the customers who want more on-line services, but also from several stakeholders within the bank itself. Assume that in this exercise all five of the requirements elicitation techniques described in this chapter are to be used. In your analysis, you and your team should consider the following questions:

- How would you combine effectively the five requirements elicitation techniques in this exercise?

- When setting up a brainstorming session, what type of stakeholder would you invite to participate?

- For the brainstorming session, what would the specific theme be for the session? How would you refine the results of the session into a usable list?

- Who would you recommend as likely candidates for interview?

- How many people would you interview, and what questions would you ask of them?

- When using the 5W2H technique, what specific questions would you ask for each of the five "W" and two "H" questions? Who would you pose these questions to?

- When planning for the Requirements Workshop, what agenda would you draw up? What stakeholders would you invite to the workshop, and what resources do you think you will need?

- Who would your audience be for a survey in this case?

- What types of questions would you ask in the survey and how would you analyse the responses?

When you have completed each of the five techniques above, first compare how each technique has worked and what (if any) requirements were elicited by each technique. Compare the results of each technique and examine how each technique may have yielded a different set of results. Finally, consider how you will document your findings and how you would confirm the elicitation results.

Reflection

At the beginning of this chapter you set out to learn about Requirements Elicitation and the techniques used by the Business Analyst. Requirements Elicitation is one of the most important tasks in the role of the Business Analyst, it is therefore important that you develop the skills necessary to conduct this activity. The key to the successful use of Requirements Elicitation techniques is to ensure that you are well prepared, and that you document and confirm all the requirements that have been elicited from stakeholders.

In your Learning Journal, answer the following reflective questions:

- What have you learned in this chapter?

- In large or small projects that you have been involved in, who were the key stakeholders?

- Look back at both successful and unsuccessful projects in your organisation. What were the reasons that the project succeeded or did not succeed? Did the project deliver exactly what the customer needed?

- Look around your own organisation and see if there are even small improvements that can be made. How would you elicit the requirements to improve these processes?

- What other analysis tools will help you in your efforts to elicit requirements?

Try to think of everyday problems that you might encounter and how you would use Requirements Elicitation techniques to help solve the problem. For example, interview one of your organisation's technical support people to find out what the requirements would be to add a new printer to your office, or survey your fellow employees to find out what type of coffee machine is best suited for the staff canteen. Whenever you see a problem that needs to be fixed, a process that you think can work better, or a new opportunity, make sure that you keep in mind the skills that you have acquired and the techniques you have learned for Requirements Elicitation so that you can approach all problem-solving efforts in a structured and carefully planned way.

5

REQUIREMENTS ANALYSIS

"It isn't that they can't see the solution. It is that they can't see the problem." – G. K. Chesterton

Introduction

Requirements Analysis allows the Business Analyst to examine all the requirements that have been documented during Requirements Elicitation. At the end of the Requirements Elicitation process you will have two major sets of outputs: confirmed requirements, and confirmed stakeholder concerns. These documents should describe the stated requirements from the perspective of the stakeholder and should also confirm that the Business Analyst has a clear understanding of the problem and the stakeholders' needs and concerns.

By now you will have lots of material as a result of Requirements Elicitation. You may have interviews notes, survey results, workshop proceedings, lists of ideas from brainstorming sessions, and answers to a series of 5W2H questions. Even after you summarise and confirm all the requirements you may still have a lot of data and information. Requirements Analysis is a set of tasks and techniques which are used to analyse all the requirements in order to establish potential solutions that will meet stakeholder needs. Requirements Analysis is often referred to as Needs Analysis.

Requirements Analysis Tasks

The Business Analysis Body of Knowledge (BABOK®) outlines the process of Requirements Analysis in six main tasks: prioritise, organise,

specify and model, define assumptions, verify, and validate the requirements. These tasks have a series of inputs and outputs which are summarised in Figure 5.1. The six inputs to the Requirements Elicitation process
(case, need, scope, process assets, management plan, and roles and responsibilities – see Figure 4.3), are also inputs into Requirements Analysis.
These inputs, plus the two outputs from Requirements Elicitation (confirmed requirements, and confirmed stakeholder concerns) make up the
eight inputs into the Requirements Analysis process. At the end of the six
analysis tasks, you will have established the necessary requirements for a
solution that can be presented to the project stakeholders for final approval
before development of the solution can go ahead.

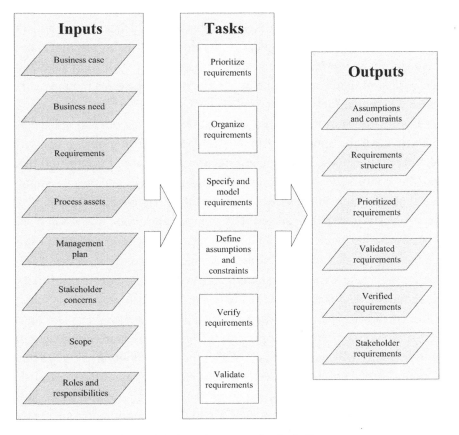

Figure 5.1: Requirements Analysis Process

Source: Adapted from the Business Analysis Body of Knowledge (BABOK®).

Prioritise Requirements

Most Requirements Elicitation efforts will yield several requirements – some of which are more important or urgent than others. One feature of good requirements is that they are prioritised clearly. The first thing the Business Analyst must do is to rank the importance or prioritise the requirements. Unless you are working on a small project, it may not be feasible to implement all the requirements in any proposed solution. In software development you will need to establish which requirements are implemented in version 1, and which ones will be implemented in version 2 or later versions. For any project with limitations of resources, such as time and cost, you must have criteria in place to determine the relative importance of each requirement in order to prioritise them. Prioritisation helps the Business Analyst resolve conflicts that may arise, plan for staged deliveries of products or services, and make any necessary trade-off decisions. If resources are limited and there is a short schedule, you will want to ensure that the product or service features the most critical and essential functions.

Before you start to prioritise the requirements you need to make sure that you have the appropriate inputs in place. From Figure 5.1 you will need five inputs: case, need, management plan, roles and responsibilities, and the confirmed requirements. The business case and need reminds you that the priorities must be aligned with the goals and objectives of the project stated at the outset. The management plan will outline the procedures that you should follow for prioritising requirements, while the list of roles and responsibilities helps you to determine which stakeholders will take part in, or should be consulted, as part of prioritising the requirements. You are now ready to start prioritising.

In small projects, the Business Analyst and the stakeholders can often agree casually on requirement priorities. Bigger projects need a structured approach, this will remove much of the "he who shouts loudest" factor, emotions, office politics, and guessing that can sometimes affect prioritisation. Prioritisation is often based on the value, cost, and risk associated with each requirement, for example – the highest priority requirements are those that provide the best value for the least total cost. Many criteria other than value, cost, and risk can be used to prioritise requirements – the Business Analysis Body of Knowledge (BABOK®) outlines eight criteria that may be used as a basis for prioritising requirements. Table 5.1 shows each of these criteria with a short description.

Criteria	Description
Value	Prioritise based on business value so that the most valuable requirement is targeted for development first. Use a Cost-Benefit Analysis (see Chapter 8) and Value Analysis (see Chapter 7) to help set priorities based on value.
Risk	Prioritise based on the business or technical risks that may lead to project failure.
Difficulty	Prioritise based on ease or difficulty of implementation, i.e. select requirements that are easy to implement rather than ones that are difficult to implement.
Success	Prioritise requirements in order to gain a "quick-win", this helps to get buy-in from stakeholders and users.
Compliance	Prioritise based on legal or regulatory requirements.
Relationships	Some low priority requirements may need to be implemented if they are closely related to more urgent priorities.
Stakeholder	Prioritise based on agreements from the stakeholders as to which requirements are high priority.
Urgency	Prioritise based on time sensitivity.

Table 5.1: Criteria for Prioritising Requirements

Source: Adapted from the Business Analysis Body of Knowledge (BABOK®).

All requirements are important, but prioritising them can be a challenging process as it is often very difficult to get agreement on what are high, medium, or low priorities. You may even have customers who insist that certain requirements are non-negotiable and must be implemented – regardless of priority. A Business Analyst must use structured techniques to set priorities. When prioritising the requirements you will need some stakeholders to be involved. A Subject Matter Expert (SME) may be invited to use the benefit of their experience to help you set priorities. There are two types of SME: a domain SME who can help to assess the business needs/goals and negotiate their importance in relation to requirements, and an implementation SME who can evaluate the complexities of implementing any requirement as part of a potential solution. The project manager is equally important in that priorities need to be fed into the project plan. Finally, the project sponsor should also be invited to take part as they are accountable for the solution to be implemented and they may also make a deciding call where there is disagreement over priorities.

Some of the analysis techniques discussed later in this book, such as Pareto Analysis, Value Analysis, Cost-Benefit Analysis, and the Importance-Performance Matrix, describe in detail how you can identify improvement priorities. Here, you will look briefly at two easy to use techniques that you can use with the criteria for prioritising requirements: MoSCoW Analysis, and Weighted Scoring Model. What ever techniques you use, the output of this process should be a formal list where each requirement is assigned a priority.

MoSCoW Analysis. MoSCoW is a prioritisation technique commonly used by Business Analysts. It will help you and your stakeholders reach a common understanding on the relative importance to be placed on the development of each requirement. You and your team should categorise each requirement according to the MoSCoW method. MoSCoW is explained as follows:

- M: **Must** have this requirement

- S: **Should** have this requirement

- C: **Could** have this requirement

- W: **Won't** have this requirement.

The "Must" requirements should be regarded as non-negotiable, without them the project will fail. It is imperative to get agreement on what these requirements are. The "Should" requirements are those that should be implemented if at all possible. While they are high priority they sometimes can be satisfied in different ways. The "Could" requirements are those that are nice to have, but that should only be included if appropriate resources are available. The "Won't" requirements are those that will not be implemented, though they may be at a later time. Drawing up a list of requirements that won't be implemented can be just as important as drawing up a list of those that must be implemented. Identifying as requirement as a "Won't" demonstrates that while it is important, it can be included in a later version of a product or service.

To see how MoSCoW analysis can be used to set priorities, let's take a look at a simple example concerning five requirements for users to be able to manage their accounts on a web site. Table 5.2 illustrates each of the five requirements with a MoSCoW rating assigned. The results for the MoSCoW analysis in Table 5.2 show that requirements A and C must be implemented, and are therefore of high priority. Requirement B should be implemented if possible, while D is a nice to have requirement that can be implemented assuming resources are available. Finally, requirement E has the lowest priority and may be excluded altogether or included in later versions.

	Requirement	MoSCoW
A	Users can log onto the web site.	Must
B	Users should be able to avail of a "Forgotten Password" utility if they forget their password.	Should
C	Users can change account details.	Must
D	A user can send an email to the system requesting a change to the account page on the web site.	Could
E	When a user clicks on a phone number on the web page a call is made automatically from their desk phone to that number.	Won't

Table 5.2: MoSCoW Analysis for Website Requirements

Weighted Scoring Model. When prioritising requirements it is sometimes useful to be able to rank the requirements according to a predetermined scale. A weighted scoring model is a tool that gives Business Analyst a systematic process for prioritising requirements based on several criteria. Creating a weighted scoring model allows you to first assign a percentage weighting to each criteria, then to assign a numerical value (out of 100) for each requirement, and then to calculate the weighted scores by multiplying the weight for each criteria by its numerical value and adding the resulting values.

A weighted scoring model based on the eight criteria for prioritising requirements, shown above (Table 5.1), can be used for setting priorities. Table 5.3 shows weightings for each of the criteria, scores for each of the five requirements (A to E), and total weighted scores for each of the five requirements. Based on the total weighted scores, requirement B with a score of 60.0 has the highest priority, while requirement D with a score of 38.0 has the lowest priority. The priorities in descending order in this example are B, A, E, C, and D.

		Requirement Score				
Criteria	*Weight*	*A*	*B*	*C*	*D*	*E*
Value	20%	80	45	40	15	35
Risk	20%	60	85	30	20	75
Difficulty	15%	55	80	50	15	25
Success	10%	30	60	55	65	30
Compliance	5%	35	50	60	50	50
Relationships	5%	80	70	50	85	80
Stakeholder	15%	25	50	45	60	60
Urgency	10%	60	25	40	65	80
Weighted Scores	100%	54.8	60.0	43.3	38.0	52.3

Table 5.3: Weighted Scoring Model for Five Requirements

Great care should be taken when assigning weightings to the criteria for assessing each requirement. Prioritisation of requirements can be based on many different criteria – establishing what these criteria are can be the subject of debate within project teams. Further debate can ensue when assigning weightings to each of the criteria, and also when setting a score. Consensus and consistency are vital to ensure best practice when using the weighted scoring model.

Organise Requirements

Now that you have a list of requirements with a priority attached to each one, it is time to start organising the requirements based on their interrelationships and dependencies. Despite assigning a priority to each requirement, you may still have a long list of uncategorised requirements that is awkward to work with – they need to be organised. The main purpose of this activity is to organise the requirements in such a way that you will impose a structure on the requirements that will lead to a user requirements document. This structure must be understood and agreed by all stakeholders – as in prioritising the requirements, the domain SME, the implementation SME, the project manager, and the project sponsor should all be involved in deciding on what structure will be applied to the requirements.

It can be difficult to organise requirements. The Business Analyst and the stakeholders must decide as a group how to organise the requirements and how many levels of abstraction to include, in other words – how detailed it should be. It is often better to focus on getting the top levels of abstraction done well to avoid being distracted by too many levels of detail. The inputs into the organise requirements process from Figure 5.1 in addition to the requirements themselves are; organisational process assets such as existing methodologies, corporate governance standards, and templates for the project deliverables. You will also need the project scope as an input so that you can decide whether requirements are in or out of scope when you set about organising them.

In order to organise requirements effectively, you will need to have a clear set of standards and rules to work with. If none exist in your organisation, you must research and select the most appropriate standard. Keep the language simple and make use of consistent terminology that is easily understood by all involved in the project. Where there are relationships or dependencies between two or more requirements, you must clearly indicate where these exist. What you are looking for is a logical hierarchy with several levels of abstraction for the requirements – for example you could break the requirements down into four main headings: user, content, systems, and owner requirements. Each of these can be broken down into further levels of abstraction – for example, the system requirements could be further broken down into specific technical requirements such as: web server, client desktops, network, security, and bandwidth requirements – each of these in turn can be broken down into more detailed requirements, e.g. client desktops. These breakdowns can be organised into hierarchical diagrams as shown in Figure 5.2.

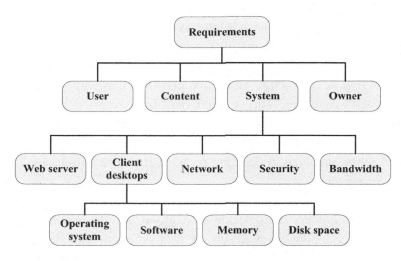

Figure 5.2: System Requirements Breakdown

Several analysis tools described later in this book can be used to organise requirements. Use Cases are an excellent way to both elicit and organise requirements – Chapter 10 describes Use Cases in detail. Other tools such as Flow Charts and SIPOC diagrams (see Chapter 9), and Project Network Diagrams (Chapter 10) will also help you to organise requirements by examining in detail the processes involved. This allows you to organise the requirements around relevant processes and sub-processes from a top-level right down to low-level user activity. Whatever method you choose to organise the requirements you should end up with a structured requirements document that organises the requirements into a logical hierarchy that makes it easy for the Business Analyst and other stakeholders to find each requirement. The list of structured requirements is now ready to be moved to the next stage of the requirements analysis process.

Specify and Model Requirements

Once priorities and structure have been placed on the elicited requirements, the next step is to write the specification for each requirement in a way that conveys the capabilities of the solution in a simple, clear, and concise way. For this step all you need as the input are the structured requirements from the organise requirements step. Any stakeholder involved in the project can be involved in helping to specify the requirements. The output of this process is normally a requirements specification document – Figure 5.3 outlines a sample structure for a typical software requirements specification document.

```
Software Requirements Specification for Project X

1. Background of Proposed System
        1.1    Goals of the Project
        1.2    Document Conventions
        1.3    Audience
        1.4    Stakeholders
        1.5    Scope
        1.6    References/Reading
2. Description of Proposed System
        2.1    Overview of Product
        2.2    Features
        2.3    Environment
        2.4    User types
        2.5    Constraints
        2.6    Dependencies and Assumptions
        2.7    Documentation
3. Features of Proposed System
        3.1    Feature 1
        3.2    Feature 2
        (Continue as needed)
4. Functional Requirements
        4.1    User Interfaces
        4.2    Software Interfaces
        4.3    Hardware Interfaces
        4.4    Communications Interfaces
5. Non-functional Requirements
        5.1    Performance
        5.2    Safety
        5.3    Security
        5.4    Quality
6. Other Requirements
        6.1    Migration to New System
        6.2    Legal requirements
        6.3    Political and Cultural Requirements
        6.4    Maintenance and Support
Appendix A: Glossary Terms
Appendix B: Stakeholder Issues List
Appendix C: Analysis Models Used
```

Figure 5.3: Software Requirements Specifications Document Outline

The simplest way to specify requirements is to use a simple text-based model. In this model you should use simple language and grammar to describe each requirement – remember that whoever reads your document may not have expertise in the area. The document will also need to be easily understood by members of the project team – especially those involved in later stages of the project. Avoid jargon and only use terminology that is both consistent and familiar to stakeholders. Make sure that you describe one requirement at a time and keep complex conditional statements to a minimum. Using simple text descriptions helps you to document the capabilities, conditions, assumptions, and constraints associated with each requirement. Figure 5.4 illustrates a simple text version of some sample requirements for client desktops. For convenience, requirements will often be numbered – this improves both the organisation and traceability of each requirement.

3   Features of Proposed System
3.1   Client Desktop
3.1.1 Operating system
3.1.1.1   Personal computers
Windows Vista Business SP1 (32Bit) with
Media required for all PCs
3.1.1.2   Mac computers
Marketing Department requires Mac
OS X v10.4.11 or later on each computer
3.1.2 Software
3.1.2.1   Browser software
Minimum versions of browser are:
Internet Explorer version 7 or above
Mozilla Firefox version 2 or above
3.1.2.2   Office Applications
Install Microsoft Office 2007 on all desktops
Install Lotus Notes v6 for email
3.1.3 Memory
3.1.3.1   Each computer must have a minimum of
2 GB RAM
3.1.3.2   Each computer must have a minimum of
2 GHz processing speed
3.1.4 Disk space
3.1.4.1   250 GB hard drive is required for each desktop

Figure 5.4: Numbered Requirements for Client Desktops

Several other methods can be used to specify requirements. In software development, Unified Modeling Language (UML) is a standard methodology used to specify, document, and construct the requirements of a system. Flow Charts, Use Cases, and Project Network Diagrams will also be useful in helping you to specify requirements. You may also use measures of performance such as Key Performance Indicators (KPI) – see Chapter 12. At the end of this process, you should have a full set of analysed requirements in the form of a requirements specification document.

Define Assumptions and Constraints

During Requirements Elicitation you will have elicited some concerns from stakeholders in the form of a stakeholder concerns document. Part of Requirements Analysis is to examine these concerns even though they do not make up part of the requirements themselves. These are issues that may affect which potential solutions are viable and which are not. Several assumptions and constraints may have been identified by stakeholders – these may pose an unacceptable risk to the project and will need to be investigated further so that they can be confirmed and addressed. Just as requirements need to be confirmed, assumptions and constraints will also have to be confirmed – the output of this process will be a clear statement of confirmed assumptions and constraints that can be managed and monitored throughout the project. While all stakeholders may be involved, as they are the people who have made assumptions and highlighted constraints, the project manager and the implementation SME have a key role to play. The project manager has overall responsibility for any project risk which may affect the time, scope, and cost of a project. The implementation SME must take into account any assumptions and constraints, which must be confirmed, when designing a solution. Both assumptions and constraints should be documented with dates, times, owners, risks, and requirements affected.

An assumption is something that is taken for granted – for example, in relation to requirements, an assumption may be a factor that is thought to be true, but is not confirmed. For example, in software development assumptions are often made as to how the software will be used and what environment it will operate in. Assumptions must be documented by the Business Analyst who should make every effort to confirm the accuracy and risks associated with each assumption. A constraint in the context of requirements is a factor that limits or restricts some or all of a potential solution. For example, a new business system to be developed can only be used by the employees of an organisation, and not by anyone else. There are two main types of constraints – business, and technical constraints. Business constraints could result in a restriction on a project due to cost or time resource limitations, while technical constraints may result in limitations based on the available software and hardware within the organisation's IT architecture. These must also be documented and confirmed so that the project team will be aware of what they can or cannot consider as part of a potential solution.

Verify Requirements

Requirements verification is a final quality assurance check conducted to ensure that the requirements provide an adequate basis to proceed with the development of the solution. This ensures that you have defined the requirements correctly. The input into this process is the list of all requirements – all stakeholders may once again be involved in verifying the requirements. The Business Analysis Body of Knowledge lists eight characteristics of high quality requirements that you should consider when verifying any requirements. These characteristics are listed in Table 5.4. A checklist is one of the most useful and effective ways to verify requirements from a quality control point of view. At its simplest, a checklist can ensure that you have not omitted anything important from the list of requirements. Checklists are also useful to ensure that there is consistency of standards and approach across all aspects of a project. Table 5.5 shows a list of checklist items for the "Unambiguous" characteristic of requirements quality – similar checklist items can be drawn up to check for the other seven characteristics described in Table 5.4.

Any requirements that do not meet quality standards can be considered to be inadequate and must therefore be revised. Many organisations will have their own standards for verifying requirements. However, the most important consideration at this stage is that after the prioritisation, organisation, specification, and verification of all requirements, an appropriate high standard has been reached so that the requirements are stated in a form that can now be used effectively to guide further development on a project.

Characteristic	Description
Cohesive	Ensures that overall business goals and objectives are met.
Complete	Ensures that all requirements are documented in full and that no functions required by the customer are missing.
Consistent	Ensures that there are no conflicts in the requirements
Correct	Ensures that all requirements are correct and that no defects exist.
Feasible	Ensures that the requirements can be implemented given available budget and technology.
Modifiable	Ensures that when requirements are organised into a logical hierarchy that they are grouped together to more easily allow modifications.
Unambiguous	Ensures that every requirement has only one interpretation.
Testable	Ensures that there is a way to test that a requirement has been fulfilled.

Table 5.4: Characteristics of Requirements Quality

Source: Adapted from the Business Analysis Body of Knowledge (BABOK®).

Criteria		Yes/No/ Not Applicable
Unambiguous	Are all the requirements specified understandable enough so that they can be passed over to the implementation group?	
	Are requirements specified in such a way to avoid the likelihood of more than one valid interpretation?	
	Are the functional and non-functional requirement separated from each others?	
	Are there any requirements that conflict with other requirements?	
	Is the language used easy for all to understand?	
	Are there any ambiguous terms such as "user-friendly", "easy-to-use", "fast", and "flexible" being used?	

Table 5.5: Checklist Criteria for Quality Unambiguous Requirements

Validate Requirements

The final task in Requirements Analysis is to validate the requirements. Up to now the Business Analyst has elicited, prioritised, organised, specified, and verified the requirements. In this final step you need to validate all the requirements to ensure that they meet three key criteria:

1. The requirements must support the delivery of value to the organisation

2. The requirements fulfil the goals and objectives of the organisation

3. Each requirement meets a stakeholder need.

Many requirements may have been elicited that do not meet some or all of the above criteria. It is also possible that some of the requirements may conflict with each other, or that customers and stakeholders have different expectations from each requirement. Validation is therefore crucial to the success of any Requirements Analysis process. This is necessary so that you can identify and correct problems before precious resources are committed to implement the requirements. To validate the requirements you will need three inputs from Figure 5.1: business case, scope, and the requirements (verified). The business case is essential in that it will tell you what the overall business goals, objectives, and measurements that the product or service is expected to produce. Scope gives you a clear indication of what should be in the solution. To be valid, a requirement must contribute to the business case and be within scope for the project. All stakeholders may be involved in the requirements validation process.

There are several key activities involved in requirements validation. The first is to identify and validate any assumptions. Several of the requirements may not yet have a clear understanding of how the solution will work – these may need to be identified in order to minimise any risk associated with the project. If possible, create a prototype of some of the proposed solution's components to validate requirements. This can demonstrate assumptions and understandings which will show up any conflicts between written requirements and the interpretation of these requirements developed in the prototype. A prototype is also used to get agreement with the users about what the proposed system should do.

Next, conduct reviews to reaffirm that requirements meet the characteristics of requirements quality outlined in Table 5.4. Your review should include end-user and customer representatives, in addition to the project stakeholders. Use requirements verification checklists to help you in this review process. You will also need to know how the benefits resulting from each requirement will be evaluated. Metrics such as Key Performance Indicators (KPIs, see Chapter 12) which measure criteria such as time, cost, quality/scope, resources, efficiency, and reliability are used to select appropriate performance measures for a solution.

Upon completion of requirements validation, you will now have a full set of validated requirements that meet all the criteria, standards, and models that you have set throughout Requirements Analysis. These are the requirements that will generate value for stakeholders which are aligned with the overall business goals and objectives.

At this stage, much of the work of the Business Analyst is done as the requirements are often passed to the Project Manager and the development team who will implement the solution. Sometimes Business Analysts will be involved in assessing and choosing the most appropriate solution, though often this task will be conducted by experts in the domain in which a solution will operate. Even when work to elicit and analyse the requirements has been completed, the Business Analyst may still be involved in a project in the event of a requirement needing further clarification, or there is a change in business need, or a change in scope is requested.

Exercise – Online Course Delivery

ABC Publishing Ltd is a successful book and magazine publishing business that is looking to expand its capabilities into other publishing media such as radio, television, and on-line. As part of this expansion process, management at ABC Publishing have proposed a training programme to improve basic computing skills in word-processing, spreadsheets, presentation software, databases, email, and Internet usage, for all employees of the organisation. Assume that you have issued a Computer Skills survey to all employees to elicit training requirements, and that you have collated responses from 100 employees within the organisation. The 10 survey questions and responses are listed in Figure 5.5. For the purposes of this exercise there are no other requirements elicited using any other technique.

Use the data provided in the survey results to analyse the training requirements for ABC Publishing. Decide for yourself what level of expertise that this organisation should have for each of the six applications listed in the survey – for example, you may want all employees to be at a minimum of Advanced level for Word, Outlook, and Internet Explorer, and at a minimum level of Intermediate for PowerPoint, Access and Excel. For your analysis you should consider the following details:

- In addition to the requirements elicited by the survey, what other inputs would you require in order to carry out the tasks in the Requirements Analysis process?

- What methods would you use to complete the six tasks that make up the Requirements Analysis process?

- Who are the key stakeholders that you will need to consult during this process?

- Critique the survey itself – can you identify strengths and weaknesses in this survey as a method of eliciting requirements?

- What measures of performance do you suggest should be used to evaluate the requirements?

- For more detailed Requirements Analysis, what other techniques would you recommend could have been used to elicit requirements?

- What assumptions and constraints do you envisage in this project?

- What would your main recommendations be as a result of your Requirements Analysis of training needs in ABC Publishing?

Question 1: What is your role within ABC Publishing?	Response %	Response Count
Executive/Manager	5%	5
Project Manager	6%	6
Team Leader	13%	13
Systems Analyst	2%	2
Business Analyst	1%	1
Web Developer	35%	35
Graphics Designer	25%	25
Administrator	10%	10
Other	3%	3
	Answered question	100

Question 2: Which of the following qualifications do you have?	Response %	Response Count
European Computer Driving License (ECDL)	11.0%	9
One or more ECDL modules	12.2%	10
ECDL Advanced	2.4%	2
Microsoft Office Specialist (MOS)	0.0%	0
Certificate in a Computing discipline	13.4%	11
Diploma in a Computing discipline	14.6%	12
Degree in a Computing discipline	24.4%	20
Other	22.0%	18
	Answered question	82
	Skipped question	18

Question 3: *What standard do you consider your-self to be for each of the following:*	Beginner	Intermediate	Advanced	Expert	Guru	Count
Microsoft Word	4.0% (4)	47.0% (47)	42.0% (42)	5.0% (5)	2.0% (2)	100
Microsoft PowerPoint	22.4% (22)	49.0% (48)	25.5% (25)	3.1% (3)	0.0% (0)	98
Microsoft Access	50.0% (46)	32.6% (30)	15.2% (14)	1.1% (1)	1.1% (1)	92
Microsoft Excel	12.5% (12)	53.1% (51)	28.1% (27)	6.3% (6)	0.0% (0)	96
Microsoft Outlook	18.4% (18)	44.9% (44)	29.6% (29)	6.1% (6)	1.0% (1)	98
Microsoft Internet Explorer	11.1% (11)	35.4% (35)	42.4% (42)	6.1% (6)	5.1% (5)	99
					Answered question	100

Question 4: *How many years' experience do you have in each of the following:*	None	Less than One	One to two	Three to four	More than four	Response Count
Microsoft Word	0.0% (0)	3.0% (3)	1.0% (1)	15.0% (15)	81.0% (81)	100
Microsoft PowerPoint	12.0% (12)	13.0% (13)	17.0% (17)	11.0% (11)	47.0% (47)	100
Microsoft Access	31.6% (31)	28.6% (28)	11.2% (11)	5.1% (5)	23.5% (23)	98
Microsoft Excel	4.0% (4)	6.0% (6)	15.0% (15)	8.0% (8)	67.0% (67)	100
Microsoft Outlook	14.1% (14)	10.1% (10)	12.1% (12)	12.1% (12)	51.5% (51)	99
Microsoft Internet Explorer	0.0% (0)	7.0% (7)	8.0% (8)	14.0% (14)	7% (71)	100
					Answered question	100

Question 5: *How often do you use each of the following:*	All the time	Often	Sometimes	Hardly ever	Never	Count
Microsoft Word	77.8% (77)	16.2% (16)	6.1% (6)	0.0% (0)	0.0% (0)	99
Microsoft PowerPoint	10.1% (10)	17.2% (17)	38.4% (38)	23.2% (23)	11.1% (11)	99
Microsoft Excel	46.5% (46)	26.3% (26)	20.2% (20)	3.0% (3)	4.0% (4)	99
Microsoft Access	9.3% (9)	7.2% (7)	14.4% (14)	34.0% (33)	35.1% (34)	97
Microsoft Outlook	53.1% (52)	11.2% (11)	7.1% (7)	10.2% (10)	18.4% (18)	98
Microsoft Internet Explorer	66.3% (65)	20.4% (20)	9.2% (9)	2.0% (2)	2.0% (2)	98
					Answered question	99

Question 6: *The HR Dept has secured courses in Microsoft Office applications. What type of training do you require:*	Beginner	Intermediate	Advanced	I don't need training in this application	Count
Microsoft Word	1.1% (1)	9.5% (9)	51.6% (49)	37.9% (36)	95
Microsoft PowerPoint	14.9% (14)	21.3% (20)	42.6% (40)	21.3% (20)	94
Microsoft Access	36.8% (35)	22.1% (21)	25.3% (24)	15.8% (15)	95
Microsoft Excel	6.3% (6)	17.7% (17)	59.4% (57)	16.7% (16)	96
Microsoft Outlook	13.4% (13)	12.4% (12)	34.0% (33)	40.2% (39)	97
Microsoft Internet Explorer	4.1% (4)	14.4% (14)	36.1% (35)	45.4% (44)	97
				Answered question	99

Question 7: *Please select from the following list typical tasks that you perform in your job (tick all that apply):*	Response %	Response Count
Writing reports	90%	90
Writing letters	47%	47
Statistical analysis	50%	50
Collecting data	75%	75
Desktop publishing	7%	7
Making presentations	55%	55
Keeping records	70%	70
Sending and receiving emails	97%	97
Looking up information on the Internet	81%	81
Backing up data	33%	33
Creating web pages	49%	49
Other	18%	18
	Answered question	100

Question 8: *Please select your preferred method of training:*	Response %	Response Count
e-Learning only	8.0%	9
Classroom only	15.2%	15
Blend of e-Learning and Classroom	76.8%	76
	Answered question	100

Question 9: *Indicate what time frame you would like to have training take place for each of the following:*	Urgent	Within four weeks	Within three months	Anytime - I'm flexible	Response Count
Microsoft Word	0.0% (0)	14.7% (11)	26.7% (20)	58.7% (44)	75
Microsoft PowerPoint	1.3% (1)	13.8% (11)	28.8% (23)	56.3% (45)	80
Microsoft Excel	10.3% (9)	16.1% (14)	29.9% (26)	44.8% (39)	87
Microsoft Access	1.2% (1)	14.5% (12)	26.5% (22)	59.0% (49)	83
Microsoft Outlook	1.3% (1)	13.3% (10)	25.3% (19)	60.0% (45)	75
Microsoft Internet Explorer	2.7% (2)	8.0% (6)	24.0% (18)	65.3% (49)	75
				Answered Question	100

Question 10: *Please list any others areas of training that you would like to participate in.*	
Human Resource Management/ Statistical Analysis	Multimedia
Advanced PL/SQL	HTML
Presentation Skills i.e. preparing and giving a presentation.	Training in web design and project management
Oracle, Websphere, Javascript	Graphics packages
Microsoft Project	Statistics packages such as SPSS
UML	Flash
Microsoft Visio	Programming
Advanced database usage	Mobile technologies

Figure 5.5: Responses for Computer Skills Survey

Reflection

At the beginning of this chapter you set out to learn about Requirements Analysis and the tasks used by the Business Analyst. You should always ensure that analysing the detailed requirements that have been elicited should be carried out in a careful sequence of six tasks: prioritise, organise, specify and model, define assumptions, verify, and validate the requirements. The key to the successful execution of Requirements Analysis tasks is to ensure that you are well prepared, and that you adhere to the sequence of tasks that lead ultimately to requirements that have been validated carefully.

In your Learning Journal, answer the following reflective questions:

What have you learned in this chapter?

- How would you apply Requirements Analysis tasks in your own working environment?

- What projects (if any) have you been involved in where the results of interviews, surveys, brain-storming or workshops have been analysed?

- If possible, ask to see old requirements documentation in your organisation – what can you learn from this documentation?

- Within your organisation try to identify any Requirements Elicitation initiative, such as a survey, which was not followed up or acted upon. What were the reasons for this?

- What other analysis tools will help you in your efforts to analyse requirements?

It is likely that as a Business Analyst you will rely on familiar and trusted techniques to analyse requirements. You should practice and cultivate these techniques so that you become an expert at using them in a variety of situations. It may also be a good idea to examine how others both elicit and analyse requirements – getting tips and best practices from expert practitioners is an excellent way to improve your own skills. You should also keep in mind that there are several techniques not discussed in this book for eliciting requirements and that you may find yourself in a position of analysing requirements elicited through unfamiliar techniques. Therefore, you should look to expand your range of knowledge and skills about using as many techniques as possible so that you can be prepared to analyse any type of requirement.

6

ANALYSIS TOOLS FOR PROBLEM IDENTIFICATION

"It's so much easier to suggest solutions when you don't know too much about the problem." – Malcolm Forbes

Introduction

As a Business Analyst, you will need to have strong problem solving skills. These skills give you a good starting point for any type of problem solving, where other people might just feel helpless and intimidated by the situation. Being able to identify problems is not an easy skill to acquire, in this book you will learn about many analysis tools that will help you to analyse problems from many different viewpoints. Sometimes you will encounter problems and you may have little or no understanding of what is causing the problem. In this case you will have to try to identify what all the possible causes of the problem are. Once you understand what is causing the problem, you will be in a much better position to recommend solutions. A clearly defined list of problems is the most suitable basis for identifying potential solutions.

In this chapter we will take a look at two analysis tools that will help Business Analysts to establish the causes of a problem. The first, Cause and Effect diagrams, is used to establish all the possible root causes of a problem. The second, Check Sheets, is designed to record and quantify facts and data over a period of time.

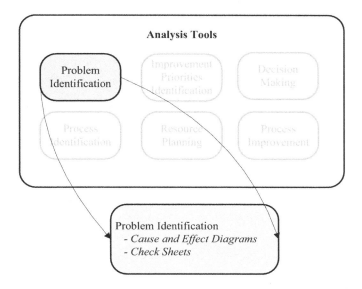

Cause and Effect Diagrams

A Cause and Effect Diagram is a structured tool that will help you to think through causes of a problem (the effect) thoroughly. Their major benefit is that they force you to consider all possible causes of the problem, rather than just the ones that are most obvious. They are also known as Fishbone Diagrams or Ishikawa Diagrams. Cause and Effect Diagrams were first developed by Kaoru Ishikawa in 1943 where he used it to explain to a group of engineers at the Kawasaki Steel Works how various factors could be related and sorted. The purpose of the diagram is to relate causes and effects. It is simple to use and an effective tool for problem identification.

The Cause and Effect diagram typically displays major categories such as people, methods, materials, equipment, measurement and environment that cause an effect, often perceived as a problem.

When to Use a Cause and Effect Diagram

Cause and Effect diagrams can be used to help identify the root causes of almost any problem. Drawing a Cause and Effect diagram can be learned easily by people at any level of an organization as they are straightforward to use. While you can draw the diagram as an individual, it is much more effective to do so in small teams of people. Cause and Effect diagrams are very useful in helping teams reach a shared understanding of a complicated problem. They will enhance your team's judgement and will force the team to consider all potential causes, no matter how trivial.

Cause and Effect diagrams are helpful when you need to define the major categories or sources of root causes. In a graphical format they can help you and your team to organize and analyze relationships between the causes of a problem. Ultimately, the team can identify factors that could improve a process or resolve the problem.

How to Draw a Cause and Effect Diagram

A Cause and Effect diagram is relatively easy to construct. But first, you have to identify what the problem is that you are considering – you and your team must agree on this. If you identify two or more problems, use a separate diagram for each problem. Once agreed, write the problem statement in a box on a large sheet of paper or whiteboard. This problem statement is the Effect. Next, draw an arrow pointing to this box from the left hand side of the diagram. You now need to identify the main causes of the effect – usually about four to six main categories is sufficient. You and your team should agree what these categories are, as they will not be the same for every diagram. Be careful not to overload the categories, you can always add another one if you need more detail. Draw and label the categories as arrows pointing to the main arrow – your diagram will now start to resemble a fish bone skeleton.

Once you have drawn the main categories, you and your team should then use an analysis method such as brainstorming or 5W2H to list all the possible causes of problems in each of the main categories already identified. These should be added as second level causes and drawn as new arrows pointing to the main category arrows. It is not unusual to find that a possible problem could be causing an effect in more than one area – be sure to note this and discuss any relationship with your team. Keep identifying second and third level causes by asking "Why" a problem is occurring, until you have identified all the possible root causes of the problem. As your diagram fills up, it is important to discuss each item with your team in order to clarify and combine causes where appropriate.

Tip:
Take care to identify causes rather than symptoms.

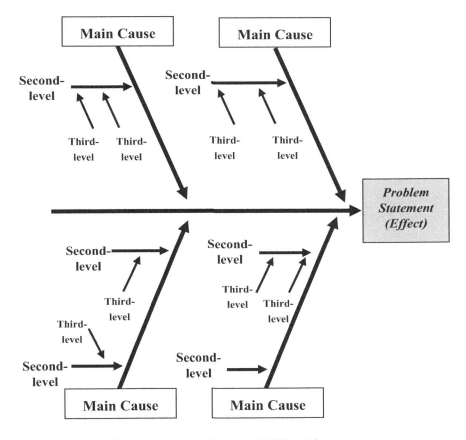

Figure 6.1: Basic Cause and Effect Diagram

Figure 6.1 shows an outline of what a basic Cause and Effect diagram should look like. Each of the main causes has a direct relationship with the Effect. Each of the second-level causes has a direct relationship with a main cause, while the third-level causes are related to the second-level causes. There is no limit to how many arrows you can draw to represent causes at any level, or to how many levels you can go to. However, you will get to a point where the diagram will become very cluttered and possibly confusing. When you are finished, you should have a diagram that identifies all possible root causes of the effect stated at the beginning of the exercise. You can now investigate each of the causes to determine if in fact they are causing or contributing to the effect. This may involve setting up an investigation, and interviewing or carrying out surveys.

Cause and Effect Diagram Example – Technical Support

In the following example you will see how a Cause and Effect diagram can be used to identify the root causes of problems at an e-Learning company. The company records all customer complaints with its e-Learning courses through a Technical Support Department. Recently, there has been a significant increase in the number of calls being logged on the Technical Support database. There is no direct evidence as to why this is happening as there are several possible causes to the problem (effect) of an increased number of complaints. The first thing to do in drawing a Cause and Effect diagram for this situation is to identify what the effect is. In this case it is relatively simple – the problem is "Increase in customer complaints". Next, identify the main categories for the diagram – the ones chosen here are: Content, Technical, Platform, Grammar, and Tests. This will give us a simple Cause and Effect diagram for the first level as shown in Figure 6.2.

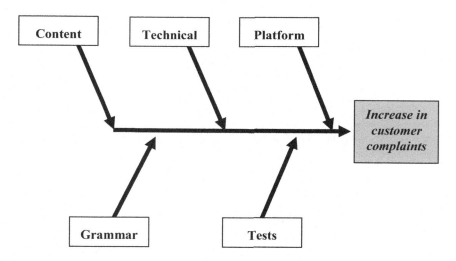

Figure 6.2: Cause and Effect Diagram – Level 1

Under each of the five main causes above, possible second and third-level causes of problems in each area are brainstormed and added to the diagram. Let's take a look in more detail at the first main cause "Content". The Technical Support Team now lists every possible cause of customer complaints related to content, for example – Content Error,

Audio, Level of Difficulty, Out-of-date. These second-level causes are now added as arrows pointing to the "Content" cause. Each in turn is now discussed for what might be causing these problems. Complaints relating to "Graphics" are listed as "Missing", "Out of sync with text", and "Corrupt files". These third-level causes are now added to the diagram. Other second-level causes, such as content being "Out-of-date" are similarly broken down into third-level causes – in this case, the course could be "Too old" or simply not being "Updated". The remainder of the "Content" main cause is then completed. Once this is done, the other main causes are worked though by the team. Figure 6.3 shows a completed diagram representing all the possible root causes of the effect of an increase in customer complaints.

Many of the causes listed in Figure 6.3 could be broken down with further analysis. Additional second and third level causes could also be added. Building a diagram like this can help you and your team in several ways. First, your teamwork will improve and your users will be educated in a simple problem solving technique. Secondly, the diagram will guide debate and discussion on the root causes of problems, and will help show a clearer picture of a problem before resolution. Cause and Effect diagrams can be fun to use and can be a valuable tool for Business Analysts that can be used for almost any problem they will encounter.

What Do You Do Next?

Once you and your team have completed the Cause and Effect Diagram, discussed and clarified all issues, and exhausted all possible root causes, you are now in a position to verify how many of the possible root causes are in fact causes of problems that are contributing to the effect. You can do this through several ways. For example, in the e-Learning Cause and Effect diagram (Figure 6.3) you could investigate if there has been an increase in any of the individual causes identified. The overall increase in customer complaints could, for example, be due to a sudden rise in wrong scores being recorded in tests. You may then investigate further as to why this is happening.

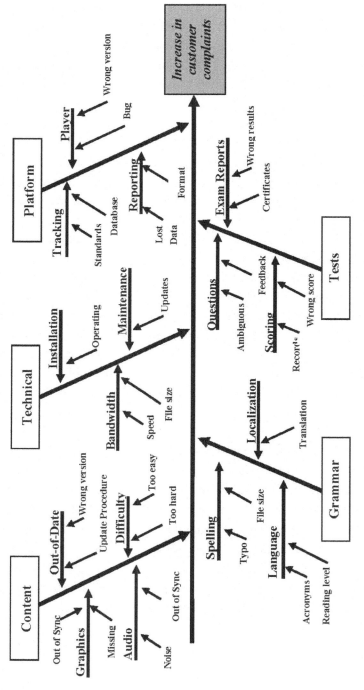

Figure 6.3: Cause and Effect Diagram for Increase in Customer Complaints

Gather data about the relative frequencies of each root cause – Check Sheets are a useful tool to help you here. You may also use Pareto Analysis on your results to identify the most important issues to be addressed as part of your process improvement. Whatever you do next, you will be in a much better position once you have identified possible problems.

Exercise – Long Queues at the Post Office

The Post Office is experiencing long delays in dealing with customers between the hours of 5.00 pm and 6.00 pm. Queues are much longer on average during this time than at any other time of the day. Prepare a Cause and Effect diagram to establish all the possible root causes of this problem. This exercise will be most effective if carried out by a team – most people will be familiar with queues in the Post Office and should be able to contribute to the analysis.

During this exercise, you and your team should discuss the following:

- What is the problem statement (Effect) in this exercise?

- What are the four to six main categories of causes to use here?

- What method(s) will you use to generate possible root causes?

- To what level of detail should you go to?

- Are there any causes duplicated in more than one category? If so, how will you deal with them?

- How would you go about verifying the root causes that you have identified?

- What other analysis tools would you use in conjunction with a Cause and Effect diagram to give you a clearer picture of the problem?

Check Sheets

A Check Sheet is a simple analysis tool that can be used to collect almost any type of data. A well designed Check Sheet is an excellent starting point for problem identification where raw data can be used as meaningful information. They are used to record and quantify data over time in a uniform manner – this can be historical data or observations as they occur. Trends and patterns can be observed and analysed to help in the problem solving process. They are useful if you want to collect data on items such as the location of defects, frequency of defects, and frequency of activities and events.

The simplest type of Check Sheet uses tallies (most commonly written as groups of five lines) to total occurrences under clearly defined categories. Tallies have been used since ancient times when Stone Age man first used pebbles, hash marks on bones and on walls, even their fingers, to count. Check Sheets are easy to design and use, and is an effective tool for Business Analysts to help identify problems.

When to Use a Check Sheet

Check Sheets are most useful when you want to gather data about a problem over a period of time. Quite often you will be aware that problems exist, but you may be unsure as to what problems are occurring, when they are occurring, and how frequently they are occurring. While you can use Check Sheets to analyse historical data, they are more commonly used to record observations over a short period of time. Once you establish a list of events or conditions, you can use the Check Sheet to count occurrences, measure activities, and locate defects or problems.

Tip:
Cause and Effect diagrams can be used as Check Sheets. You can tick or mark an arrow to indicate when a root cause of a problem occurs.

Check Sheets can be used by an individual as well as in teams – much will depend on how much data you will need for an effective analysis. Consider using a team of people if a lot of data are to be gathered. Your aim here is to create a clearer picture of factual problems, not just the obvious or most common ones. You should aim to answer the following questions:

- What event is occurring?

- Who is responsible the event?

- When and where does the event occur?

- How often does the event occur?

- How long does it take?

By asking these questions you will establish a set of criteria that will help you to confirm that the data collected will help you to address the problems under investigation.

How to Create a Check Sheet

As with many of the analysis tools described in this book, one of the first things you must do is to define clearly what it is that you are analyzing. If you are working in a team, get a agreement on the descriptions of the activities, conditions, and events that you are measuring. Next, design the Check Sheet – it is important that the sheet is designed in such a way as to make data capture quick and easy. There are two main types of Check Sheet that you can use. The simplest form is the Tally Check Sheet, while a Defect Map Check Sheet is a graphical version of this tool. Both are described here.

Tally Check Sheet. In this type of check sheet you will simply count occurrences of an event or activity. In one column, list events that are likely to occur. In the second column, show some space to count – typically so called five-barred-gates. Finally, a third column is used to write a numerical total. Figure 6.4 shows a simple Tally Check that can be used to count events.

	Count	Score
Event A	ǁ̶H̶ ǁ̶H̶ ǁ̶H̶ ‖	17
Event B	ǁ̶H̶ ǁ̶H̶ ǁ̶H̶ ǁ̶H̶ ‖‖	23
Event C	ǁ̶H̶ ‖‖	8
Total		**48**

Figure 6.4: Simple Tally Check Sheet

Defect Map Check Sheet. In this type of check sheet a diagram is drawn so that the location of defects or errors can be mapped and recorded. A diagram makes it easier to identify a problem area that may otherwise be difficult to illustrate. It is usually used in combination with a tally Check Sheet. For example, Figure 6.5 shows a simple diagram of a photocopier that you could use to record the location of where paper gets jammed. Figure 6.5 also shows the number of occurrences in a Tally Check Sheet.

These types of Check Sheets provide a good summary of the problems encountered and can now be used to further analyse a problem. It can help you identify what potential problem should be addressed first, and can also be useful in confirming existing knowledge about a problem.

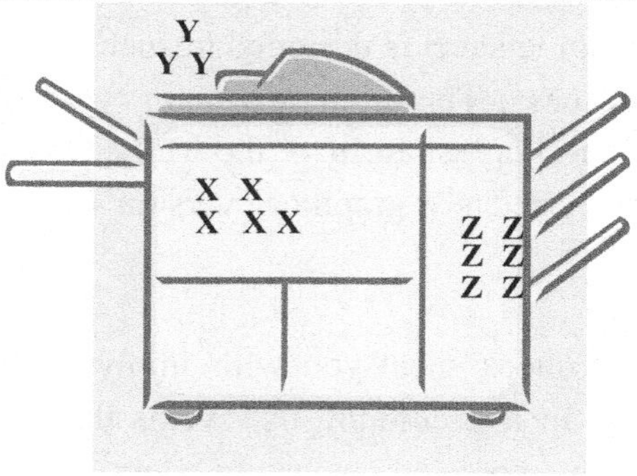

	Count	Score
Defect X	⊪⊪	5
Defect Y	⊪⊪	3
Defect Z	⊪⊪⊪	6
Total		14

Figure 6.5: Defect Map and Tally Check Sheet for a Photocopier

Check Sheet Example – Mortgage Application Form

A mortgage company uses a standard application form for people wishing to take out a mortgage. The form requires the applicant to fill in some personal details as well as financial details about the property being purchased. Experience has shown that a high level of rejection occurs because the forms have not been completed correctly. Rejected applications due to incorrect form filling causes unnecessary delays and anxiety for clients. Typical errors that occur are:

- Some fields being left blank

- Incorrect format for some items, e.g. date fields

- No signature given

- More than one item ticked

- Fields being mixed up, e.g. first name and surname.

While some people are not good at filling out forms, very often the reason why forms are not filled out correctly is that they are not well designed, or instructions are not clear. Figure 6.6 shows a simplified mortgage application form. A Tally Check Sheet can be used to record error types as they occur. The period of time over which this study will take place is two weeks (ten working days). For each day, a tally mark is recorded for each error, at the end of the two week period a clearer picture of what are the most common errors will result. Designing a Check Sheet for this study is straight-forward. A simple list of each of the form's fields provides an adequate list of possible errors. Figure 6.7 shows a Check Sheet design suitable of gathering information on errors that occur in form filling. You could also print the application form and use it as a Defect Map Checksheet.

What Do You Do Next?

Once you have gathered all the data over the period under investigation, you should now have more information to help you decide what to do next. In the Mortgage Application form example, you can see from Figure 6.7 that some features have higher scores than others. You'll need now to investigate why this is happening. For example, the highest score for any field is 84 errors occurring in the Date of Birth field over the two week period. A redesigned field for easier use, with clear instructions may help to reduce errors in this area. You'll also note from Figure 6.7 that there is a higher rate of errors on Fridays. This could be because applicants are rushing to get an application in before the end of the week, or that there are not enough staff available to check through application forms before submission.

Personal Information

Title (tick one)   Dr ☐   Mr ☐   Mrs ☐   Ms ☐   Miss ☐

First name   [   ]

Surname   [   ]

E-mail   [   ]

Preferred Contact No. [   ]

DoB (dd/mm/yy)   [   ]

Address   [   ]

Employment Status   [   ]

Annual salary   [   ]

Mortgage Details

Customer Type   First Time Buyer   ☐
(tick one)   Moving Your Mortgage   ☐
                    Buying a Bigger House   ☐
                    Topping up   ☐

Property Value   [   ]

Loan Amount   [   ]

Mortgage Term   10 ☐   15 ☐   20 ☐   25 ☐   30 ☐

Signature   [   ]

Figure 6.6: Mortgage Application Form

Error	Score Week 1					Score Week 2					Total
	M	T	W	T	F	M	T	W	T	F	
Title											20
First name											26
Surname											53
E-mail											74
Contact Number											64
Date of Birth											84
Address											27
Employment Status											19
Annual salary											29
Customer Type											57
Property Value											29
Loan Amount											34
Mortgage Term											33
Signature											65
Total	48	57	51	52	97	45	65	51	52	96	614

Figure 6.7: Tally Check Sheet for Mortgage Application Form Errors

A Check Sheet can be a really powerful tool if you use it in conjunction with other tools such as a Pareto Chart. With lots of data gathered, you will need some form of further analysis to help you prioritize improvement opportunities. It is also a good idea to keep the Check Sheets and use scanning software to upload Tally and Defect Map sheets to a central location for future reference. Remember also that your analysis is only as good as the data you have gathered – a Check Sheet may not reveal a particular source of a problem. In this case you may need to revisit the design of your Check Sheet, or gather data over a longer period.

Exercise – Car Assembly Paint Shop

A car assembly factory paint shop has rigorous procedures for checking the quality of paint work on the body, doors, boot, and bonnet of the cars. In particular, if there are any scratches, bubbles, scuff marks, paint runs, uneven paint, or unpainted sections, the paint work is rejected and the parts must be repainted. Your job here is to design both Tally and Defect Map Check Sheets to record occurrences of any of these faults. Your Check Sheets should record these data on a daily basis for a period of four weeks, and should also record the number of parts checked.

Reflection

At the beginning of this chapter you set out to improve your problem identifications skills. Cause and Effect Diagrams and Check Sheets are two simple tools that you can use to develop these skills. The key to successful use of these tools is to ensure that they are well designed and easy to use. While these tools may not reveal any surprises, it is important to remember that how often what is very obvious to you is less than clear to other people – hence they are very effective tools for teams.

In your Learning Journal, answer the following reflective questions:

- What have you learned in this chapter?

- Can you identify situations in your organization where a Cause and Effect diagram could be used?

- Are there opportunities for you to gather data on a problem using Check Sheets?

- What other analysis tools will help you to identify problems?

- What are your next steps after identifying problems using these tools?

Try to think of everyday problems that you might encounter and how you would use these tools to help identify the problem. For example, draw a Cause and Effect diagram to try to find the root cause of why your car doesn't start in the morning. Design a Check Sheet to gather data on the different types of deliveries to reception at your place of work. It is a good idea to keep practicing using these tools to enhance your problem identification skills.

7

ANALYSIS TOOLS FOR IDENTIFYING IMPROVEMENT PRIORITIES

"It's all knowing what to start with. If you start in the right place and follow all the steps, you will get to the right end."
– Elizabeth Moon

Introduction

Knowing where to start is obviously a key point in problem-solving. Sometimes it is easy to identify what the problem is – for example, if you can't go anywhere because your car has a puncture in one wheel, you will know exactly what needs to be done in order to solve the problem. On the other hand, if your car won't start the problem could be caused by a myriad of possibilities – no petrol, electrical fault, broken ignition, and so on. In business, as a Business Analyst you will be faced with many problems – some easy to identify, but many will not be so easy to figure out. If there are several problems to be addressed, the chances are that you will not be able to resolve them all in one step. You will want to know what the most important issues to tackle first are – in other words, you will have to be able to identify improvement priorities.

In this chapter we will take a look at two simple tools that will help Business Analysts to look at the causes of problems in a different way. The first, Pareto Analysis, will help you to identify the critical few from the trivial many causes of a problem. The second, Value Analysis, will help you to identify needed improvements in a product or process based on functionality and value for each function.

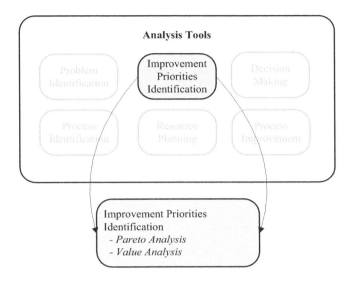

Pareto Analysis

Pareto Analysis is based on the Pareto Principle which states that, for many events 80 per cent of the effects come from 20 per cent of the causes. The Principle is named after Vilfredo Pareto, who was a lecturer in economics at the University of Lausanne in Switzerland. In 1906, in a study of income and wealth, he made the observation that twenty percent of the population owned eighty per cent of the property in Italy. In further studies, he found that this 80:20 principle also applied in surveys of income and wealth in other countries.

The Pareto Principle is best used in business as a "rule of thumb". It is often referred to by different names: Pareto chart, Pareto Law, ABC analysis, the 80–20 rule, and the law of the vital few. The Principle is not an exact rule in that variations such as the 90/10, 70/30, and 95/5 rules can also be applied. The main benefit of the Pareto Principle is to be able to determine the critical few from the trivial many causes of a problem. This tool can be used in a variety of ways by the Business Analyst.

Putting the Pareto Principle into business practice, you can apply Pareto Analysis to almost anything, from the science of management to the physical world:

- 20 per cent of your inventory takes up 80 per cent of your warehouse space

- 80 per cent of your inventory comes from 20 per cent of your suppliers

- 80 per cent of a company's income is generated by 20 per cent of its customers

- 80 per cent of a company's business will be generated by 20 per cent of the sales team.

The value of the Pareto Principle for a Business Analyst is that it reminds you to focus on the 20 per cent that matters.

When to Use Pareto Analysis

Many problems are caused by more than one factor. Before you attempt to solve a problem you may need to separate the critical few from the trivial many causes of the problem. Business Analysts need to be able to prioritise potential causes of a problem – this will then enable them to determine what problems need to be addressed first, and what problems can be dealt with later. So if 80 per cent of problems are due to 20 per cent of causes you need to be able to establish and verify what those 20 per cent of causes are – they are not always obvious. This in turn can help you identify improvement priorities as you can now concentrate on solving the 20 per cent of causes. Pareto Analysis is often used in quality control and can be used to measure the success of problem solving actions. For example, you could carry out quarterly Pareto Analyses to track progress over a period of time.

How to do a Pareto Analysis

Before you carry out a Pareto Analysis it is first of all important to identify the source of your data. Where possible, use data such as number of defects or rate of returns. Ensure that your data are as accurate as possible.

Tip:
First, determine how long the study should be. Would a week's worth of data be enough, or a month, or a quarter? You need sufficient data to draw a Pareto chart, but don't overdo it.

There are seven basic steps to carrying out a Pareto Analysis:

1. Create a table listing all the causes and their frequency as a percentage

2. Rank order the data in the decreasing order of percentage of the causes, i.e. the highest percentage first

3. Add a cumulative percentage column to the table

4. Plot the names of the causes on the x-axis and the cumulative percentage on the y-axis of a graph (put the y-axis on the right side of your graph)

5. Join the above points to form a cumulative curve

6. Using the same graph, plot a bar chart with the same causes on the x-axis and actual frequency on the y-axis (put this y-axis on the left side of your graph)

7. Establish where the curve in step 5 above reaches a value of 80 per cent and draw a line at this point until you intersect with the x-axis. This point on the x-axis separates the important causes on the left and less important causes on the right (see Figure 7.1).

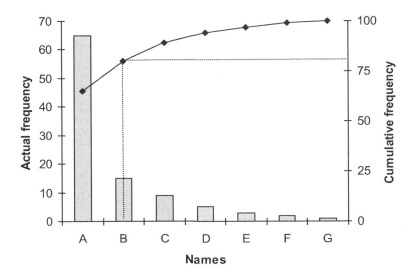

Figure 7.1: A Basic Pareto Chart
(dotted vertical line represents 80 per cent mark)

Pareto Analysis Example – Hotel Room Complaints

The Pareto chart is a type of bar chart where the values being plotted are arranged in descending order of importance from left to right. Let's take a look at a simple example which shows data for a high level of complaints about rooms in a hotel for the first quarter of the year.

Table 7.1 shows the number of complaints received in several different categories. Data such as these can be gathered using customer survey forms that are common in many hotel rooms. A glance at the figures shows us that the Room Service and Reservations categories appear to have the most complaints. A Pareto chart will give us more detail as we want to know what 20 per cent of effects are causing 80 per cent of the problems.

	Number of Complaints
Heating	10
Reservations	155
Décor	2
Room Service	287
TV set	23
Internet	17
Bed linen	16
Pillows	5
Towels	4
Furniture	9
Telephone	6
Cleaning	111
Noise	42
Documentation	1
Other	3

Table 7.1: Hotel Room Complaints (Q1 2009) by Category

Table 7.2 shows the ranked hotel rooms complaints data with these calculations. The data are now in order to draw a Pareto chart. The left side of the chart should show the actual number of complaints (column 2 in Table 7.2). The right side of the chart should show the cumulative percentage for each category (column 4 in Table 7.2). Finally, the bottom of the chart will display the names of each category.

	Number of Complaints	Cumulative	% Cumulative
Room Service	287	287	41.5
Reservations	155	442	64.0
Cleaning	111	553	80.0
Noise	42	595	86.1
TV set	23	618	89.4
Internet	17	635	91.9
Bed linen	16	651	94.2
Heating	10	661	95.7
Furniture	9	670	97.0
Telephone	6	676	97.8
Pillows	5	681	98.6
Towels	4	685	99.1
Décor	2	687	99.4
Documentation	1	688	99.6
Other	3	691	100.0

Table 7.2: Cumulative Number and Percentage of Complaints by Category for Hotel Room Complaint

Figure 7.2 represents a Pareto chart for the data in Table 7.2. From this chart you can see that 80 per cent of complaints are represented by three causes – Room service, Reservations, and Cleaning, which represents 20 per cent of the causes. The chart now helps us to prioritise potential causes of the problem of a high level of customer complaints. From the chart we can identify improvement opportunities and reach a consensus on what needs to be addressed first. Clearly, tackling the issues of Room

Service, Reservations, and Cleaning will have most effect in reducing the overall number of complaints. On the other hand, a major effort at reducing complaints about Heating will have little effect on reducing the overall number of complaints.

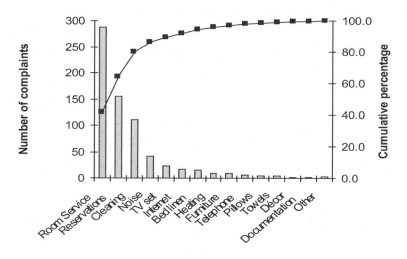

Figure 7.2: Pareto Chart for Hotel Room Complaints

What Do You Do Next?

Once you have prepared a Pareto chart you can see at a glance what the priorities for your attention are. However, sometimes you need to carry out further analysis in order to get to the real core of the problem. Let's take a look at the Hotel Room Complaints data, where Room Service represents 287 (41.5 per cent) out of 673 complaints. Obviously, there will be complaints made about several aspects of room service. You can create a second Pareto chart based on the precise nature of each of these complaints. Table 7.3 shows the number of room service complaints in descending order, with cumulative values, and percentage cumulative values calculated.

	Number of Complaints	Cumulative	% Cumulative
Delays in delivery	96	96	33.4
Reduced menu	65	161	56.1
Food too cold	39	200	69.7
Drinks too warm	22	222	77.4
Not available at certain hours	20	242	84.3
Wrong items delivered	14	256	89.2
Reception	11	267	93.0
Wrong charge applied to bill	9	276	96.2
Untidy trays	6	282	98.3
Other	5	287	100.0

Table 7.3: Cumulative Number and Percentage of Room Service Complaints

Figure 7.3 shows a Pareto chart representing the data in Table 7.3. In this case you can see first that the Pareto Principle does not apply – 80 per cent of the problems are not caused by 20 per cent of the effects. However, it still gives you some valuable information – the first three categories represent almost 70 per cent of all problems and clearly tackling theses issues will have most effect on the overall problem being analysed. So, in this case, tackling the issues of delays in delivery, perhaps expanding the menu, and ensuring that food is kept warm, will have an effect on the Pareto chart in Figure 7.3. This in turn will have the effect of reducing the overall level of complaints. On the other hand, an effort by staff to keep trays tidy will have a negligible effect on the overall level of complaints. Your Pareto analysis doesn't have to stop here. In our example there are 98 complaints related to "Delays in delivery" – you could analyse these data further.

Finally, be sensible when using Pareto Analysis. While it is an excellent method for identifying improvement priorities, it does not tell you how difficult or easy any individual problem will be to resolve. Let's take a look again at the Hotel Room Complaints data. Heating accounts for only about 1.4 per cent of all complaints which would be a low priority for improvement using the Pareto Principle. However, it might be very easy to fix – perhaps as simple as changing a thermostat setting. Simple problems can sometimes turn into more difficult problems to resolve. In that case, solve it by all means – it is easy to do. However, Pareto Analysis now gives you some facts to know what the impact of resolving any particular issue is on overall performance.

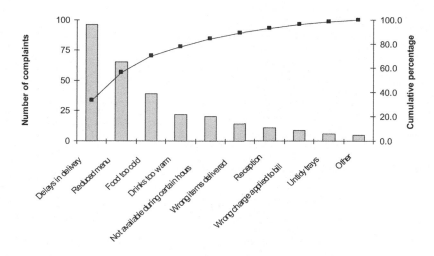

Figure 7.3: Pareto Chart for Room Service Complaints

Exercise – Warehouse Inventory Control

John Clark is a warehouse manager in a large DIY store. He has just completed a stock take of all inventories in the store warehouse. He has long suspected that some items are over-stocked and others are under-stocked. He wants to know if there is a better may to manage the warehouse inventory. Recently, he heard about the Pareto Principle that states *"20 per cent of your inventory takes up 80 per cent of your warehouse space"* and wondered if this applied to the DIY store warehouse. He was also worried about whether he is correctly forecasting stock levels to meet demand on a yearly basis. He wanted to know if the agreed re-order quantities from suppliers were adequate to meet demand, and to ensure that no over-stocking was taking place due to larger than necessary re-order quantities. In particular, he wanted to concentrate on the Hand Tools Department as the stock take showed that some items had high levels of stock, while others had very low levels.

Clearly, some items will be more important to the DIY store than others. This is because some items will sell better than others, so that if there are no or very few best-selling items in stock – many customers will be disappointed. Such items have a high value. On the other hand, low value items might be those that have a high inventory level, but do not sell very well. The concept of "usage value" (number of sales multiplied by price) is often used as a way of discriminating between different stock items. Inventory for those items with a high usage value should be controlled carefully, while items with a low usage value need not be controlled as closely.

Table 7.4 shows a selected range of hand tools sold in the DIY store. Also provided are the price, annual sales, inventory, and re-order quantity of each tool. In order to be able to draw a Pareto chart you will first have to complete the following:

- Calculate the usage value for each item

- Rank each item in descending order according to usage value

- Calculate the cumulative usage value

- Calculate the percentage cumulative usage value

Once you have done this, draw a Pareto chart to represent these data. The left side of the chart should show the usage value. The right side of the chart should show the percentage cumulative value. Finally, the bottom of the chart will display the names (or part numbers) of each item. Once you have completed the Pareto chart, answer the following questions:

- Does the Pareto principle apply to usage value in this case?

- Which items would you recommend to John Clark that he concentrates his efforts at controlling the stock level most closely?

- What items would you recommend to John that do not need close control?

- How could John forecast the correct levels of stock for each item?

- What changes in re-order quantities would you recommend as a result of your analysis?

- What minimum level of stock would you recommend be maintained at all times for items with high usage value?

Part number	Description	Unit Price	Annual sales	Inventory 31/1/2009	Re-order quantity
BHZ155	Phillips Screwdriver	€1.29	780	10	50
UYT764	Slotted Screwdriver	€1.49	1030	60	50
ERM835	Hammer	€9.99	1980	360	250
LKW331	Vice-Grip	€15.99	1750	150	20
PWU792	Pliers	€14.99	2150	60	5
BVT657	Snips	€9.99	580	220	25
SWP234	Flat File	€3.99	140	800	250
PWA399	Smoothing Plane	€12.99	80	10	10
POU889	Chisel	€2.49	320	15	10
BQH129	Hand Saw	€9.99	200	80	5
BNM711	Utility Knife	€3.49	880	60	50
PLM908	Hacksaw	€9.99	320	220	20
UIL019	Spirit Level	€10.99	100	170	50
UWN682	Adjustable Wrench 250mm	€7.49	150	120	100
WEJ778	Tape Measure	€9.99	2250	155	300
HEG601	16mm Spanner	€4.99	80	25	80
SAU791	Clamp	€5.99	90	9	10
XZQ770	Trowel	€7.99	200	186	60
VMN482	Jigsaw Blade	€1.09	300	30	50
HXY650	Nail Claw	€7.99	100	98	20
OIP889	Wire Stripper	€14.99	560	120	10
RTW254	Hex Key Set	€9.49	140	231	75
BTY667	Heavy Duty Saw	€10.99	54	55	25
WPL990	Nail Punch	€2.99	23	98	25
MBY327	Brick Cutter	€11.99	60	21	5

Table 7.4: DIY Warehouse Inventory Analysis

Value Analysis

Value Analysis is a tool that can be used by Business Analysts to help identify needed improvements in a product or process based on functionality and value for each function. It is also known as Value Method, Value Engineering, Value Methodology, or Value Management. Lawrence D. Miles, an engineer at General Electric, developed Value Analysis concepts during World War II when innovation was required because of shortages of some materials for building B-17 and P-47 military aircraft. Some critical materials were difficult to obtain, and a great many of substitutions had to be made. Miles and his team determined the function of each part in the aircraft engine's turbocharger and found more cost effective materials to achieve the necessary functions.

According to the Canadian Society of Value Analysis (www.scavcsva.org), Value Analysis is defined as *"a systematic and function-based approach to improving the value of products, projects, or processes"*. Put simply, Value Analysis improves value. Knowledge of Value Analysis will improve your ability to manage projects, solve problems, innovate, and communicate. In this section, you will analyse the functionality of a product, state an estimated cost for each function, and compare each function with that of a competitor, in order to improve value.

When to Use Value Analysis

All business activities are performed with the objective of providing value. Before you decide to do a Value Analysis, you must first understand the concept of value. Value is a combination of the benefits gained from an activity and the cost of achieving these benefits. There are many measures of value, but a simple one will suffice here. Value can be measured as follows:

$$Value = Worth/Cost$$

Using this formula, any value greater than 1.0 is considered "good value", while any value less than 1.0 is considered "poor value". Good value is therefore achieved when worth is delivered at the lowest cost.

As a Business Analyst, you will often look to identify needed improvements, lower the cost, and prioritise redesign activities of a product, project, or process. To do this you will need to determine the real value of each component or function. A Value Analysis program in your organisation will provide you with a useful tool to improve value in any product, project or process. Savings on cost, reduction of risk, improved schedules, and even improved job satisfaction can result from the outcomes of Value Analysis studies.

Tip:

Market the philosophy of Value Analysis to your peers and other colleagues in your organisation; you will need their support throughout all improvement efforts.

How to Do a Value Analysis

The fundamental concept underlying Value Analysis is function – ask yourself "What does an object do?" rather than "How is an object made?" The primary concern is to determine what functions have a high cost associated with them – these functions can then be targeted as a priority for redesign. Before considering costs, let's take a look at a simple example to illustrate the concept of function. A pencil is sometimes used to explain this concept. As you can see in Figure 7.4, a basic pencil can be shown to have five separate components, each with its own function.

The primary function of a pencil is to make marks on paper – all other functions are secondary to this. All pencils have graphite as a primary component, not all pencils will have the other secondary components. A customer using a pencil will definitely want to make marks, but may not necessarily want to make use of the secondary functions – they are therefore of different levels of importance to the customer. If one of the components accounts for a disproportionately high cost, for example the metal band, this can be targeted for redesign. A lower cost metal may be available that will provide the same function.

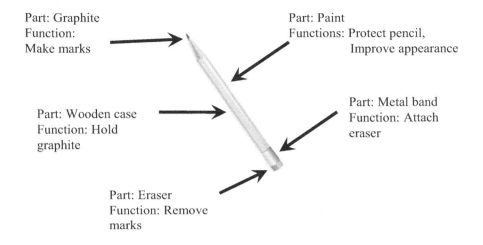

Part: Graphite
Function:
Make marks

Part: Paint
Functions: Protect pencil,
 Improve appearance

Part: Wooden case
Function: Hold
graphite

Part: Metal band
Function: Attach
eraser

Part: Eraser
Function: Remove
marks

Figure 7.4: Functions of Components of a Pencil

Value Analysis Example – Building a Better Mousetrap

To illustrate in more detail how to do a Value Analysis we will take a look at the classical case of "Building a Better Mousetrap". This example will show how a Business Analyst can identify improvement opportunities by looking at a problem from the viewpoint of function. In this example you will also look at the functions, the importance of each function to customers, competitor's design, and cost of the mousetrap in order to identify which components are prioritised for redesign. In this way you will be able to increase the value of the mousetrap.

First, you need to identify the functions of each component of the mousetrap (see Figure 7.5). Each component will have one or more functions associated with it. You may need expert help from manufacturers to draw up an accurate list of all the functions of each component. Next, compare the design of the mouse trap with those of a competitor. At its simplest, judge the performance standard of your product's functions as either better, the same, or worse than your competitor's. See Chapter 12 for a more detailed discussion on performance standards. Criteria that you should investigate include functionality, design, and innovation. It will not always be possible to compare every function as competitor's designs and functionality will not be the same for every function. For example, in the mouse trap example here, it may be impossible to compare the "Instant kill" function with a competitor. Therefore, you will not always have a complete set of data when comparing functions in two or more products, projects, or processes. Be careful with your analysis in this case.

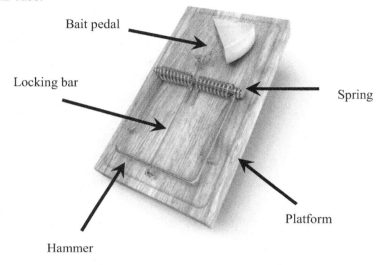

Bait pedal

Locking bar

Spring

Platform

Hammer

Figure 7.5: A Typical Mousetrap

Next, survey customers on the importance of each function to them – a customer satisfaction survey is an ideal way to do this. What you are looking for here is to determine how important each function is to the customer – this will have an impact later on redesign decisions. A simple measure used here is to determine if a function is of high, medium, or low importance to a customer.

Once you have identified all the functions of the product, compared the functionality with competitor's designs, and determined the importance of each function to customers, it is time to allocate an estimated cost to each function. Once again you may need expert advice on determining costs – the product manufacturer should be able to provide you with the necessary financial information. Use exact costs where available and ensure that where you estimate costs that you are using the most accurate information from reliable sources. In our example, the overall cost of the mouse trap is €2.00 – a cost is now assigned for each of the functions of the mouse trap that must total up to €2.00. The final step is to then assign a percentage of the overall total cost to each function.

Table 7.5 is a summary of the information that will have been gathered for the Value Analysis of the Building a Better Mousetrap project. This table identifies the three most important functions for redesign. In the table you can see how each of the functions of the mousetrap components compares with a competitor's design. Where there is no information or not enough evidence available, N/A (not applicable) is applied. Following a customer survey, you now know whether each function is of high, medium, or low importance to customers. Costs and percentage of overall cost for each function has also been determined. This analysis shows that the three functions which have the highest percentage of overall costs are:

1. Swing hammer

2. Hold bait

3. Easy to set.

While "Swing hammer" is only of medium importance to customers, it does account for 17.5 per cent of the overall cost and is therefore the primary target for redesign. Priority number 2, "Hold bait", is of high importance to customers and accounts for 11.5 per cent of the overall cost. The "Kill mouse" and "Easy to set" both account for the same percentage each (10 per cent) of overall cost. Both are of equal importance (High) to customers, but the competitor's design for "Easy to set" is rated as "Better", while the competitor's design for "Kill mouse" is rated as the "Same". Therefore the "Easy to set" function will have a slightly higher priority for redesign due to the competitor's design being better – this is priority number 3.

Project: Building a Better Mouse Trap

Component	Functions	Competitor's Design	Importance	Cost (€)	%	Priority
Platform	Support other parts	Same	Low	0.12	6.0	6
	Resist overturning	Worse	Medium	0.07	3.5	12
	Hold trap	Same	Medium	0.08	4.0	11
	Display manufacturer name	Same	Low	0.06	3.0	13
Bait pedal	Hold bait	Better	High	0.23	11.5	**2**
	Attract mouse	N/A	High	0.04	2.0	15
	Easy to bait	Better	High	0.10	5.0	8
Spring	Swing hammer	Same	Medium	0.35	17.5	1
Hammer	Kill mouse	Same	High	0.20	10.0	4
	Instant kill	N/A	High	0.15	7.5	5
	Hold dead mouse	Same	Medium	0.05	2.5	14
	Prevent escape	Better	High	0.02	1.0	17
Locking bar	Hold hammer in place	Better	Medium	0.03	1.5	16
	Easy to set	Better	High	0.20	10.0	**3**
	Easy to un-set	Better	Medium	0.10	5.0	9
	Finger safe	Better	High	0.11	5.5	7
	No slippage	Worse	Low	0.09	4.5	10

Table 7.5: Value Analysis for Building a Better Mouse Trap Project

What Do You Do Next?

You now have a list of priorities for redesign based on function. It is always a good idea to re-check your data – any assumptions you've made, or areas where you have insufficient data could be revisited. Refine your findings where possible to ensure a more focused analysis. At this stage you will not have factored in the cost of redesigning each function, or the level of difficulty in any redesign project. Some functions will have a low level of importance for customers, perform worse than competitors, and account for only a small percentage of overall cost – yet may be simple and cheap to redesign. Use your findings carefully to ensure that they make sense. With Value Analysis you are attempting to identify the highest priority for redesign so that you can add most value to your product, project, or process.

A Cost-Benefit Analysis is imperative before embarking on a redesign process for any function. While a Value Analysis will prioritise functions for redesign that will add value, a Cost-Benefit Analysis may reveal a different picture. Using these two tools together will provide you and your clients with carefully identified and costed improvement opportunities before a decision on what to do next will be made.

Exercise – Office Alarm System

Juniper Alarms is a company specialising in providing security systems for medium to large sized offices. In a highly competitive market, Juniper Alarms is seeking to improve the value of its leading Business Monitored Alarm System (BMAS) product for customers. You and your team have been employed to identify improvement opportunities for a possible redesign of the BMAS product. To get you started, the basic BMAS product consists of the following components:

▪ Control panel	▪ Cabling
▪ Security keypad	▪ Video camera
▪ Motion detector	▪ Video monitor
▪ Door contact	▪ Digital recorder
▪ Window contact	▪ Backup battery
▪ Glass break sensor	▪ Swipe card
▪ Siren	▪ Swipe card reader

A full alarm system will have many of each of the above components – for example, every window in the building will have a window contact. For the purposes of this exercise, concentrate on only one of each component. In your research for this exercise you may also find alarm systems with other components. Your task now is to determine the following:

- The function(s) of each component

- Comparison with a competitor's product

- The importance of each function to customers

- The cost associated with each function

- The percentage cost associated with each function

- A priority list for redesign

Reflection

At the beginning of this chapter you set out to find out how you would know where to start in your problem-solving efforts. With Pareto Analysis and Value Analysis you now have two powerful and easy to use tools to help you identify the critical few from the trivial many causes of a problem, and to identify needed improvements in a product or process based on functionality and value for each function.

In your Learning Journal, answer the following reflective questions:

- What have you learned in this chapter?

- Can you identify situations in your organisation where the Pareto principle will apply?

- What processes or products in your organisation would benefit from a Value Analysis?

- What other analysis tools will help you to identify process improvement opportunities?

- What are your next steps after identifying process improvement opportunities using these tools?

Discuss the use of Pareto charts with your colleagues. Use examples of Pareto charts that you have drawn and ask them to provide feedback. Use this feedback, especially if from a more experienced colleague, to improve your Pareto and Value Analysis skills. Check if people in your team, or in the wider organisation, have already used Pareto charts or Value Analysis, and ask to see the results. Did these efforts lead to process improvement? Your organisation may have a Knowledge Management System that documents all projects, including ones that have failed or have not been completed. If possible, see how these tools were used as part of a process improvement project – in this way you will learn from the experience of others in your own organisation.

8

ANALYSIS TOOLS FOR DECISION-MAKING

*"Whenever you see a successful business, someone once made
a courageous decision."* – Peter Drucker

Introduction

Making good decisions is almost never an accident. Decision making
should always be the result of setting good objectives, having intelligent
direction, making honest effort, and to use skillful execution. A decision
represents the wisest choice of two or more alternatives. When decision
making is very difficult or the issues at stake are vital, sometimes we are
not sure how or what to decide to do. In business analysis we cannot afford to resort to informal decision making techniques such as tossing a
coin or guessing what the best decision will be. It is the job of managers
to make decisions. When managers turn to you as a Business Analyst for
help in making a decision, you need to have the right techniques to be
able to analyse a situation and provide alternatives so that informed decisions can be made.

In this chapter you will look at three tools that are useful in helping
to make the right decision. The first, SWOT Analysis, is an effective tool
to define a situation currently faced by an organisation. The second,
PEST Analysis, considers macro-environmental factors when making
decisions. Using PEST and SWOT together can be used as a basis for the
analysis of business and environmental factors. The third tool, Cost-
Benefit Analysis, provides financial assistance in the decision making
process.

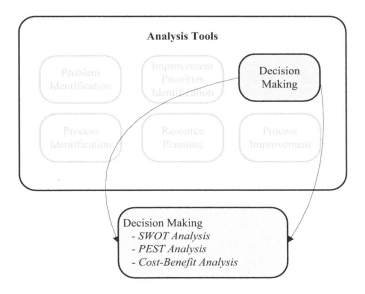

SWOT Analysis

SWOT Analysis is a planning tool used to understand the **S**trengths, **W**eaknesses, **O**pportunities, and **T**hreats involved in a project or business. Albert S. Humphrey of the University of Stanford is credited with developing SWOT Analysis in the 1960s. He first developed a team method for planning called SOFT (Satisfactory, Opportunity, Fault, and Threat) – this was changed to SWOT in 1964. SWOT Analysis can be used for all sorts of decision-making, it is a well known tool and is easy to use. SWOT Analysis is also sometimes known as Situation Analysis.

At its simplest, SWOT Analysis defines a situation currently faced by an organisation, and allows us to do four things which are sometimes placed in a SWOT quadrant (see Figure 8.1). This type of analysis also helps us to identify, and distinguish between, internal (Strengths and Weaknesses) and external (Opportunities and Threats) environmental characteristics. It is very effective if you want to evaluate overall organisational health.

An organisation's Strengths are the resources and capabilities available to meet its strategic business goals. Examples include:

- Patents

- Brand recognition

- Market share

- Financial reserves

- Location

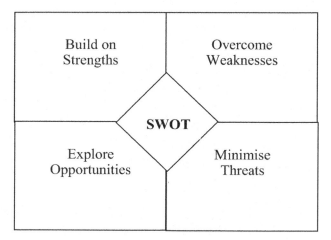

Figure 8.1: SWOT Quadrant

Weaknesses are the deficiencies within an organisation that may restrict or limit meeting these goals. Examples include:

- Gap in capabilities

- Poor reputation with customers

- Cash–flow difficulties

- High cost structure

- Legacy IT systems.

Opportunities can occur when changes happen in the organisation's external environment. It is a chance to introduce a new product or service that can add value to your organisation. Examples include:

- New technologies

- Customer needs

- A new or favorable trend
- New market opportunity
- Partnerships.

Threats are changes that happen in the external environment that could become a barrier to attaining your organisation's business goals. Examples include:

- Emergence of a competitor with cheaper product or service
- New rules from a Regulatory Agency
- Change in market demand
- Tax changes
- Interest and/or exchange rates.

When to Use SWOT Analysis

SWOT Analysis's four headings provide a good framework for reviewing strategy, position and direction of an organisation, or a business proposition. You can use SWOT Analysis for lots of things such as:

- Business and strategic planning
- Evaluating competitors
- Marketing efforts
- New product development
- Research reports
- Team building.

A SWOT Analysis will give you the information you need to match your organisation's resources and capabilities to the environment in which it operates. It can also be used in goal-setting to help you identify goals that will give you the most benefit. Use SWOT Analysis to assess all the relevant characteristics within your organisation in order to confirm its internal strengths and weaknesses. SWOT Analysis will also give you a good understanding if you want to study external factors such as the opportunities available and what the threats are that could cause you problems.

How to Do a SWOT Analysis

Carrying out a SWOT Analysis does not require any specialist hardware or software tools. You can use a flip-chart, whiteboard, or basic pencil and paper, to create your SWOT quadrant. The first thing to do is appoint a facilitator who is experienced in organisational analysis. The facilitator can set the scene for the SWOT Analysis by providing the background to the analysis and setting the ground rules. Next – you and your team should draw the four SWOT headings and make sure that everyone understands what each heading means. Now identify items under each heading. Combine other analysis techniques such as Brainstorming to help you and your team to identify the relevant characteristics. Concentrate on processes – i.e., things that you can do. Avoid listing people under any heading.

Start by completing an organisational scan and look first at the internal environment. Identify the organisation's Strengths – remember, you want to build on these. Some questions that you might ask here to help with your analysis are:

- What resources are available?

- What skills and capabilities does your organisation have?

- What specialist internal tools can you use?

- What is already working well in this area?

Next, identify the organisation's Weaknesses – these must be overcome. Questions to ask that might help here are:

- What are the skills and capabilities that you need, but don't have?

- What are the resources (people, time, money) that you don't have access to?

- What is not working well in this area at this time?

- What is the financial situation – i.e., is there enough money to help overcome a particular weakness?

Now it is time to look at the external environment. First, identify Opportunities that the organisation may be able to explore and take advantage of. Helpful questions to get you going here are:

- Is there any vulnerability in our competitors?

- Are there new market opportunities?

- Is there a technological innovation that you can take advantage of?

- If you can overcome some of your weaknesses, what opportunities would become available?

Finally, identify the Threats to the organisation. Ask the following questions to help you with this:

- Are there substitute products and services available that compete with your organisation?

- Are there new laws or regulations that will have a direct effect on your business?

- Are your suppliers able to keep up with your demands?

- Is your organisation vulnerable to fluctuations in currency exchange rates?

Once you and your team finished identifying items in each of the four quadrants, review them for appropriateness and completeness.

Tip:
It is often helpful to carry out a PEST analysis prior to a SWOT analysis – PEST measures an organisation's market and potential according to external factors.

SWOT Analysis Example – Tourism Ireland

The see how effective a SWOT Analysis can be, let's take a look at an example. Tourism Ireland is responsible for marketing the island of Ireland overseas as a holiday destination. In a Business 2000 Case Study, the "Ireland experience" was assessed using SWOT Analysis (see

www.business2000.ie for more details on this study). In assessing the
market, Tourism Ireland targeted the family market in Great Britain, the
luxury segment in Europe, and business tourism in all key markets as
key emerging markets. The SWOT Analysis was conducted in order to
maximise Tourism Ireland's ability to compete and to identify possible
future opportunities.

Strengths	Weaknesses
• People • Landscape • Heritage • Music • Food • Sport and outdoor activities • High levels of investment • Good access to island	• Weather • Transport • Infrastructure • Internal access/traffic • Lack of national conference centre • Lack of iconic landmarks
Opportunities	**Threats**
• Increased access to the island • Develop business from Eastern Europe, China and Asia • Further develop business from Nordic countries and southern Europe • Development of the conference market • Development of products for age 55+ market	• Changes in consumer behaviour • New EU accession states • Changes in Irish lifestyle • Continued growth in shorter stays

Figure 8.2: SWOT Analysis for Tourism Ireland Marketing Plan

Source: adapted from "Marketing the Ireland Experience – Business 2000 Case Study:
Tourism Ireland".

Figure 8.2 summarises the findings of the SWOT Analysis. This identifies the internal Strengths, such as "Music", "Sport", and "access", and
internal Weaknesses such as "Weather", "Infrastructure", and "traffic".
Externally, opportunities such as "Develop business" in new markets, and

the "55+ market" have been identified, while the external Threats "consumer behaviour" and "shorter stays" have also been identified.

Tourism Ireland focused first on the Great Britain target market which in 2004 accounted for 62% of all visitors to the island of Ireland – however, this represented a decline on previous years. Based on the findings of the SWOT Analysis, it was decided to launch a "Project Britain" initiative to identify reasons for the decline and to develop a strategy to restore growth. The main conclusions from the analysis were:

- Emphasise the friendliness and hospitality of the people

- Focus on winning a greater share of the fast growing four to seven night holiday segment

- Develop a more sophisticated image for Dublin that positions it as a cosmopolitan city with plenty to see and do

- Identify and promote the top ten attractions in each region of Ireland

- Develop niche activity products in rural areas such as wind-surfing, cookery, and health farms

- Promote the ease of touring the island and highlight the range of internal transport options available.

What Do You Do Next?

SWOT Analysis is a starting point for many decision making processes. After this type of analysis you will be in a much better position before deciding what to do next. A SWOT Analysis will usually identify several options for improvement in each of the four SWOT categories. A detailed analysis may reveal so many possible projects that it is important to prioritise what are the most urgent or important issues to tackle first. Once you have prioritised projects for improvement, you may need more information about each process identified. Use other tools such as SIPOC Diagrams, Flow Charts, Cause and Effect Diagrams, and Pareto Charts to give you a better understanding of how each process works so that improvements can be made. Whatever Opportunities you identify, ensure that you complete a Cost-Benefit Analysis for each opportunity.

It is important to investigate all items in each of the four quadrants. Don't be complacent with Strengths – they could become a Weakness if not built upon. There is often a temptation to concentrate on overcoming Weaknesses to the detriment of the other three components of the SWOT quadrant. Some Weaknesses will be difficult to overcome. For example, in the Tourism Ireland case described above – "Weather" is listed as a Weakness, Ireland is not a "sun" destination. We all know that there is very little we can do about the weather, but we can overcome this weakness by insuring that there are all-weather activities for tourists to engage in. There is equally a temptation to ignore or at best pay little attention to Threats on the grounds that they are outside your organisation's control. In the Tourism Ireland case, "New EU accession states" are listed as a Threat – they are among the fastest growing destinations in Europe, are becoming more accessible, and are able to compete strongly on price.

Finally, identifying external Opportunities can sometimes be the hardest part of conducting a SWOT Analysis. One way of coming up with new ideas is to look at what opportunities will present themselves if you can overcome identified Weaknesses and minimise potential Threats. Carrying out a regular SWOT Analysis will also help you to manage and monitor progress on all your improvement initiatives.

Exercise – Golf Club Expansion

Woodhaven GC is a nine-hole golf club based in a rural area. It has 450 full members, 50 juvenile members, and 35 country members. Recently, a farm adjoining the golf club lands has been put up for sale by its owner. The club committee has decided to investigate the possibility of purchasing the land in order to expand the golf club to 18 holes. You have been hired as a Business Analyst to carry out a feasibility study on expanding the club, and to report back to the club committee. The first step in this study is to carry out a SWOT Analysis. An organisational scan has revealed the following:

1. Woodhaven GC was founded in 1912 and has set up a small committee to plan for centenary celebrations in 2012.

2. Full membership has been growing by an average of 10 new members a year.

3. Full membership is expected to reach the club's capacity of 475 members in three years.

4. Juvenile membership has remained steady at an average of 50 players over the past 10 years.

5. Country (part-time) membership fluctuates by year – in some years it can be as high as 50 members, in others as low as 10 members.

6. Membership fees at all levels have increased at a rate of 5 per cent, 10 per cent 12 per cent, and 15 per cent over the past four years respectively.

7. The clubhouse is 25 years old and is in need of some refurbishment. The men's changing room in particular needs attention.

8. The club does not have a driving range and has only a small putting green for players to practice on.

9. The clubhouse has a profitable bar which is popular with club members.

10. A private joke between employees of the club implies that if you want a day-off from work that you should order an egg sandwich from the restaurant, which has operated at a loss for the last three years.

11. The club has applied for and expects to receive a grant from the National Lottery to build a modern practice area to include putting greens and sand bunkers.

12. The club's course is widely acknowledged as one of the best nine-hole courses in the country.

13. Income from green fees has doubled over the past two years.

14. The club's green keeper recently won the Green Keeper of the Year award.

15. Woodhaven GC has struggled to attract national and regional competitions due to the fact that it does not have 18 holes.

16. The club has a poor record in attracting sponsors for its local competitions.

17. The club has a part-time professional who manages the small, but well stocked Pro Shop.

18. A new hotel is being built in a local large town and is expected to be complete in 18 months.

19. Some of the land on the adjoining farm is prone to flooding in extremely wet weather.

20. A new 18-hole championship golf club is almost ready to open 25km away. The new club has already started a high profile marketing campaign to attract new members.

21. Some of the local Golf Societies are considering moving to the new club.

Draw a SWOT quadrant and place each of the 21 items above in its appropriate position on the quadrant. To keep your diagram simple you may use the number of each item on the quadrant. Some items may need to be split into two parts, while others may be positioned in more than one quadrant. Once you have completed the quadrant, answer the following questions in order to identify improvement opportunities:

- What can you suggest to build on the Strengths identified in the organisational scan?

- What potential projects can you identify to overcome the highlighted Weaknesses?

- What are the most urgent Weaknesses that must be overcome as soon as possible?

- What Weaknesses, if overcome, can create new Opportunities?

- What are the Opportunities that the club could explore in order to identify new business opportunities?

- What are the main Threats to the club and what would you recommend to minimise these Threats?

- In your opinion, what are the top five priorities for improvement in this case?

PEST Analysis

PEST Analysis is an examination of the macro-environment that affects all businesses, sometimes called "the big picture". It is most often used to consider an organisation's environment before embarking on a marketing process. This analysis involves considering **P**olitical, **E**conomical, **S**ocial, and **T**echnological factors that affect a business. Many of these factors are often beyond the control or influence of the business; however they are important to be aware of when doing new product development, and business or strategy planning.

The origin of PEST analysis is unclear. Francis J. Aguilar of the Harvard Business School in 1967 was the first person to discuss ETPS: Economic, Technical, Political, and Social factors. This was later rearranged to STEP, and since the 1980s there have been several modifications such as STEPE (extra "E" for Ecological), and PESTLE (extra "L" and "E" for Legal and Ecological respectively).

It is very important that a business considers the environment that it operates in before embarking on a marketing process. Environmental analysis should be considered as a continuous process and feed all aspects of planning. This environment can be divided into three components:

- The internal environment

- The micro-environment

- The macro-environment.

The internal environment is made up of resources such as an organisation's staff, internal customers, office technology, salaries, and finance. The micro-environment is made up of resources such as external customers, distributors, suppliers, and competitors.

Tip:
Use a SWOT analysis to examine an organisation's internal and micro (external) environment.

PEST Analysis is an excellent tool for examining the macro-environment where you will need to consider political factors, look at economic factors, compare technological competitive advantage, and review social and cultural influences. These are called the PEST factors.

When to Use PEST Analysis

PEST analysis can be used for marketing and business development assessment, as well as decision-making. It can also be used to review a strategy, new direction of an organisation, or a new idea for products and services. PEST analysis is similar to SWOT analysis - it's simple, quick, and uses four key perspectives. As PEST factors are essentially external, it is recommended that you complete a PEST analysis before completing a SWOT Analysis. While there is overlap between PEST and SWOT, PEST can help identify SWOT factors even though similar factors will appear in each type of analysis.

Use a PEST Analysis when you are considering any of the following options:

- Entering a new market

- Launching a new product or service

- Considering a potential acquisition

- Investigating a potential partnership

- Examining an investment opportunity.

It is important to identify clearly the goal of a PEST analysis. The number of macro-environmental factors is practically unlimited, so be clear about using PEST to analyse a particular situation.

How to Do a PEST Analysis

Carrying out a PEST Analysis, as in SWOT Analysis, does not require any specialist hardware or software tools. You can use a flip-chart, whiteboard, or basic pencil and paper, to list your PEST factors. Draw the four PEST headings and make sure that everyone understands what each heading means. Now identify items under each heading.

First, consider the Political factors such as government and local authority laws, regulations, and legal issues. Examples to watch out for include:

- Employment laws

- Environmental regulations

- Tax policy

- Trading agreements

- Government stability

- Product labeling requirements

- Health and Safety regulations

- Funding (e.g. grants available for investment)

- Home market lobbying and pressure groups.

Next, look at the Economic factors. In marketing, you need to consider the state of a trading economy in the short and long-terms - especially true when planning for an international marketing campaign. Issues to look out for include:

- Interest rates

- Exchange rates

- Rate of inflation

- Employment levels

- Gross Domestic Product (GDP)

- Consumer spending power

- Trade tariffs

- Seasonal issues (e.g. weather).

The third factor to consider is the social and cultural influences that make up part of the macro-environment. These will vary considerably from country to country, and even from region to region within countries

– it is very important that these issues be considered. Issues to consider include:

- Ethnic and religion issues

- Attitudes to foreign products and services

- Language

- Consumer leisure time

- Roles of men and women

- Demographics (e.g. age, gender, race, family size)

- Living standards

- Education standards.

Finally, as Technology is vital for competitive advantage and is a major driver of globalisation, you must consider technical factors in your analysis. Factors to look out for include:

- Technology legislation

- Access to Internet and broadband availability

- Computer usage and availability in the home

- Quality and standard of technology

- Communications infrastructure

- Rate of technological change

- Outsourcing.

While identifying the PEST factors that you should examine in the macro-environment is relatively straight-forward – getting the information you need is not so easy. There are several sources of information and the World Wide Web is a good place to start. Web sites such as the Central Intelligence Agency (CIA) World Factbook (www.cia.gov), and on-line encyclopedias such as Wikipedia (www.wikipedia.org) and Britannica (www.britannica.com) are excellent sources of general information. Search engines such as Google and Yahoo! can be used to find all sorts of information, though you need to be careful about how you use your search results. Also, most newspapers such as *The Irish Times* (www.irishtimes.com), now publish on-line and many have archive material freely available. Your local library may also have access to on-line databases such as Lexis-Nexis (www.lexisnexis.com).

Many countries will have a government agency responsible for dissemination of statistics – a good example is the Central Statistics Office Ireland (www.cso.ie). The CSO makes statistics about such factors as people and society, labour market and earnings, environment and climate, economy, and business sectors, freely available to the public on-line. Other countries provide similarly huge amounts of information on-line, for example the UK Statistics Authority (www.statisticsauthority.gov.uk), the US government's official web portal (USA.gov), and the Statistics Bureau in Japan (www.stat.go.jp) – if you search for such offices on-line you will find them for most countries. Finally, Eurostat (ec.europa.eu/eurostat) is also an excellent source of information for countries in the European Union.

PEST Analysis Example – Mobile Phone Company

Mobile phone companies operate in a very competitive market and are continually looking to develop, roll out, and enhance both personal and business offerings. They are always on the lookout for opportunities to create demand for new data services. In early 2004, 3G was launched in Europe, and mobile phone companies moved to 3G in order to enhance customer experience and productivity. In an environmental scan for a PEST Analysis, Figure 8.3 is a summary of the main PEST factors that affect such a company's operation in a new 3G market.

Here you can see the Political factors such as governmental and legal issues that affect how the company operates. For Economic factors, we find issues that influence the purchasing power of customers and the company's cost of capital. For Social factors, we find several demographic and cultural aspects of the environment which influence customer needs and market size. Finally, for Technological factors we find several technologies which can impact what products and services you can provide.

What Do You Do Next?

A PEST analysis is often used simply as a tool to establish the "big picture". This helps us to find out where a business's products and services are in the context of what is happening in the macro-environment that will at some point affect what is happening inside the business. The four PEST factors form a framework for reviewing a situation, and can also be used to review a strategy or position, direction of a company, a marketing proposition, or idea. This provides important information for your decision making process.

Political	**Economic**
• Highly regulated • Laws • Infrastructure • Ban on mobile phone use in certain situations	• Expensive 3G licenses • Competition from other mobile phone companies • Reduced calls cost • Economic downturn • Developing countries
Social	**Technological**
• Ubiquity • Health concerns • Mobile etiquette • Demographics • Cultural trends • Video and picture phones • Social networking	• Mobile broadband • 3G • UMTS (2.5G) • GPRS/WAP • SMS/MMS • Coverage

Figure 8.3: PEST Analysis for a Mobile Phone Company

Completing a PEST analysis can be a simple or complex process, it often depends how comprehensive you need to be. Make sure you get more than one person's view and that you have sourced your information from several reliable sources. It is a good idea to get an expert to review your findings. It is also important to ensure that your information is kept up to date and that you recheck your PEST factors on a regular basis. Decide which trends should be monitored on a continuing basis.

Analyse your PEST Analysis findings carefully – most, if not all of these factors will be outside you and your organisation's control. Identify the most important issues and strategic options. Finally, prepare a report in order to circulate your findings.

Exercise – Soft Drinks Company Marketing Campaign

An international soft drinks company is considering developing a new brand of sugar-free fruit flavoured waters aimed at young, sporty, and health conscious people. The company wants to consider a pilot release of their new products in one country before a more widespread launch. The company has selected three countries with similar sized populations and you have been employed as the Business Analyst to carry out a PEST Analysis in order to determine the macro-environmental factors to consider before deciding in which country to launch the new drinks range. The countries are: New Zealand, Croatia, and Costa Rica.

Carry out a PEST analysis for each of the three countries above. Once you have completed your analysis, answer the following questions:

- What sources of information did you use for your analysis? How reliable are these sources?

- What is happening politically in each of three countries? Factors to consider here are:
  - o tax policies
  - o employment laws
  - o environmental regulations
  - o trade restrictions and reform
  - o tariffs
  - o political stability.

- What is happening within the economy of each country? Factors to consider here are:
  - o economic growth or decline
  - o interest and exchange rates
  - o rate of inflation
  - o wage rates (including minimum wage)
  - o working week
  - o unemployment levels
  - o credit availability
  - o Gross Domestic Product (GDP).

- What is occurring socially in each of the countries in which you might operate or expect to operate? Factors to consider here are:
    o cultural norms and expectations
    o health consciousness
    o rate of population growth
    o age distribution
    o attitudes to career development
    o emphasis on health and safety
    o global warming.

- What is happening technology-wise in each country? Factors to consider here are:
    o mobile phone penetration
    o web 2.0 (blogs, wikis, social networking websites)
    o communications infrastructure
    o broadband availability
    o distribution networks.

- What are the most important issues to consider from your analysis?

- Based on your findings, which of the three countries (New Zealand, Croatia, or Costa Rica) would you recommend as a most suitable location for launching the new brand of soft drink?

Cost-Benefit Analysis

At some stage in every project after meticulous planning and analysis of all possible solutions, you will need to make a decision as to which solution to implement. Whether you have proposed several possible solutions or just one, you will need to know from a financial point of view if the solutions are worth implementing. Quite often, selecting a solution is based on financial factors such as which solution has the lowest cost, or will return the greatest profit. Cost-Benefit Analysis is a simple to use tool that will help the Business Analyst decide which solution makes the most sense from a financial point of view. In other words, it is a decision making tool.

Jules Dupuit, a French economist and civil engineer was one of the first people to suggest using Cost-Benefit Analysis in an 1844 study on deciding what the best toll to apply to a bridge was. Since then, economists and accountants have used Cost-Benefit Analysis as a methodology to measure costs and benefits as an aid to help decide if a project is worthwhile or not. It is an important tool to use when several options need to be analysed for financial impact.

When to Use Cost-Benefit Analysis

Several sections in this book describe tools and strategies for problem solving. Whatever solution or solutions are proposed, as a Business Analyst you will need to get an accurate estimate of the benefits that your proposed solutions will deliver, as well as how much they will cost. In financial terms, the final solution should return the greatest benefit for the cost that is incurred. We all use Cost-Benefit Analysis almost every day. For example, if you need to purchase petrol for your car and Station A is selling petrol for €1.10/litre and Station B is selling it for €1.12/litre – it makes most sense to go to station A. In this simple example, the benefit (a tank full of petrol) will be the same, but the cost is lower in Station A – therefore you will get a greater return for your money by buying your petrol in Station A.

Decision makers need to understand all the financial implications of each of the proposed solutions. Many projects, such as fixing a leaking pipe, will have an immediate benefit, but others, such as moving an office to a new cheaper location, may take longer for the benefit to be realised. Many businesses will want to know how soon they will get a return on their investment (ROI), and when in time this will occur (payback). Cost-Benefit Analysis will help you to provide the financial data that that you need to help you make the best decision. However, you need to be careful that you do not always use Cost-Benefit Analysis as the sole decision making tool. Other non-financial factors may need to be considered. For example, it will be relatively easy to calculate the costs of refurbishing an office, but very difficult to calculate the benefits gained from employees working in a more comfortable environment. In its simplest format, Cost-Benefit Analysis concentrates on tangible costs and benefits (e.g. saving money), and does not take into account intangible costs and benefits (e.g. saving time).

How to Do a Cost-Benefit Analysis

When you decide to do a Cost-Benefit Analysis, you will need to be careful how you go about doing it. Financial data are not always readily available, so you should get your data from the most reliable sources and get advice from your Finance Department. It doesn't matter what order you calculate the costs and benefits, but most of the time costs are calculated first. When calculating costs, you should use real costs for material and labour. Most of the time you can establish these by determining pay rates for labour, and prices for materials. Remember, your conclusions are as good as the data that you base them upon.

Tip:

When labour and material need to be procured from a third party, use quotations given by suppliers in your costs.

First, identify the costs from a qualified source associated with every activity within the proposed solution. In your team, discuss each option, compare prices, and select the options that offer the most potential. Finally, add up all the costs to get a total cost for each solution selected. For example, a company that is investigating the potential of buying some new software that will improve productivity would estimate costs based on the following factors:

- Actual price of software

- Cost of installation

- User training

- Annual maintenance   .

Once all costs have been calculated, it is time to get an estimate of the benefits of each solution – make sure you do this for each of the solutions that you have costed. Estimate all the financial benefits that the solution will generate – many of these will be reduced costs. In our example here, the benefits of buying new productivity software to be considered are based on cost–reducing factors such as:

- More efficient business processes

- More efficient staff

- Better customer information

- Better data management.

When you have calculated all the costs and benefits of each solution, it is time to use this information to help make a decision. A useful way to compare each option is to use a Cost-Benefit ratio which is simply to divide the benefits by the costs. The solution with the highest ratio is the one that should be selected. Consider the cost-benefit data for three solutions in Table 8.1. In this example, you can see that Solution A has the lowest cost (€10,000), but that Solution C generates the highest benefit (€23,000). However, when you compare the Benefits/Costs ratio you can see that Solution B offers the best benefit for the cost incurred with a ratio of 1.27. Another option to consider is the concept of "payback". This is the time taken for the benefits to out-weigh the costs – in other words, it is when the project starts to pay for itself. The formula for the calculation of payback is the reverse of the Cost-Benefit ratio: Costs/Benefits. In the example, Solution B has a payback value of 0.79 which is the equivalent of 9.5 months (0.79*12) over a year – this is a shorter period of time compared to the other solutions. Finally, the Return on investment (ROI), which is expressed as a percentage, also shows that Solution B offers the best rate (26.67%) of return, while Solution C offers the lowest rate (15.0 per cent). On the basis of all these data, Solution B is the one that should be selected as it has the highest ratio value, the shortest payback time, and the highest ROI.

	Solution A	Solution B	Solution C
Total Costs	€10,000	€15,000	€20,000
Total Benefits	€12,000	€19,000	€23,000
Cost-Benefit ratio	1.20	1.27	1.15
Payback	0.83	0.79	0.87
ROI (%)	20.00	26.67	15.00

Table 8.1: Cost-Benefit Analysis Comparing Three Solutions

When you are measuring costs and benefits over a long period of time, there is another important factor that you need to consider – this relates to the time value of money (TVM). €100 is worth more today than it will be in five years time as you would expect to be able to purchase more with this money today than in the future – mostly due to factors such as inflation which will de-value money over time. In a Cost-Benefit Analysis you may need to take TVM into account. Consider the data in Table 8.2 for two alternative solutions to be implemented over a four-year period.

Solution X	Year 1	Year 2	Year 3	Year 4	Total
Benefits	€ 0	€ 20,000	€ 40,000	€ 50,000	€ 110,000
Costs	€ 45,000	€ 20,000	€ 10,000	€ 5,000	€ 80,000
Cash flow	-€ 45,000	€ 0	€ 30,000	€ 45,000	€ 30,000
Solution Y	**Year 1**	**Year 2**	**Year 3**	**Year 4**	**Total**
Benefits	€ 10,000	€ 15,000	€ 35,000	€ 50,000	€ 110,000
Costs	€ 30,000	€ 25,000	€ 15,000	€ 10,000	€ 80,000
Cash flow	-€ 20,000	-€ 10,000	€ 20,000	€ 40,000	€ 30,000

Table 8.2: Cost-Benefit Analysis for Alternative Solutions X and Y

The total costs and benefits are calculated for each year. At the end of the four year period the Cost-Benefit ratio for each solution is the same (1.38), and the net benefit is also the same (€30,000). So, these data as they stand cannot help us to decide which solution to implement. However, on closer inspection you will note that although both solutions end up with the same total values, there are differences in the costs and benefits for each year. Net Present Value (NPV) is a technique for calculating the expected net financial gain or loss for a proposed solution by discounting all expected future costs and benefits to the present point in time. NPV will account for the time value of money for each solution – for example, money earned in year 1 is worth more today than money earned in year 4

Let's take a look at Table 8.3 where the data from Table 8.2 are expanded to take account of the time value of money by calculating NPV.

Discount rate (r): 0.05					
	Year				
Solution X	**1**	**2**	**3**	**4**	**Total**
Benefits	€0	€20,000	€40,000	€50,000	€110,000
Discount factor	0.95	0.91	0.86	0.82	
Discounted benefits	€	€18,141	€34,554	€41,135	€93,829
Costs	€45,000	€20,000	€10,000	€5,000	€80,000
Discount factor	0.95	0.91	0.86	0.82	
Discounted costs	€42,857	€18,141	€8,638	€4,114	€73,750
				NPV =	**€20,080**
	Year				
Solution Y	**1**	**2**	**3**	**4**	**Total**
Benefits	€10,000	€15,000	€35,000	€50,000	€110,000
Discount factor	0.95	0.91	0.86	0.82	
Discounted benefits	€9,524	€13,605	€30,234	€41,135	€94,499
Costs	€30,000	€25,000	€15,000	€10,000	€80,000
Discount factor	0.95	0.91	0.86	0.82	
Discounted costs	€28,571	€22,676	€12,958	€8,227	€72,432
				NPV =	**€22,066**

Table 8.3: Net Present Value (NPV) Calculations for Alternative Solutions

First, you need to set a rate at which you will discount both the costs and the benefits over time – in Table 8.3 this is set at 5 per cent (0.05). Next, you need to apply a discount factor to each cost and to each benefit in order to calculate the discounted costs and benefits. This is done by using the following formula:

$$Discount\ factor = 1/(1 + r)^t$$

In this formula, "r" is the discount rate and "t" is the year. For example, the discount factor for year 1 using a discount rate of 5 per cent is 0.95, i.e. $1/(1+0.05)^1$. Each cost and benefit is multiplied by the corresponding discount factor to determine the discounted values. Next, add up the total discounted costs and benefits for each solution. To calculate NPV for each solution simply subtract the total discounted costs from the total discounted benefits. This gives an NPV value of €20,080 for Solution X, and an NPV of €22,066 for Solution Y. Solutions with higher NPVs are preferred to solutions with lower NPVs. So even though Table 8.2 shows no difference between Solutions X and Y, you can see that in Table 8.3, Solution Y has a higher NPV. Therefore, on the basis of discounted costs and benefits, the analysis shows that Solution Y should be the preferred solution.

Cost-Benefit Analysis Example – Training Programme

A large multi-national company is introducing a new on-line system for dealing with customer complaints. The company has over 1,000 employees who deal with customers on a regular basis. A new two-day (14 hours) training programme is to be developed to provide these employees with the necessary skills to operate the new customer complaints system. Traditionally, the company uses instructor-lead training (ILT) in the classroom to provide most of the company's internal training needs. However, as there are so many employees who need this training, an alternative to classroom training needs to be investigated. A media rich e-Learning option to deliver the training on-line is to be considered, and in order to determine whether to continue with ILT or develop an e-Learning solution, a Cost-Benefit Analysis needs to be performed.

The first step in Cost-Benefit Analysis is to measure all of the direct and indirect costs involved in creating ILT and e-Learning versions of the training program. Costs and benefits will not be the same for every comparison, so we need to create some assumptions to get started. Table 8.4 outlines some basic assumptions for the Cost-Benefit Analysis.

Item	Assumptions
Life Span of Course	1 year
Total Number of Students	1,000
Student Learning Time in Classroom	14 hours (2 days)
Reduction in Seat Time for e-Learning	50%
Burdened Compensation for Trainer (per day)	€391
Burdened Compensation for Student (per day)	€209

Table 8.4: Assumptions for Training Development Cost-Benefit Analysis

In Table 8.4, the Cost-Benefit Analysis assumes that there will be a 50 per cent in seat time for e-Learning compared to ILT, in other words

– a 14 hour ILT course will correspond to a 7 hour e-Learning course. We also need a daily cost for both the trainers and the students. Trainers are paid €75,000 per year. Add 20 per cent to cover taxes, insurance, and other benefits. There are 230 working days in a year, so a daily cost per trainer works out at €391. A similar calculation for the employees (students) works out at €209 based on an average salary of €40,000. We can now apply these figures in our calculations.

Table 8.5 shows a detailed breakdown of costs for each program. This table is based on a model developed by Kevin Kruse (2002). The benefit for both solutions is the same – training 1,000 employees on a customer complaints program. The final calculations show that the cost of creating and delivering an ILT version to 1,000 employees will cost €1,308,146. The cost for providing equivalent training using media rich e-Learning is €512,206. Therefore, the conclusion here is that based on cost alone, the decision should be to choose the e-Learning solution as it will save €795,941 over a year.

What Do You Do Next?

Now that you have the finance figures to help you make a decision, you should examine all aspects of the costs to see if they are accurate or can be reduced on a factor by factor basis. The training programme example illustrates that there is a very high costs for developing the e-Learning program – however, these costs remain the same whether 50 or 500 employees are trained. Clearly, ILT costs would be significantly reduced if fewer students were trained. You can investigate your options by modifying the costs and changing the numbers. In this example, the high number of students (1,000) swings the balance in favour of an e-Learning solution by a large margin. Using the same calculations for 500 students, the margin is reduced to a saving of €274,984. While this is still a significant saving, it is a lot less than for 1,000 students and makes the final decision less obvious. In fact, these figures will show that the e-Learning solution only makes sense if a minimum of 237 students are trained in this way.

	ILT	e-Learning
Development costs per hour	€2,750	€35,000
Number hours	14	7
Total Create Courseware	**€38,500**	**€245,000**
3-day course	€3,000	€0
Number of trainers	5	0
Burdened Compensation for Trainer (3 days x 5 trainers x €304 per day)	€5,870	€0
Total Train the Trainer	**€8,870**	**€0**
Number of ILT Sessions (12 students/class)	83	0
Instructor Time in Days (includes preparation)	2.5	0
Instructor Costs (83 x 2.5 days x Burden Cost)	€81,522	€0
Student time in days (includes 1 day travel)	3	1
Cost of Student Salaries (1000 x days x €164)	€626,087	€208,696
Airfare (Rate = €300 per student)	€300,000	€0
Hotel (Rate = €150 per student)	€150,000	€0
Transportation (Rate = €40 per student)	€40,000	€0
Meals (Rate = €50 per student)	€50,000	€0
Total Delivery	**€1,247,609**	**€208,696**
Location Fees	€0	€0
Facilities Fees	€0	€15,000
Manual (@ €8 each)	€8,000	€0
CD-ROM (@ €5 each)	€0	€5,000
Total Equipment	**€8,000**	**€20,000**
Student Registration	€5,168	€10
Technical Support	€0	€20,000
Updates to Content	€0	€5,000
Updates to Technology	€0	€13,500
Total Maintenance	**€5,168**	**€38,510**
Final Costs	**€1,308,146**	**€512,206**

Table 8.5: Cost-Benefit Analysis of ILT vs e-Learning Based on Training Programmes

Source: Based on Kruse (2002).

There are other options that you might consider that will affect your calculations. You could reduce costs further by outsourcing some options. For example, development costs of €35,000 per hour are quite high due to the high cost developer's salaries. Outsourcing to a lower cost location may make sense and be worth investigating. You could also consider using virtual classroom on-line tools to reduce travel and its associated costs – many companies are now making use of Virtual Learning Environments to replace or augment classroom training.

Finally, the training program example above takes place over one year. You could also consider running the training program over two or three years in which case you will have to account for the time value of money by discounting your costs over the duration of the training.

Exercise – Motorway by-pass

The Shamrock Transport Company (STC) specialises in providing all forms of road transport throughout Ireland. John Smith is the General Manager of STC and the company has a fleet of vehicles ranging from articulated trucks to small vans. Its most profitable route is the Dublin to Galway road – every day, STC trucks and vans travel this busy road. Recently, a well known traffic black spot – the large town of Gatestown was by-passed by a 20 kilometre dual-carriageway that is designed to reduce the Dublin to Galway trip by up to 30 minutes during peak times, and by at least 15 minutes during off-peak times. The by-pass is 5km longer than going through Gatestown. John knows that his drivers have been looking forward to this new by-pass for several years. However, controversially – the new by-pass is tolled and some drivers are suggesting that it would be cheaper to go through the town than to pay the toll. Many transport companies, including STC, are complaining about the high tolls - especially for trucks. The tolls on the Gatestown by-pass are as follows:

18 wheeled trucks	€8.00
6 wheeled trucks	€6.00
Large van	€6.50
Small van/car	€3.50

John is not sure if he should tell his drivers to use the by-pass and save a lot of time, or to continue to go through Gatestown as before though it will take longer. He wonders which option is best as STC is particularly vulnerable to fuel costs. He is also curious to know if all STC vehicles should use the by-pass, or only some. Finally, he also wants to be able to compare options over the next two years.

You have been engaged to carry out a Cost-Benefit Analysis to help John decide what advice he should give his drivers. Assume the following points:

- All vehicles in the company's fleet have diesel engines except cars

- Diesel is priced at 135.9 cent per litre

- Petrol is priced at 142.9 cent per litre

- All fuel will rise by 10% at the end of year 1

- Tolls will increase by 20% at the end of year 1

- National statistics indicate that accident rates on by-passes are 60 per cent lower when compared to the older roads

- The number and frequency of STC vehicles using the Dublin to Galway road on an annual basis is as follows:

Vehicle Type	Number Using Road	Frequency (return trips)
18 wheeled trucks	2	One per week
6 wheeled trucks	5	Two per week
Large vans	10	Three per week
Small vans	10	Five per week
Cars	5	One per week

For each vehicle type, calculate the costs and benefits of going through Gatestown, and the costs and benefits of using the tolled by-pass. Once you have done this, consider the following questions:

- What would your recommendation to John Smith be for each type of vehicle, i.e. should the drivers use the by-pass or go through the town?

- Can you add figures to your calculations for the benefits of using the by-pass such as:
  o Reduced driver stress
  o Less wear and tear on vehicles
  o Reduced accident rate
  o Less impact on environment (e.g. reduced carbon emissions)?

- What other intangible costs and benefits should you consider when reporting back to John Smith?

- What effect will using discounted costs and benefits, and using NPV calculations, have on your decisions?

Reflection

At the beginning of this chapter you set out to develop the right techniques to be able to analyse a situation and provide alternatives so that informed decisions can be made. SWOT, PEST, and Cost-Benefit Analysis are essential tools that will help you in the decision-making process.

In your Learning Journal, answer the following reflective questions:

- What have you learned in this chapter?

- Can you identify situations in your organisation where SWOT, PEST, and Cost-Benefit Analysis can be used to help making decisions?

- Are there decisions that you are aware of already made in your organisation where SWOT, PEST, and Cost-Benefit Analysis were not used? If so, could these tools have helped make better decisions?

- What other analysis tools will help you to in the decision-making process?

- What are your next steps after using these tools for the decision-making process?

It is always a good idea to get some colleagues or experts to review your findings. For SWOT Analysis, get a colleague who is very knowledgeable about the organisation that you are conducting the SWOT Analysis on to review thoroughly your findings – ask yourself if you are comfortable with your work, as your findings may be used in making important strategic decisions for your organisation. Getting someone knowledgeable to review your PEST Analysis findings will be more difficult as you will need a person with a macro-environment view of your analysis. At the very least, look back on your findings and reflect on the sources of all your information to ensure that you have gathered the best information available. For Cost-Benefit Analysis, it is imperative that when your are reflecting on your findings that you ensure that your financial data are reviewed by finance experts.

SWOT, PEST, and Cost-Benefit Analysis are tools that you can use over and over again. Practice using them to improve your analysis techniques. Always consider using them in some form whenever you are involved in making decisions. Finally, if you are the decision maker you should determine if SWOT, PEST, and Cost-Benefit Analysis has been carried out on all alternatives presented to you.

9

ANALYSIS TOOLS FOR IDENTIFYING PROCESSES

"When a problem comes along, study it until you are completely knowledgeable. Then find that weak spot, break the problem apart, and the rest will be easy."
– Norman Vincent Peale

Introduction

Before you can embark upon any process improvement effort, it is essential that as a Business Analyst, you have a thorough understanding of how a process currently works. This applies for processes that may only need minor improvement, as well as more complicated processes where there is a lot of room for improvement. You and your team will often be faced with fixing a problem that you may not have much knowledge of, or expertise in. The chances are that you won't have the benefit of a lengthy familiarisation session to gain a detailed understanding of a process – you will need a quick way to get as much detail as possible about a process so that later you can make more informed decisions.

In this chapter we will take a look at two tools that will help Business Analysts to look at how a process can be described prior to any improvement efforts. The first, Flow Charts, will help you to graphically illustrate a process as it currently works. The second, SIPOC Diagrams, will also help you to graphically identify the key inputs and outputs of a process that will lead to identifying all the suppliers and customers of any process.

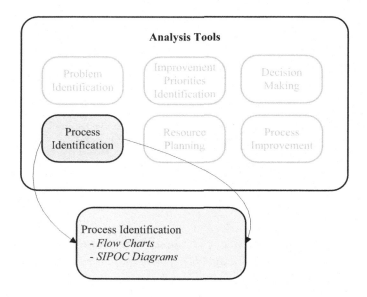

Flow Charting

Flow Charts are diagrams that illustrate the sequence of operations to be performed to get to the solution of a problem. They are very effective in determining how a process works prior to improvement. They are also known as Process Charts or Process Maps. Flow Charts can provide Business Analysts with a common language or reference point when dealing with projects or processes. They provide an excellent form of documentation for a process, and quite often are useful when examining how various steps in a process are sequenced and how they work together.

Flow charting have been around for a very long time. In fact, Flow Charts have been used for so long that no one individual is specified as the "creator of the Flow Chart". However, Frank Bunker Gilbreth, Sr. is credited with introducing the first process charts in a presentation entitled "Process Charts – First Steps in Finding the One Best Way" to the American Society of Mechanical Engineers (ASME) in 1921. Gilbreth is also better known as the father and central figure in the book and film *Cheaper by the Dozen* written by his son, Frank Jr. and his daughter Ernestine.

For the Business Analyst, Flow Charts provide an easy way to illustrate the workings of a process "at a glance" – you don't need complicated software, a pencil and paper will often suffice. There are some rules about how Flow Charts should be drawn, but once mastered – Flow Charts are an essential tool that if used either on their own, or in conjunction with other tools, such as Pareto Analysis and Cause-and-Effect diagrams, adds greatly to your business analysis skills.

When to Use Flow Charts

A Flow Chart is a great tool, which if used correctly, can give you a detailed understanding of a process prior to any improvement efforts. Flow Charts let you see the process flow at a glance, so therefore can provide an excellent "snap shot" of any business process that you are analysing for improvement opportunities. You can discover a lot about the complexity (and simplicity) of many business processes just by looking at a Flow Chart of them – even without reading the text or understanding the symbols on the chart.

Use Flow Charts to see easily the flow of information and materials, the number of steps in a process, branches in the process, opportunities for infinite loops or processes going nowhere, inter-departmental operations, and much more. They can show up badly organised flows and therefore help clarify improvement opportunities. You can also use Flow Charts to highlight problem areas where no procedure exists to cope with a particular set of events.

How to Create a Flow Chart

Flow Charts are usually drawn using a set of standard symbols. There are four basic symbols on a Flow Chart as shown in Figure 9.1. A round-edged rectangle that represents the start or end of a Flow Chart, standard rectangles that represent activities or tasks, diamonds which represent decision points, and arrows which represent flow of control.

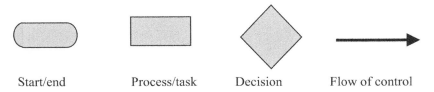

Start/end   Process/task   Decision   Flow of control

Figure 9.1: Basic Flow Chart Symbols

The vast majority of Flow Charts rely on these four symbols – in fact, if you use other flow charting symbols, many people won't know what they mean. With these basic symbols you can describe almost any process – for each step on a Flow Chart you can ask yourself "Why is this done?" First, let's look at a simple example of using a Flow Chart to describe the process of making a decision on whether you can afford to go out for the night. Figure 9.2 illustrates a Flow Chart that uses all four of the basic symbols. In this Flow Chart you can see that after the Start symbol, the first process is to count your money to see if you have enough to go out for the night. Assume that you need at least €50.00 for a good night out. Once the money is counted, you have to decide if you have more than €50.00. If the answer is "Yes" – then you have sufficient money to go out for the night. If the answer is "No", then you do not have enough money to go out, and must stay at home for the night. As the Flow Chart shows, you can repeat this process until you have less than €50.00, at which point the process ends.

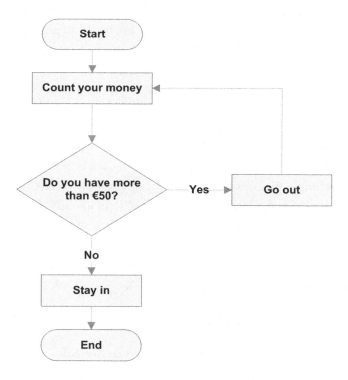

Figure 9.2: A Simple Flow Chart

There are also many other types of symbols, such as off page connectors (for when your diagrams get too big) and input/output symbols to represent printed reports and data storage options. Table 9.1 provides an overview, with short descriptions and meanings, of the most common Flow Chart symbols. The symbols used here are the standard symbols used in Microsoft Office applications.

Symbol shape	Symbol Name	Short Description
	Terminator	Used to show the start and end points in a process.
	Process	Show a process or action step. This is the most common symbol in process flow charts.
	Alternate process	Shows when the process flow step is an alternate to the normal process step. Flow lines into an alternate process flow step are typically dashed.
	Decision	Indicates a question or branch in the process flow. A decision shape is used when there are two or three options.
	Data (I/O)	Indicates input to and output from operations of a process.
	Predefined process	A marker for another process step or series of process flow steps that are defined elsewhere. Commonly used to represent sub-processes.
	Internal storage	Used in programming to mean information stored in RAM memory, instead of in a file.
	Document	A process flow step that produces a document.
	Documents	A process flow step that produces more than one document.
	Preparation	A process step that is a preparatory process flow step, e.g. a set-up operation.

	Manual input	A process step where the user is prompted for information that must be manually input into a system.
	Manual operation	Process steps are not automated.
	Connector	Used as a connector to show a jump from one point in the process flow to another. Connectors are usually labelled with capital letters to show matching jump points.
	Off-page connector	Shows a continuation of a flow chart onto another page.
	Stored data	A process step that stores data.
	Magnetic tape	Data storage location where data is usually stored on a backup tape.
	Database	Data storage location where data is stored in a database.
	Direct access storage	A computer hard disk.
	Display	Indicates a process flow step where information is displayed to a person.

Table 9.1: Description of the Most Commonly Used Flow Chart Symbols

Special symbols can also be developed when required. The following guidelines should be used when drawing Flow Charts:

- Describe the process to be charted – keep this short, a one line statement will suffice

- Start with a "trigger" event – for example, "Count money" in the example above

- The usual direction of the flow of a process is from left to right or top to bottom

- Only one flow line should enter a decision symbol, but two or three flow lines, one for each possible answer, should leave the decision symbol

- Only one flow line should come out from a process symbol

- Only one flow line is used in conjunction with terminal symbol

- Ensure that the Flow Chart has a logical start and finish – Flow Charts can only have one Start terminal symbol, but may have more than one Terminator symbol

- Follow the process through to a useful conclusion (i.e. end at a target point).

Tip:
Many people who do not use Flow Charts will not know what all the symbols mean, so it is a good idea to add a shape symbol key to your Flow Chart.

To help you draw a Flow Chart you should make use of other analysis tools. For example, you could brainstorm for possible problems in the process; use Cause-and-Effect diagrams to identify all possible problems in the process, or use SIPOC diagrams to identify the suppliers, inputs, outputs, and customers of the process.

Flow Chart Example – Customer Support Line

To understand how Flow Charts can be used effectively to describe a process, let's take a look at a more detailed example. In this example you will look at the process of managing incoming telephone calls for a Customer Support Line where there have recently been a lot of complaints from customers, in particular from key customers, about long waiting times and calls not being dealt with efficiently. Your task is to review the Support Line's process for handling calls and to suggest ways to improve the quality of service. The Support Line operates from 8:00 am to 8:00 pm with a goal that 95 per cent of incoming calls would wait less than two minutes for a Customer Support Representative (CSR).

A recent customer survey has shown that only 75 per cent of calls are being answered in less than two minutes and that many customers are hanging up before they are put in contact with the most appropriate CSR. You decide to investigate why some customer's problems are not being solved quickly enough, or in some cases not at all. You decide first of all to draw a Flow Chart to identify the current process for dealing with incoming calls.

Figure 9.3 gives a Flow Chart specifying the process of answering incoming customer calls. From the chart you can see that the process of handling calls is a relatively straight-forward one. A customer calls and immediately enters a queue. When a Junior CSR becomes available the customer call is then answered. Sometimes a customer hangs up if they are waiting too long. If the Junior CSR understands the problem and can solve it over the phone, the process jumps to the end of the chart where the CSR checks if the customer is satisfied and closes the call. If the Junior CSR cannot solve the problem it is escalated to a Senior CSR who will also attempt to solve the problem over the phone. If the problem is solved over the phone, the process jumps to the end of the chart where the CSR checks if the customer is satisfied and closes the call. If the problem is not resolved over the phone, the Senior CSR can arrange a visit from a Technician to the customer, then check if the customer is satisfied and close the call.

However, you can see immediately from the chart that there are three problem areas that may be contributing to the high level of customer complaints. These three areas are shown on the chart with a question mark. First, if a customer hangs up, there is no information being recorded. Secondly, if a customer declines an offer of a visit from a Technician, there is no process for dealing with this situation. Thirdly, no information is being recorded if a customer is not satisfied. Finally, no information is being recorded anytime if a customer is key or not. This Flow Chart, which can be quickly drawn, shows up immediately areas for process improvement. You are now ready to proceed to investigate possible solutions to improve quality of service in this Customer Support Line.

What Do You Do Next?

Once you have drawn an accurate Flow Chart, you should now have a detailed understanding of the process prior to improvement efforts. You are now in a stronger position to address the issues revealed by the Flow Chart. In the example above there are several deficiencies highlighted – steps can now be taken to improve the situation.

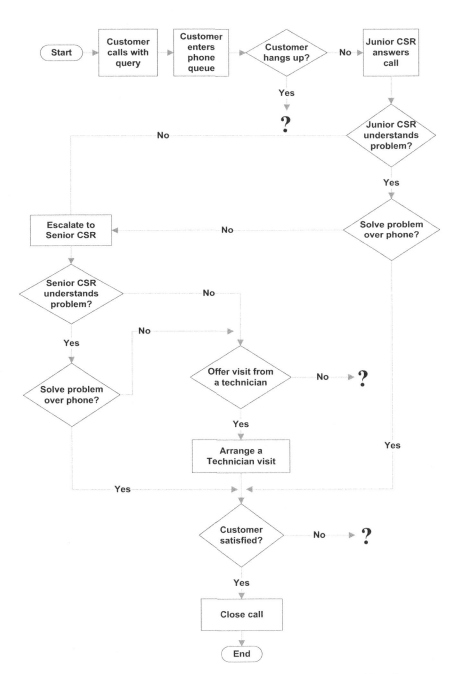

Figure 9.3: Flow Chart of Customer Support Line Call Handling Process

Some further analysis will be helpful. For example, what types of problems are callers reporting? A Pareto Analysis may give you more information about which types of calls are most common and that are taking up more of the CSR's time. This may give you a clue as to why some calls are not successful, for example – problems that rarely occur may lead to long calls that involve Junior and Senior CSRs, plus possibly making an appointment for a visit from a technician. This may lead to frustrated customers.

Staffing levels may also be an issue; wait times will be long without adequate staff. This happens because companies that provide customer support lines have allocated inadequate staffing to handle the incoming calls. Carrying out a Capacity Planning analysis will help you determine the appropriate staffing levels on the Customer Support Line.

Exercise – New Hire Recruitment

Jane Smyth is a Recruitment Manager in medium sized supermarket chain that is about to expand its number of stores nationwide. A new recruitment drive is needed to fill up to 250 vacancies that will arise as part of the expansion. Up to now, the company had an informal recruitment process that was managed by Jane and her team, and there has been little attention to detail paid to activities in the recruitment process. Recently, there have been cases where positions were advertised when there were no approval from management to fill vacancies, and some new recruits arrived for work on their first day with nobody expecting them. Jane decides that a review of current processes should take place and plans to introduce new procedures and improve on the current recruitment process.

The current recruitment process can be summarised as follows:

- Vacancies are advertised in local newspapers and on the company web site as they arise

- Applications are received by post and processed by Jane and her team

- Each application is forwarded to Store Manager

- Store Manager shortlists applications for interview

- Candidates are invited for interview

- Shortlisted candidates are interviewed by Store Manager

- Successful candidates are offered position

- Successful candidate accepts position

- Recruitment Manager draws up contract of work

- Candidate signs contract of work

- Candidate starts work.

Draw a Flow Chart to represent the situation described above. You should need only to use the four basic flow charts symbols in your diagram. Ensure that you use a decision box every time a decision has to be made by either the Recruitment Manager or the Store Manager. Look for areas of poor process flow or where no information is being recorded.

Once you have completed your Flow Chart you are in a good position to consider some improvements. Jane has suggested some improvements that she and her team want to introduce into the process, as follows:

- Make use of the Internet for on-line recruitment

- Introduce standard applications forms (non-standard applications will not be considered)

- All vacancies must now be approved by both the Store Manager and the company Financial Controller before they can be advertised

- All applications will be processed first by the recruitment team to ensure that they meet a minimum set of requirements as specified by the Store Manager for each position

- Interviews will now be over two rounds – a final shortlist of three candidates is recommended for each position

- Second round interviews are to be conducted jointly by the Store Manager and the Recruitment Manager

- All offers are to be approved by Financial Controller before contracts are signed

- The IT department, Payroll, and HR departments are to be notified a minimum of fours weeks in advance of a new employee taking up a position.

Update your original Flow Chart to include these suggestions to show how the new recruitment processes will work. When complete, ask your self the following questions:

1. Are there sufficient approval activities in the new process?

2. What alternatives should there be if there are a low number of applicants?

3. What other improvements can you suggest be added to Jane's suggestions?

4. Does the new process as outlined make sense?

SIPOC Diagrams

Before beginning a project to improve a process, you must first identify all the relevant elements of that process. A SIPOC diagram is a good starting point to help define these – SIPOC stands for **S**uppliers, **I**nputs, **P**rocesses, **O**utputs, and **C**ustomers. Throughout the process, the suppliers (**S**) provide input (**I**) to the process (**P**). The process you are looking to improve adds business value, this results in output (**O**) that should meet or exceed a customer's (**C**) expectations.

A SIPOC diagram is also called a high-level process map. It is used commonly in the Six Sigma methodology to show only the major steps of a process. The SIPOC diagram helps Business Analysts and their teams to visualise the five key components of a process which will give them a more comprehensive understanding of various areas in a process that could lead to improvement. SIPOC diagrams can also be used to define a complex project that may not be well scoped.

When to Use SIPOC Diagrams

SIPOC diagrams should only be used to describe the existing process "as is" and not the "to be" process. It is a particularly useful tool when you need to answer the following questions:

- What are all the **I**nputs to the **P**rocess?

- Who supplies the **I**nputs to the **P**rocess?

- What requirements are placed on the **I**nputs?

- What are all the **O**utputs of the **P**rocess?

- Who are the real **C**ustomers of the **P**rocess?

- What are the requirements of the **C**ustomers?

The purpose of mapping an organisation's current process in a SIPOC diagram is to provide a high-level answer to these questions. As the process you are looking to improve may not be familiar to you, you will need to interview the stakeholders of the process to establish all the elements of your SIPOC diagram. A SIPOC diagram is simple to do, but it is a great source of information that allows all the participants in a process to learn together and come to a consensus about the components of the diagram. A SIPOC diagram gives you a broad view of the process you are investigating. These diagrams show complex processes in a simple flow chart, helps teams stay on course, and ensures that all team members are viewing the process in the same way.

How to Draw a SIPOC Diagram

The SIPOC diagram's purpose is to provide a clear, simplistic illustration of the process under investigation. Figure 9.4 shows a simple template for using a SIPOC diagram. Drawing a SIPOC diagram involves completing five steps that allow you to complete the five parts of the diagram in the following order:

Step 1 – Identify the Process. Begin with the Process. First, give the process a name that identifies the process you and your team are examining. It is also important to establish the process boundaries which involve defining where the process begins and ends. This helps prevent your team from straying into other unrelated processes. You only need four to six high level steps to describe the process – these should be the key functions that the process performs. If there is more than one process, or if a process is divided into sub-processes, draw a separate SIPOC diagram for each.

Step 2 – Identify the Outputs. Next, identify the all Outputs of the Process described in the above step. This involves listing the products and/or services that result from the process. Examples of outputs would be reports, ratings, products, and documents.

Step 3 – Identify the Customers. Identifying the customers involves listing all the recipients of the outputs described in step 2 above. In many cases the recipients will be a person or a group of people, but it may also be another system.

Step 4 – Identify the Inputs. Next, identify all the Inputs required for the Process. What resources such as data, supplies, systems, and tools, are required for this process to function properly?

Step 5 – Identify the Suppliers. Finally, identify all the Suppliers of the Inputs identified in step 4. Include internal as well as external suppliers to the process. Who or what organisation, system, report, or database supplies whatever it is that is needed as an input into the process?

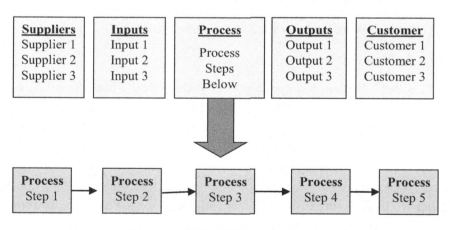

Figure 9.4: SIPOC Diagram Template

Tip:

Include all inputs, outputs, and customer requirements, even if they are apparently insignificant.

Once you have completed the SIPOC diagram you and your team should review all aspects of the resulting diagram. Ensure that you have agreement among the team that the diagram is an accurate high-level view of the process under investigation.

SIPOC Diagram Example – Prescribing Medicines

To understand how a SIPOC diagram can be used in business as a starting point for process improvement, let's take a look at how free medical prescriptions are processed in a public hospital. The process of prescribing and dispensing medicines is a relatively straight forward one. However, assume that the hospital authorities are looking to cut the costs associated with this process and at the same time reduce errors or duplicate prescriptions that might occur with a view to improving how medicines are supplied and controlled in the hospital. Before embarking on any attempt to improve this process you decide first to draw a SIPOC diagram to describe the situation as it currently stands.

Following the five step procedure described above for creating a SIPOC diagram, the process of prescribing and dispensing medicine is first described. A high-level description in six steps of this process is as follows:

- Hospital patient first meets a doctor

- Doctor makes a diagnosis

- Doctor prescribes medicine

- Hospital pharmacist dispenses medicine

- Patient history file is updated

- Medicine reordered to maintain supply.

This process has a clearly defined beginning and end. Other processes associated with this, such as making payments to suppliers for the medicines, are excluded in this analysis. The first part of the SIPOC diagram can now be drawn – see Figure 9.5.

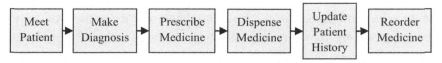

Figure 9.5: High-level Process for Prescribing and Dispensing Medicine

This process will vary from hospital to hospital, so it important to ensure that you have identified the key steps in the process before moving on to the next step.

Outputs

Medicine
Dose
Frequency
Recommendation
History file
Payment request
New order

There are several outputs to this process, most obviously the medicine itself. Each prescription will also have instructions, such as dose and frequency, and recommendations, such as "avoid alcohol", to the patient about taking the medicine. As this is a public hospital there will also need to be payment request documentation produced to ensure that the hospital will be paid by the Health Authorities for each medicine dispensed. The patient's history file is also updated. Finally, the dispensed medicine is replaced by issuing a new order to the supplier.

Now that the outputs have been identified, the next step is to list all the customers of these outputs. The patient that receives the medicine is the most obvious customer of this process. However, as you have already identified several outputs of the process – these outputs must all have a customer associated with them. A hospital administrator will update the patient history file. The Health Authority will be the customer for the documentation that will include payment details. Finally, the order for a replacement medicine will be sent to a drug company for re-supply.

Customers

Patient
Administrator
Health Authority
Drug company

Inputs

Medicines
History file
Guidelines
Regulations
Internal procedures
Training

Next, it's time to look at the inputs and suppliers to the process. Medicines are the main input to the process, but there are also other inputs. The patient history file will need to be provided so that the hospital doctor can examine it for past diagnoses. Drug companies will also issue guidelines and recommendations for usage of each medicine. As Health is a highly regulated business, there will be laws and regulations which can also be regarded as input into this process. Internal procedures will also dictate how internal processes are to be conducted – this should also be included as an input. Finally, training in the process is an important input.

Identifying the suppliers into the process of prescribing and dispensing medicines is the final step to complete the SIPOC diagram. For this process, medicines will be supplied by drug companies and distributors. Regulatory agencies will

Suppliers
Drug Company
Distributor
Regulatory agency
Government

also supply the regulations that govern healthcare. Finally, the Government will supply the laws under which the legislation for providing free medical prescriptions in hospitals. The final SIPOC diagram is now ready to be drawn – see Figure 9.6.

Once completed, review with your team all the steps that you have taken in creating this diagram. You will also need to consult with the hospital staff to ensure that your diagram accurately reflects the process as you have described it. This should also highlight any issues with the current process that may be of value to you when you move on to explore improvement opportunities for this process.

What Do You Do Next?

A SIPOC diagram allows you and your team to review all the processes in a manner in which next steps in a project for process improvement can be identified. You may still need to conduct a further analysis to more fully understand the causes of problems in the current process. A Cause and Effect diagram, used in conjunction with a SIPOC diagram can be used to help find the root causes of problems quickly and accurately. This is especially true when a Business Analyst has only limited experience in the process under investigation. In order to understand the process in more detail, a flow chart breaking up the high-level steps in the SIPOC diagram will give you a clearer understanding of how the process works. To reduce costs, you may need to re-design one or more steps in the process – conducting a Value Analysis will be useful here so that you are in a better position to reduce costs and add value to the process.

Finally, you should keep referring back to your SIPOC diagram throughout your process improvement efforts. It will provide you and your team with a good reference point in any process improvement initiative. New members joining your team will benefit greatly from viewing the SIPOC diagram.

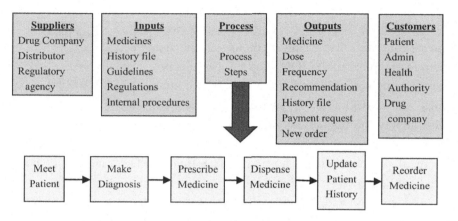

Figure 9.6: SIPOC Diagram for the Process for Prescribing and Dispensing Medicines

Exercise – Annual Performance Appraisal

Robert Walsh is an IT Manager in a financial organisation and has fifteen IT Support staff working in the IT Department. Every year he needs to conduct performance appraisals for all employees in his department. Due to new guidelines from the Financial Regulator he is required to ensure that all employee performance in his department is appraised correctly. In particular, clear performance objects are to be set and measured for each employee. You have been hired as a Consultant to review the existing annual performance appraisal process and to suggest how Robert and his department can improve this process in order to be compliant with the new guidelines.

Robert has provided you with a high-level overview of how he conducts performance appraisals for his staff as follows:

- Review job description

- Review/feedback on performance objectives from last appraisal

- Outline training and development needs

- Discuss salary increase

- Set performance goals for next year.

Draw a SIPOC diagram to describe the above process and identify all the Suppliers, Inputs, Outputs, and Customers of this process. Use your own experience of performance appraisals and you may need to consult with your Manager or your organisation's HR department for more detail if you are not familiar with how performance appraisals are conducted.

Once you have completed the SIPOC diagram, ask yourself the following questions:

1. Does the SIPOC diagram accurately reflect the process as described by Robert Walsh?

2. Have you identified all outputs, and customers for those outputs, of the process?

3. Have you identified all inputs, and suppliers for those outputs, of the process?

4. What improvements based on your analysis can you suggest to Robert for improving the performance appraisal process?

5. What other analysis would you suggest conducting to add value to your findings?

Reflection

At the beginning of this chapter you set out to find out how you could gain a thorough understanding of how a process currently works. With the Flow Chart and SIPOC diagram tools you now have two very effective methods to describe a process before embarking on any improvement projects. In your Learning Journal, answer the following reflective questions:

- What have you learned in this chapter?

- Can I apply Flow Charts and SIPOC diagrams to common everyday processes (e.g. buying a book, or fixing a flat tire)?

- Can you identify processes in your organisation that are suitable for you to draw a Flow Chart and/or a SIPOC diagram?

- What other analysis tools will help you to understand processes better?

- What are your next steps after describing a process with a Flow Chart or a SIPOC diagram?

Ask a colleague to review your charts and diagrams and to provide feedback. Use this feedback, especially if from a more experienced colleague, to improve your flow charting and SIPOC diagram skills. Finally, check if your organisation already uses Flow Charts or SIPOC diagrams and ask to see them – your organisation may have a Knowledge Management System that documents all projects. If possible, see how they were used as part of a process improvement project – in this way you will learn from the experience of others in your own organisation.

10

ANALYSIS TOOLS FOR
PLANNING RESOURCES

*"Most people spend more time and energy going around
problems than in trying to solve them." –* Henry Ford

Introduction

When you are faced with a problem as a Business Analyst, you will need
to equip yourself with many tools and techniques, and perhaps even a
combination of tools and techniques, which will set you on the path to
solving a problem. All problems are different, and solutions may vary
widely when it comes to fixing a problem. Therefore problem-solving
techniques are by their nature very generic. Some techniques can be used
to help solve a multitude of problems, while others may only be useful in
certain circumstances. However, all problems need resources to resolve
them. Whether you are designing a new process or improving an existing
process, you will need to understand the inter-dependencies between the
process and resources such as people. All processes are made up of activities, and many will need people and other resources to engage in
these activities at various different stages. Therefore you will need to
examine the most efficient way of planning activities and making the
best use of people resources, how people interact with an activity, and
what resource capacity is required to meet your improvement objectives.

In this chapter we will take a look at three tools that will help Business Analysts with problem-solving efforts that take resources into account. The first, Project Network Diagrams, will help you to graphically
illustrate the most efficient sequence of activities in a process. The sec-

ond, Use Cases, will help you to examine a process by expressing the interactions between the process and the people (users) in its environment. The third, Capacity Planning, will also help you to understand the resource requirements of problem-solving initiatives.

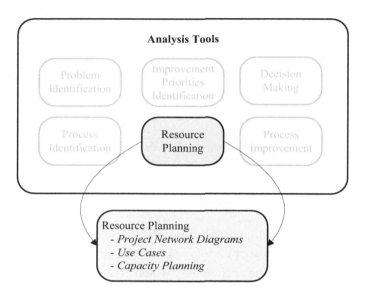

Project Network Diagrams

A Project Network Diagram is a graphical representation of a project's schedule that shows the logical relationships and sequencing of activities that make up the project. This type of diagram is useful for planning, tracking, and controlling any project from start to finish. For this reason, it is a very popular tool for use by Project Managers, but it also provides the Business Analyst with a simple to use tool that will help in the planning and controlling of many new product and program developments or improvements. It is also an ideal tool for determining the critical path through a project, i.e. the sequence of activities through the project that takes the longest time. This path will tell both Business Analysts and Project Managers the earliest time in which a project can be completed, and is therefore critical to the overall success of the project.

Project Network Diagrams were first developed in the 1950s by the United States Navy to help in the development of missile defence systems. The essential concept behind Project Network Diagrams is that some activities cannot start until others are finished. There are several different names used to describe this type of diagram such as a PERT Chart, Activity-on-Arrow Diagrams, Critical Path Analysis, and the Critical Path Method.

When to Use Project Network Diagrams

Project Network Diagrams can be used for simple as well as complex projects. As projects get more complex, it is vital that you be able to identify any relationships that exist between the activities that make up a project. This is particularly important when you want to know the logical sequence in which the activities must take place. If done correctly, a Project Network Diagram will show these relationships in a clear and concise format to ensure more efficient management of time as well as resources.

For the Business Analyst, Project Network Diagrams are a very useful problem-solving tool when you are planning a new process, or if you are involved in improving an existing process. For new processes you will have to determine the logical sequence of activities for any solution that you propose. This is because conflicts between activities often cause scheduling problems on projects, for example if you have two activities requiring the same resource they cannot be completed at the same time. For improvement efforts, a Project Network Diagram will help in mapping the sequence of activities as they currently exist and may help to point out where activities need to be divided or refined, what remedial action needs to be taken, and where resources might be better used.

How to Draw a Project Network Diagram

There are several types and formats of Project Network Diagram in use today – here, the Activity-on-Arrow (AoA) method will be used as it is a simple, but effective method that is easy to learn. This method is also known as the Arrow Diagramming Method (ADM). Other methods include Activity-on-Node (AoN) and Precedence Diagramming Method (PDM). The rules for drawing AoA diagrams are straight-forward. For this method only two symbols are required: an arrow to represent an activity, and a circle (node) to represent an event. There are two types of event – the start (tail), and the end (head) of each activity, see Figure

10.1. Each activity will have a name – e.g. "A" in Figure 10.1. If there is room on the diagram you can list the full name of the activity, otherwise a code can be used to keep the diagram simple and uncluttered. Any event (node) cannot be reached until all the activities leading to it are complete. An activity cannot start until its tail event has been reached. Finally, no two activities can have the same head or the same tail events.

Figure 10.1: A Single Activity (A), Tail (node 1), and Head (node 2)

The first thing to do before drawing a Project Network Diagram is to draw up a list of all the activities involved in the project. In project management, an Activity List will have been created from a Work-Breakdown Structure. In addition to a name, each activity will have a duration, usually measured in hours or days, which should be added to the list. Next, determine which activities have dependencies on other activities being complete before they can start. Table 10.1 shows a list of seven activities for a small project, with their duration in days, and dependencies.

Activity Name	Immediate Predecessor	Duration (Days)
A	None	1
B	None	2
C	A	2
D	A	3
E	B	1
F	C	2
G	D, E	2

Table 10.1: Activity List, Dependencies and Duration (days)

From Table 10.1 you can see that the first two activities, A and B, have no predecessors and are therefore not dependent on any other activity being complete before they can start. This means that both these activities can start at node 1, so the diagram begins with two arrows, representing activities A and B, stating at node 1. These activities are completed with the addition of nodes 2 and 3 to represent the end (head) of each activity as shown in Figure 10.2.

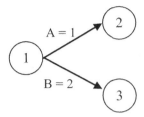

Figure 10.2: Project Network Diagram Representing First Two Activities in Table 10.1

Next, let's consider activities C, D, and E. Activities C and D are both dependent on activity A being complete, while activity E is dependent on activity B being complete. So, following the rules for drawing this type of diagram we need three arrows to represent these three activities, and three more nodes to represent the heads (ends) of each activity. Figure 10.3 shows how this will look.

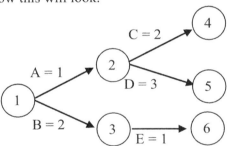

Figure 10.3: Project Network Diagram Representing First Five Activities in Table 10.1

Now there are only two activities left, F and G. However, there is now a problem. From Table 10.1 we can see that activity F is straightforward – it is dependent only on activity C being complete, but we can also see that activity G is dependent on both activities D and E being complete. According to the rules an activity can only have one start (tail), therefore we cannot start activity G at both nodes 5 and 6. The problem is overcome by merging the heads of activities D and E (nodes 5 and 6) into one head (node 5) as shown in Figure 10.4. The diagram can now be completed with activities F and G, as these are the final activities they merge at node 6.

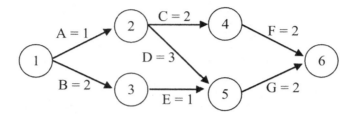

Figure 10.4: Project Network Diagram Representing All Activities in Table 10.1

Tip:
Always pay particular attention when more than one activity enters or leaves a node. This is a major source of errors.

Figure 10.4 shows the final Project Network Diagram for the activities on Table 10.1, with the logical sequence of each activity and their durations shown. When drawing diagrams like this, always work from left to right with all arrows facing towards the right side of your diagram. Avoid crossing arrows – if this does happen you will need to rework your diagram to prevent this from happening. Always be on the look-out for bursts and merges. Bursts occur when a single node is the start of two or more activities. For example, there are two bursts on Figure 10.4 from node 1 and node 2. Merges occur when a node is preceded by two or more activities. There are two merges on Figure 10.4 to node 5 and node 6. Be sure to check that your diagram shows all the activities listed on your activity list.

Finally, you can now determine the critical path through Figure 10.4. Examination of the diagram shows that there are three possible paths through the diagram. To determine which one is the critical path, add up all the durations for each path as shown in Table 10.2.

Path	Duration (days)
A, C, and F	5
A, D, and G	6
B, E, and G	5

Table 10.2: Possible Paths and Their Duration for Figure 10.4

The path A, D, and G with the longest duration, 6 days, is the critical path which tells us that the overall duration of this project is 6 days. This is the path to which most attention will be paid to by a project manager, because any delay in the activities on this path will have a more serious impact on the overall project schedule than delays in other paths. For the Business Analyst you have valuable information about the resource requirements for a solution. For example, it may be that in the example above you might want to reduce the overall project duration by one day as a result of limited resources. Therefore, you would concentrate on the critical path to see if savings can be made by altering one or more activities on that path.

Project Network Diagram Example – Marketing

To show how a Project Network Diagram can help you understand how a process works, and in what sequence the activities take place, let's look at an example where there are several activities taking place in a marketing campaign. ABC Marketing has been engaged to launch a campaign to publicise a new product line. They plan initially to send out an on-line survey to the general public and send a mail-shot to select clients as a first round of analysis. In the second round of analysis, focus group discussions will be held to get as wide an opinion on the new product as possible. The focus group discussions will take place after the survey and mail-shots are complete in order to refine the findings of these two activities. Detailed interviews will be conducted with a small number of key stakeholders while the focus groups are taking place. Time is critical on this project, so you will need to establish what the Critical Path is using a Project Network Diagram. Table 10.3 shows the full list of activities, their immediate predecessors, and their durations in days. Each activity is given a letter as a task code.

Activity	Task Code	Immediate Predecessor	Duration (days)
Plan research campaign	A	None	1
Prepare survey	B	A	5
Publish survey on-line	C	B	1
Prepare mail shot	D	A	2
Send out mail-shots	E	D	1
Analyse first round results	F	C, E	2
Prepare focus group	G	F	3
Host focus group meeting	H	G	1
Prepare interview questions	I	F	1
Hold interviews	J	I	1
Analyse second round results	K	H, J	2
Draw up final campaign plan	L	K	5

Table 10.3: Activity List for ABC Marketing Campaign

Figure 10.5 shows a Project Network Diagram for the ABC Marketing campaign project. There are twelve activities which are plotted on the diagram according to their logical sequence based on the immediate predecessors for each activity. The diagram starts with the "Plan research campaign" activity (A), which has no preceding activity.

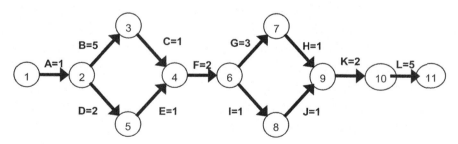

Figure 10.5: Project Network Diagram for ABC Marketing Campaign

Next, you can see from Table 10.3 that there are two activities, "Prepare survey" (B) and "Prepare mail shot" (D), which are dependent on activity A being complete. These are added to the diagram next as a burst from node 2. The activity "Publish survey on-line" (C) is dependent on activity B being complete, and the activity "Send out mail-shots" (E) is dependent on activity D being complete. These are then added to the diagram, but as both are followed by only one activity, "Analyse first round results" (F), they must merge into one node (5). Activity F is followed by two activities, "Prepare focus group" (G) and "Prepare interview questions" (I), which therefore burst from node 6. These activities are followed by activities "Host focus group meeting" (H) and "Hold interviews" (J) respectively. As activities H and J are followed by only one activity, "Analyse second round results" (K), they must merge at node 9. The final activity, "Draw up final campaign plan" (L) is dependent on activity K being complete, so it is added to the end of the diagram.

You are now in a position to determine the critical path through the ABC Marketing Project Network Diagram. From Figure 10.5 you can see that there are four possible paths through the diagram, these are listed with their total durations in Table 10.4.

Path	Duration (days)
A, B, C, F, G, H, K, L	20
A, B, C, F, I, J, K, L	18
A, D, E, F, G, H, K, L	17
A, D, E, F, I, J, K, L	15

Table 10.4: Possible Paths and Their Duration for the ABC Marketing Campaign

The path through activities A, B, C, F, G, H, K, and L at 20 days is the longest path and therefore should be monitored closely as the critical path. With this information you can monitor the tasks on the critical path which are crucial to the success of the project – any delay in any of the critical path activities will delay the whole project. Delays on any other path, though undesirable, will not impact the overall duration of the project as long as the total duration is less than that of the critical path. A Project Network Diagram tool is therefore an ideal graphical representation of a project to help the Business Analyst to:

- Determine the minimum and maximum time that activities can be started and completed

- Determine the time that the whole project will take to complete through identifying the critical path

- Show any activities that could create a possible delay

- Identify where resources, such as people, are not being used effectively.

What Do You Do Next?

The first thing to do when you have created a Project Network Diagram is to step back, examine the diagram, and follow the logical sequences on the diagram through each activity to the final deliverable. Make sure to get the opinions of others on your diagram – a Project Manager will be a great help here. If you are looking at creating a new solution to a problem, you will have a greater understanding of how the potential solution will work. If you are looking at improving an existing process, a Project Network Diagram will help you to figure out how the existing process works. You will then be able to look for improvement opportunities by looking at different possible sequences to make better use of available resources.

Using hand-drawn Project Network Diagrams is the easiest and most practical method of drawing your initial diagram. However, you should consider using project management tools when you need to modify your diagram. Tools with the ability to drag-and-drop and copy-and-paste will speed up your modifications. These also allow you to link your diagram with other project management tools such as Gantt Charts and Activity Lists.

Exercise – Project Network Diagram

In the following exercise you are required to draw a Project Network Diagram, using the Activity-on-Arrow (AoA) method, based on the 15 activities listed in Table 10.5. To get you started, the activities, their immediate predecessors, and their duration in days are given. For the purposes of this exercise, it is unimportant what the activities are – the main skill here is in being able to construct the diagram based on the information given. Once you have drawn the diagram, answer the following questions:

1. How many possible paths are there through this project?

2. What activities are on the critical path?

3. What is the overall duration of the project?

4. What other paths should you monitor?

Activity	Immediate Predecessor	Duration (days)
A	None	1
B	A	3
C	A	3
D	A	4
E	B	3
F	C	1
G	C	5
H	C	3
I	E, F	2
J	E, F	4
K	G, J	3
L	G, J	1
M	D,H	2
N	L, M	4
O	N	3
P	I, K, O	1

Table 10.5: Exercise Activities, Predecessors and Durations

Use Cases

When planning for resources you will sometimes have to think not only about the resources required to solve a problem, but also about the resources that will use the new or improved system. When eliciting requirements you will need to determine the interactions between a system and its environment, in other words: what the input into the system is, and what the output of the system is. This means that the role of the users of a system is vitally important for the Business Analyst to understand. A Use Case is a relatively simple tool that you can use to help in your requirements elicitation efforts. However, they are often either not used correctly and preparing them can be difficult. Dr. Ivar Jacobsen is credited with first developing Use Cases as a way of specifying functional requirements for software systems while working at Ericsson in Sweden in 1986, and is known as the "father" of Use Cases. While most often considered primarily as a tool for modelling software systems, Use Cases can also be used for any kind of business modelling where the requirements of the customer (user) need to be established.

A Use Case describes the possible series of interactions between a system and its environment that concentrates on providing business value. The users of a system, which are usually people or other systems, are known as actors. An actor is an entity external to the system that interacts with the system to achieve a desired goal – for example, a person using a bank automatic teller machine (ATM) is an actor who is interacting with a bank's system. By documenting how an actor uses a system you can get a greater understanding of the requirements and goals of the system. It is important to note that Use Cases concentrate only on how actors use a system, not on how the system is created or on what the components of the system are. This makes Use Cases particularly effective in communicating information about a system to its users by concentrating on what an actor will do with a system rather than how the system works.

When to Use a Use Case

There are several answers to the questions "How do we gather the requirements of a system?", or "How do we describe the user's interaction with a system?" While many tools described elsewhere in this book will help you to answer these questions, a Use Case will help you and your team to more easily elicit and be precise about the requirements of a system undergoing new development or improvement. Use Cases are especially helpful when eliciting the requirements of software systems and are unique in their power to help Business Analysts, and others involved in software development, to understand the value which the system will provide for all its stakeholders.

When you want to establish consensus between all team members about what a system will do for a user, and how the user interacts with the system, preparing Use Cases as part of the requirements elicitation process will enable the developers, testers, and technical writers who will follow to understand how the system will work. Developers will employ the Use Cases during the design and development of the system. Testers will make sure that the requirements documented in the Use Case are met by the system. Technical Writers will document how the system will be used by the user. In order to develop better solutions, all these team members must understand Use Cases. So, before you go ahead to design and develop a system, you first need to focus on whom or what will use the system (or be used by it). Writing Use Cases is therefore an essential part of software development, though they can be used for almost any business system.

How to Create a Use Case

The key to writing good Use Cases is to first identify the actors and the Use Cases, secondly draw a Use Case diagram, and thirdly write the Use Cases in simple language using a template. A Use Case diagram can be used to help illustrate how an actor can interact with a system, and helps in the understanding of a Use Case. In this type of diagram Use Cases are generally shown as oval shapes, the actors as stick figures, with lines representing associations that connect Use Cases to the actors who are involved with them. Sometimes a box is drawn around the Use Cases to emphasise the boundary between the system as defined by the Use Cases, and the actors who are external to the system. Figure 10.6 illustrates a simple Use Case diagram for a user accessing a web page. In this diagram, the actor is represented by the stick figure, the Use Case "Access web page" is represented by the oval shape, the line from the user to the oval connects the user to the Use Case, and finally the box represents the boundary of the Use Case. You can build upon this diagram by adding more users and Use Cases in order to show all interactions between users and a system.

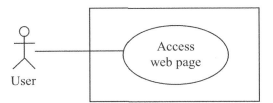

Figure 10.6: A Simple Use Case Diagram

As a Business Analyst you will encounter many different versions of Use Cases, some with different components and various levels of detail. Almost every Use Case will have seven basic components – these are described in Table 10.6. You may add other components as needed, though you should use a common template to be consistent as even small projects can have many Use Cases. Keep the language in the Use Case as simple as possible, but make each component as meaningful as possible. You may not need to use all components listed in Table 10.6 – you simply need enough components to accomplish the job to be done.

Use Case Component	Description
Name	The Use Case should have a unique name that describes the goal or event it will deal with.
Actor(s)	Each actor should be given a unique name that describes the role they play while interacting with the system. This may be a job title, but must never name an individual person.
Preconditions	Any fact that the proposed solution can assume to be true before the Use Case starts.
Basic flow of events	This is the most important part of the Use Case. It should be a short description using non-implementation specific language of the basic flow of events in the Use Case. The basic flow of events will describe the steps that the actors in the Use Case take in order to interact with the system. The basic flow of events corresponds to the most correct and simple path through the Use Case.
Alternative path(s)	This will show less common paths through the Use Case and will also deal with error handling. This section will also document some of the less common interactions between the actor and the system.
Exception(s)	Similar to Alternative Path, but actually shows what happens when an error occurs.
Post-conditions	Any fact that the proposed solution can assume to be true after the Use Case ends.

Table 10.6: Basic Components of a Use Case

An important aspect of writing a Use Case is to if possible avoid using any implementation specific language. In other words do not list any programming code or mention details of the user interface with the system.

Tip:
Only document what is relevant to the actor in each Use Case. If it is not relevant – leave it out.

For example, do not write, "The bank account holder places the ATM card into the slot of the ATM machine and types in a four-digit number on the keypad to access details of their account". Instead you should write, "The bank account holder provides a card to access details of their account". By doing this you will remove certain assumptions relating to the user interface: ATM card, slot, four-digit number, keypad, and ATM machine. As these items are implementation specific they should not be included in the Use Case.

A Use Case is useful tool to help clarify the scope of a project. If used correctly they can provide a good high-level understanding of user behaviour when using a system. They also indicate clearly what the normal situation is, what alternatives are possible, and what exception paths are available through an activity.

Use Case Example – Bank ATM

To help understand the basics of creating Use Cases, let's look again at a bank ATM as an example. Let's say you are part of a team that has been asked to review customers' use of a bank's ATM systems. First, you should identify a high-level understanding of user behaviour when using an ATM system. For the purposes of this example, let's assume that a typical bank ATM supports the following processes:

- Customer uses bank ATM for cash withdrawal

- Recording of all ATM transactions by central computer

- ATM maintenance by engineer, including replenishing cash by a security agent.

Of course modern ATMs can be used for many more activities, but the three above will suffice for illustrative purposes in the example here. From this high-level view you can determine the principle activities of the system, and the actors (people and equipment) who are external to the system that are involved in these activities. Use Cases should only represent significant activities in the ATM system, e.g. a bank customer's use of the ATM machine to withdraw cash is a Use Case. A bank customer keying in a PIN number is not a Use Case.

You now have enough information to identify three Use Cases corresponding to the processes supported by a typical bank ATM: "Withdraw cash", "Record transactions", and "Maintain ATM". The actors are: "Customer", "Central computer", "Engineer", and a "Security agent". This gives you enough information to draw a Use Case diagram, and to write the three Use Cases. So, the first step is to draw a Use Case diagram to give a graphical overview of the Use Cases in this project. Figure 10.7 shows the interactions between the actors and the three Use Cases.

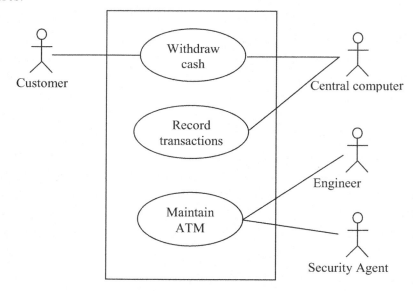

Figure 10.7: Use Case Diagram for Bank ATM

The Use Case diagram in Figure 10.7 can be interpreted easily. You can see immediately how each of the four actors interacts with each of the three Use Cases. This type of diagram will give you a good understanding of what the relationships are between each of the Use Cases and the actors. The next step is to write the Use Cases for each of the ovals in the Use Case diagram.

The Use Cases in Tables 10.7 ("Withdraw cash"), 10.8 ("Record transactions"), and 10.9 ("Maintain ATM") are based on the basic Use Case template described in Table 10.6. The Use Case "Withdraw cash" in Table 10.7 will be similar to many other Uses Cases that can be written for using the services that a bank ATM provides. For example, Use Cases could also be written for "Deposit cash/cheque", "Pay a bill", and "Top-up mobile phone".

The Use Case "Record transactions" is relatively straight-forward as the only actor is the bank's central computer. This is the second Use Case in our example in which the bank's customer is not involved – therefore there is no mention of the customer in this case.

Use Case Component	Description
Name	Withdraw cash.
Actor(s)	Customer. Central computer.
Preconditions	Customer must have a valid ATM card.
Basic flow of events	The basic flow of events in this Use Case is: 1. Customer specifies if a receipt is required 2. Customer enters amount of cash to withdraw 3. ATM machine checks with the central computer that the customer has sufficient cash on account to make the withdrawal 4. Cash is dispensed to the customer 5. Receipt is dispensed to the customer

Alternative path(s)	The alternative paths through this process are: 1. Customer does not want a receipt 2. Customer does not have enough cash on account to support the withdrawal 3. Link between ATM and the central computer is broken 4. Customer cancels transaction at any time 5. Customer forgets to take the dispensed cash
Exception(s)	The following exceptions may occur in this Use Case: 1. Customer enters incorrect PIN number, the system displays an error message and the customer re-enters a number 2. Customer enters an amount of cash that is over the daily limit for account holders. The system displays an error message and the customer re-enters an amount 3. Customer enters an amount of cash that is over account holder's balance. The system displays an error message and the customer re-enters an amount
Post-conditions	Customer account is updated by central computer.

Table 10.7: Description for the Use Case "Withdraw Cash"

Almost everything in the "Record transactions" Use Case occurs automatically, and no people actors are involved. In writing a Use Case like this it is particularly important to avoid using technical language and jargon. This can actually be hard to do and it is an important skill for a Business Analyst to use non-implementation specific language in a Use Case.

Use Case Component	Description
Name	Record transactions
Actor(s)	Central computer
Preconditions	ATM and central computer have an active connection.
Basic flow of events	The basic flow of events in this Use Case is: 1. Central computer receives communication that a customer is using the system 2. Details on each customer transaction are transmitted to central computer 3. Central computer logs all transactions in a central database 4. Customer's account is updated by central computer 5. Central computer backs up all data recorded
Alternative path(s)	If a communication breakdown occurs, back-up systems will take over using the same basic flow of events.
Exception(s)	When an error occurs, back-up systems takeover and an error message is sent to technical staff.
Post-conditions	All data are recorded and user accounts updated with details of each transaction.

Table 10.8: Description for the Use Case "Record Transactions"

In the third Use Case (Table 10.9) there are two actors involved again – an engineer and a security agent. This is the third Use Case in our example in which the bank's customer is not involved – therefore there is no mention of the customer in this case. You'll also note that there are no preconditions or post-conditions. If possible, including preconditions or post-conditions should be avoided as you need to know that they will apply in every possible circumstance in which the Use Case refers to. If they do not apply in all circumstances, leave them out – or consider writing further Use Cases to deal with preconditions or post-conditions being false.

Use Case component	Description
Name	Maintain ATM
Actor(s)	Engineer Security agent
Preconditions	None
Basic flow of events	Engineer carries out a routine maintenance check on the ATM at regular intervals. Security agent replenishes cash in the ATM when existing cash level falls below a threshold value.
Alternative path(s)	A fault occurs in the ATM outside of scheduled maintenance routine. ATM runs out of cash before security agent can replenish.
Exception(s)	Engineer carries out maintenance within a set short period to repair fault. Security agent carries out an extra delivery of cash within a set short period to re-fill ATM.
Post-conditions	None.

Table 10.9: Description for the Use Case "Maintain ATM"

The "Maintain ATM" Use Case could easily be broken into two separate Use Cases, e.g. "Maintain ATM" and "Replenish cash". For the purposes of this Use Case, both activities are considered as being part of overall maintenance and are included in this Use Case. You should be careful in deciding what should and should not be included in a Use Case, and how many Use Cases you should write. Too many Use Cases with very little detail in each will be just as impractical as too few Use Cases with too much detail – as a Business Analyst, it is important that you get the balance right. A good rule of thumb is that each project should have no more than thirty Use Cases. If there are more, consider dividing the project into two or more parts.

What Do You Do Next?

As with other analysis tools, it is always important for you to check your results. Other people, even non-experts, can provide valuable feedback since Use Cases are designed to be easily understood by users. If they are not understood, you may have to re-write them.

Be careful not to overdo Use Cases – there is a temptation to describe all of a system's behaviour using Use Cases. It may be possible to elicit all requirements with Use Cases, even in situations where they are not the most appropriate tool to use. Other requirements elicitation techniques may be better in some circumstances. Use Cases can be very helpful when planning resources as they give you a good understanding of what resources are necessary for each system. However, Use Cases do not tell you how much or how many resources are required, or for how long they are required. Other techniques such as Capacity Planning should be used in conjunction with Use Cases.

Finally, there are software tools and methodologies that can be used to help create Use Cases and to draw Use Case diagrams. Unified Modelling Language (UML) is a general-purpose language used especially in the field of software engineering. If you are involved in creating a lot of Use Cases, it may be useful to learn how to use UML.

Exercise – Library Loans

A university library contains a large selection of books, some of which can be borrowed by the university's students, academic staff, and non-academic staff (the latter includes library staff). Assume that you are part of a team that is developing a new computer system to manage all lending of books in the library. Only students and staff of the university have permission to borrow books from the library. Students may borrow up to a maximum of three books at a time, non-academic staff may borrow up to five books at a time, while there is no limit for academic staff.

The library may have more than one copy of a particular book. Most books may only be borrowed for one week at a time, though it is possible to extend a loan period for one more week. Books that are not available because they are already borrowed may be reserved. The loan periods vary from one week maximum for popular books, to three weeks for less popular books. Academic staff may borrow books for up to three months. Your task is to:

- Identify all the actors

- Identify all the Use Cases

- Draw a Use Case diagram

- Write full descriptions of each of the following Use Cases using the template in Table 10.6:
  o Borrow a book
  o Reserve a book
  o Extend a book loan.

Capacity Planning

Deciding what resources are necessary to complete a task can sometimes be a difficult decision to make. In a perfect world you will have the necessary resources available at all times to avoid performance bottlenecks, and you will have the correct number of people and systems working at any given time. An organisation's ultimate goal is to provide satisfactory levels of service in the most cost effective way. When you are designing new processes or improving existing processes, you may have to consider the capacity of your organisation to deliver the required level of service. You can use Capacity Planning to help you decide what quantity of resources (facilities, equipment, and staff) you will need to have available over a set period of time (hour, day, week, month, or year). Capacity is the maximum quantity of work that can realistically be processed during a specific period of time using the resources available. When calculating Capacity you need to distinguish between the theoretical capacity and the actual capacity of an organisation. Theoretical Capacity is the expected production rate multiplied by the number of staff, multiplied in turn by the number of working hours. However, this type of capacity is rarely reached as various factors need to be accounted for. To get the actual capacity, you need to take into account variables such as holidays, sickness, absenteeism, varying skill levels, varying production rates, training, meetings, and subtract these from the theoretical capacity.

Capacity Planning is all about measuring work. A Business Analyst should consider being able to measure work for several reasons. You will always need to know what your organisation's capacity is to deliver a solution to your problem-solving efforts. If an organisation is about to undergo a major transformation such as increased automation, re-organisation, or a major policy change, a Capacity Plan will help in the preparation and analysis of the business case for the transformation. One of the biggest costs in an organisation is people; a Capacity Plan will help to determine how these costs are distributed over products and which activities can be allocated to each product. Capacity Plans will also help in using activity-based costing for prioritising process improvement efforts, deliver performance metrics for process management, and can also be used to supplement other tools and methodologies.

Using Capacity Planning will enable your organisation to provide a better more reliable level of service to its customers, and helps ensure that timeliness standards are met. Organisations that have a culture of using Capacity Plans can maximise productivity, increase employee utilisation, and ensure better cost control through improved data on employee activity. For the employees there will be less stress and a much better Work Life Balance, resulting in fewer crisis situations. Keep in mind that measuring capacity can be a sensitive issue – one person's capacity for work will differ from another.

When to Use Capacity Planning

It is important for the Business Analyst to be able to measure work. For example, if you are preparing a business case, looking to prioritise improvement efforts, calculating process or efficiency metrics, or planning capacity – you will need to be able to determine how much work is involved. This is especially true when you are looking to make efficiency savings in a process.

There are three main scenarios where you should consider using Capacity Planning:

1. To determine level of service requirements

2. To analyse current capacity

3. To plan for future activities and requirements.

In the first scenario, where you will need to determine the level of service requirements, you must first understand the meaning of "workload" – this is usually measured as a unit time standard. This is defined as the time required for a qualified employee to complete a defined task while working at the standard rate under normal circumstances. It is important you base your measurements on this definition. Later you will learn about some methods for estimating workload, for now the key points to remember are that in order to measure workload, you need to determine *who* is doing the work, *what* type of work is being carried out, and *how* the work is being carried out. Use Case documents will be of great assistance here.

To determine if your organisation is meeting the needs of its customers, you need to analyse the current capacity. It may be that the level of service is at a high standard because you have more capacity than is needed to deliver the service. It could also be that poor levels of service could be due to under-capacity to deliver, rather than inefficient or inadequate processes. Many organisations do not have a good measure of what their current capacity is and make the mistake of under- or overestimating their capacity to get a job done. For an organisation, such as a bank with 100 branches nationwide with 750 employees, it is definitely worthwhile doing a Capacity Plan as it will simply not be possible to allocate 7.5 people per branch. In this case you would need some way to determine how the employees are distributed over the branch network.

How to Draw Up a Capacity Plan

The Capacity Planning process is made up of several steps that involve different tools and methodologies that will enable you to carry out the key activity of measuring work. For each step you need to get as accurate a measurement as possible. In some cases you will be able to determine exact figures for measuring workload, while in others you will only be able to estimate. In the case of estimates you will need to rely on scientifically proven methods to get the best estimates. Figure 10.8 summarises the steps in the Capacity Planning process.

Capacity planning is an on-going process and you should continue to look for ways to optimise capacity, operational efficiency, and employee utilisation. There are several techniques that you can use to measure work as part of your capacity planning efforts – here you will examine four of these techniques:

- Simple Estimation and Time Study

- Work Volume Measurement

- Observation

- Activity Sampling,

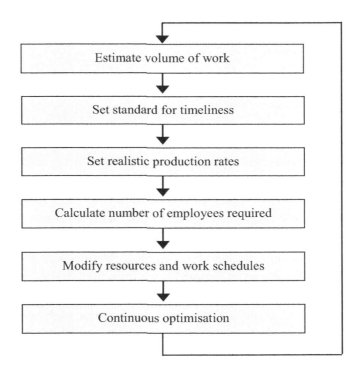

Figure 10.8: The Capacity Planning Process

This first technique, Simple Estimation, makes use of different types of estimates to give you an idea about how much work is required to complete a task. This technique also includes Time Study. The second technique, Work Volume Measurement, looks at ways in which you can estimate the time it takes to complete a task based on volume. The third technique, Observation, is a simple way to measure the capacity of people in the performance of their jobs. The fourth technique, Activity Sampling, measures work by making observations at intervals over a period of time. Let's now take a look at these work measurement techniques in more detail.

A Simple Estimation Technique. Estimating how long a task will take can often be a guessing game – for example, how long does it take a librarian to replace a book returned from a loan onto its rightful place on a book shelf? There are various ways to estimate how long this, or any other simple task, will take to complete. Some of these can be particularly useful and informative, especially when working in groups. Estimating can be divided into three types as follows:

1. Whole Estimate

2. Analytical Estimate

3. Group Average Estimate.

Each of these estimation techniques provides varying levels of accuracy listed in ascending order above – the Whole Estimate is the least accurate, while the Group Average Estimate is the most accurate. A Time Study usually follows these three estimation techniques – this is where the actual time it takes to complete the task being estimated is measured.

Let's say you want to estimate how long it will take the librarian to replace a book on a shelf – at a high level this involves checking in the returned book, taking the returned book from the library desk, walking a few meters to the shelf, placing the book on the shelf, and returning to the library desk. If you ask each person in a group, such as your team, to guess privately how long this will take off the "top of their heads" with only this high-level information – you will usually get widely varying estimates. Record the highest and the lowest estimate – no matter how different they are. As the likely result of this estimate could vary enormously, it may not be an effective method of estimation – at the very least it will show you that more accurate techniques are required.

The next estimation technique involves an Analytical Estimate. This time you provide as much detail as possible on the process being measured and ask each member of your team to do a second estimate. A Business Analyst should use documented procedures in this case. For example, an Analytical Estimating Recording sheet, which will show all the activities in the task, is necessary for this exercise. Figure 10.9 shows a sample sheet for the librarian replacing a returned book on a library shelf. Each member of your team should now estimate the time for each individual activity and add up the total time. Record the highest and the lowest estimate – no matter how different they are. You should find that the estimates are not as widely varying as in the first "top of the head" whole estimate – there should be a reduction in the difference between the highest and lowest values as members of your team now have more information on which to base their estimates.

Analytical Estimating Recording Sheet				
Prepared by: *Business Analysis Team* Description of task: *Placing loan book returns on library shelf*				
Description of Activity	**Unit of Measure**	**Quantity**	**Standard Time**	**Total Time**
Obtain book from Library desk				
Scan bar code				
Log book as returned				
Reset security tag				
Check book's Dewey number				
Look up shelf location for book				
Walk 10 meters to book shelf				
Locate correct position for book				
Place book on shelf				
Return to Library desk				
			Total time:	

Figure 10.9: Sample Analytical Estimating Recording Sheet

The next type of estimate is the Group Average Estimate, where you now ask your team to get together in pairs and for each pair to review each of their analytical estimates. Each pair should then agree on a new estimate based on this review. Record the highest and the lowest estimate – no matter how different they are. This usually results in a further reduction in the difference between the highest and lowest values.

Once the three types of estimate are completed, you are now ready to conduct an actual Time Study. This is where you and your team measure the time it will actually take the librarian to replace a returned book on the library shelf. Get each member of your team to time the librarian in action, using stopwatches or their own wrist watches. Record the highest and the lowest measures – even though there may only be a few seconds at most between the highest and the lowest measure. This should result in the most accurate measurement that you can get. Table 10.10 shows some sample data resulting from all three estimating techniques and the Time Study. You can see that there is a gradual improvement in the measurements, with a reduction in variance between the highest and lowest values, as more accurate estimating techniques are used.

Technique	Highest (secs)	Lowest (secs)	Variance (secs)
Whole Estimate	90	15	75
Analytical Estimate	45	16	29
Group Average Estimate	21	29	8
Time Study	22	20	2

Table 10.10: Sample Results for Estimating Techniques and Time Study

Note that the Time Study is done in an actual environment, but not under strict conditions. However, it should give you a more accurate measure for this work than the estimating techniques in use. A more accurate measure would be gained if you measured the librarian in action several times, measured more than one librarian, and measured the time taken to return books on different shelves. It may not always be possible to carry out a Time Study – but when you do you should determine what type of user you are going to measure as they will vary from novice to expert.

Work Volume Measurement Techniques. There are several ways in which you can estimate the time it takes to complete a task based on volume. The simplest technique is to look at historical patterns and trends on which you can base future projections. This can be an effective technique but it relies on having very accurate data. For example, if you have historical data which shows that one employee can on average create ten widgets per day over a one year period, you can project that in order to create twenty widgets per day you will need two employees. Another technique is to use your own personal insight and experience. While this is not a scientific technique, experience has a value when measuring workload and it is definitely worth getting the view of an expert to review any measures you calculate with other techniques. You could also use other techniques such as getting a group consensus on a measurement, or get an independent market research survey done.

The work volume estimating technique that you will look at here is called Simple Regression. The key principle of this technique is that it distinguishes between parts of a task that take a constant amount of time and parts that are volume related. The formula for estimating the amount of time (y) that a task will take is:

$$y = a + bx$$

where "a" is constant time, "b" is volume related time, and "x" is number of items being measured. To illustrate how this formula works, let's take a look at a simple everyday example – estimating how long it takes to copy 1,000 pages on a photocopier. Suppose you observe a colleague photocopying 10 pages and that the total amount of time taken is 30 seconds. By dividing the amount of time taken by the number of pages (30/10) it means that each page takes on average 3 seconds to copy. Therefore, based on this as a measurement for all photocopying jobs, it would take 3,000 seconds (50 minutes) for 1,000 photocopies. However, as you will see, this is not a reliable measurement.

In order to make an accurate estimate you will need to distinguish between routine constant and variable (volume related) activities in the task. In the case of the photocopy example, the task can be broken down into three different activities. In the case of photocopying 10 pages, during your observation you note that the activities can be broken down as shown in Table 10.11. Here you can see that there are two tasks that are constant – setting up the photocopier and collecting the finished pages take the same amount of time for any amount of pages. The actual copying of the pages is volume related – in this example there are 10 pages to copy (assuming that a photocopier can copy at a rate of one page per second), so this variable part of the task will take 10 seconds to complete. The overall duration in seconds is estimated using the simple re-gression formula (y = a + bx):

$$y = (15 + 5) + (10 \times 1) = 30$$

Activity	Time (seconds)	Constant/Variable
Set up photocopy machine	15	Constant
Photocopy pages	10	Variable
Collect pages	5	Constant

Table 10.11: Volume Estimate of Photocopying 10 Pages

Now let's consider how we can use this formula to estimate how long it would take to photocopy 1,000 pages. Table 10.12 provides the breakdown of activities and the time taken for each one. The overall du-ration in seconds is estimated using the simple regression formula (y = a + bx):

$$y = (15 + 5) + (1,000 \times 1) = 1,020$$

Activity	Time (seconds)	Constant/Variable
Set up photocopy machine	15	Constant
Photocopy pages	1,000	Variable
Collect pages	5	Constant

Table 10.12: Volume Estimate of Photocopying 1,000 Pages

Using the simple regression method that takes into account constant and variable activities, photocopying 1,000 pages is estimated to take 1,020 seconds – 17 minutes. This is a huge difference when compared to the time of 50 minutes estimated earlier using a 3 seconds per page measure. There are other variables in this example that you may also consider such as allowing for paper getting jammed, and running out of toner and paper. Using a method such as simple regression will give you a much more accurate measure of work.

Observation. Observation is a simple way to measure the capacity of people in the performance of their jobs. By observing a person carrying out his or her normal work duties you can get a good picture of that person's workload capacity in their normal work environment. Observation is a useful technique when you want to record details about an existing process or if you are involved in a project to change or improve an existing process. It is also one of the main Requirements Elicitation techniques (see Chapter 4). There are two types of Observation: Passive, and Active.

In Passive Observation the observer quietly observes the user carrying out their working duties recording everything in detailed notes that is observed over a set period of time (hour, day, or week). This type of observation should be invisible to the user and can be done remotely using CCTV cameras, or by simply taking a position in the user's location that does not interfere with their work. The observer does not interact in any way with the user throughout this process, and only asks questions at the end of the process. For more accurate results, the observation should take place several times until the observer is satisfied that they have a good understanding of how the process works. For example, you could observe a librarian carrying out his or her work from a discreet distance over a period of hours.

Active Observation is similar to Passive Observation except that this time the observer can ask questions and interact with the user - the observer is very visible to the user. If the observer has a question to ask, for example to clarify how part of a process works, they ask the question straight away even if it interrupts the user in their work. Obviously this type of observation needs to keep the interruptions to a minimum by ensuring that only important interruptions are made. Otherwise an inaccurate picture of how a process works, and consequently the workload capacity of the user, will arise.

Whether you choose to use Passive or Active Observation to measure workload, you should always let the person being observed know that the observation is taking place. People may be resistant to being observed and will need to be assured that they are not being investigated – rather that the observations are part of a process improvement exercise. You also need to be careful in the choice of person to observe. It may be unfair on all employees to select the organisation's star performer and base production on resulting workload measurements. Equally, using a novice user will result in less valuable information. As far as possible, observe normal users in their normal environment, under normal working conditions.

When you have completed your observations, clarify with the user any issue that you observed during the process. Provide a summary of your notes to the user and review your observations. When used correctly, a simple technique like Observation can give you a realistic and practical overview of a person's workload capacity by observing how people actually work in their normal environment. However, you should also note that even though this is a relatively simple method to use, it can be disruptive to the person or persons being observed, and can be very time consuming.

Activity Sampling. Activity Sampling is a simple and less intrusive method of measuring workload when compared to Observation. Unlike a full Observation, Activity Sampling is a technique in which observations are made at intervals over a period of time – for example, you could record what a librarian is doing at ten minute intervals throughout the day. Each observation records exactly what is happening at the time interval – these intervals can be at fixed times or at random times. Activity Sampling is used normally for collecting information on the percentages of time spent on activities. This removes the need to devote the time necessary for full Observation. A huge advantage of Activity Sampling is that it allows you to measure activities or groups of activities of long duration more economically.

Before you start sampling activities you need to document what activities the person under observation is likely to be doing during their normal routine under normal working conditions. For example, a librarian is likely to be doing several activities including lending out books, accepting returned books, using a computer, making a telephone call, taking a break, or some other activity. Table 10.13 shows an Activity Sampling check sheet for measuring the workload of a librarian for a three hour period at 10 minute intervals. As the table shows, the observer simply ticks the activity that the librarian is doing at the exact instant at each 10 minute interval. If there are a lot of ticks under activities listed as "Other", you should consider re-designing your Activity Sampling check sheet to include more activities. Using a simple check sheet like this you can get a good picture of activities over a period of time.

Tip:
The number of activities should not exceed 10, as more than this will slow down your study.

Time interval	Lending	Returns	Using Computer	Using phone	Break	Other
0						√
10	√					
20			√			
30			√			
40		√				
50				√		
60					√	
70						√
80	√					
90		√				
100			√			
110						√
120			√			
130		√				
140				√		
150			√			
160				√		
170			√			
180	√					

Table 10.13: Activity Sampling Check Sheet for Library Workload

Let's now take a look at an example where the activities of a personal assistant (PA) are being sampled over a 35 hour week (2,100 minutes) period of study. Table 10.14 summarises the results of this Activity Sampling exercise using the data collected from an Activity Sampling check sheet similar to the one in Table 10.13.

Activity	Number of Observations	% of Total Time	Time Equivalent (minutes)	Minutes per Unit of Work	Number of Units
Word processing	90	42.9	900	12 per page	75 pages
Phone calls	50	23.8	500	3 per call	167 calls
Queries	30	14.3	300	1 per query	300 queries
Filing documents	25	11.9	250	2 per document	125 documents
Other	15	7.1	150	1 per "other"	150 "others"
Totals:	210	100	2,100		

Table 10.14: Activity Sampling Results for PA Workload

Observations were made at 10 minute intervals throughout the study with a total of 210 observations made. The figures for observations in each activity are then converted to percentages to show the amount of total time that each activity represents. Using the total time taken figure of 2,100 minutes you can work out the time equivalent in minutes for each activity as a proportion of the time taken.

The number of minutes per unit of work is based on average industry standards for each activity – each determined separately with work measurement techniques. The figure of 12 minutes per page for word processing is based on a typing rate of 50 words per minute for an average page with 600 words. The figure of 2 minutes per document for filing includes time to file documents in different locations. Three minutes per call is a common standard in Call Centres for dealing with queries. One minute is allocated to each of handling queries and dealing with "other" activities not recorded on the Activity Sampling check sheet.

By dividing the time equivalent by the number of minutes per unit of work, the total number of units of work that the PA can manage over the period of study can be calculated. For example, based on the sample data and calculations, it is estimated that a PA can produce 75 word processing pages in 15 hours (900 minutes) based on the fact that the PA is spending 42.9 per cent of the time word processing. In total, based on this Activity Sampling process, the workload of a PA per week works out at 75 word processed pages, handling 167 calls, dealing with 300 queries, filing 125 documents, and dealing with 150 other types of activity.

Finally, Activity Sampling will not give you 100 per cent accuracy, so you will want to know how confident you can be with how accurate your estimates are. In general, the more observations you make, the more accurate your estimates should be – so how many observations do you need to make to achieve a specific level of confidence? A formula can be used to calculate the number of observations needed for different levels of confidence as follows:

99% Confidence	$N = (2.58)^2 P(100-P)/D^2$
95% Confidence	$N = (1.96)^2 P(100-P)/D^2$
90% Confidence	$N = (1.645)^2 P(100-P)/D^2$

where N is the number of observations needed, P is the proportion occurrence, and D is the margin of error. Both P and D are expressed as percentages. A 95 per cent confidence level is generally considered to be a reasonable compromise between reliability and precision. Suppose you want to achieve a 95 per cent confidence level with a margin of error of ±10 per cent. Using the proportion figure for the word processing activity from Table 10.14, P will have a value of 42.9 per cent, and D will have a value of 10 per cent. When these are inserted into the formula, N will have a value of 94.1. This means that to achieve a 95 per cent confidence level with a margin of error of ±10 per cent you will need to make at least 94 observations. If you want to reduce the margin of error further down to ±5 per cent, you will need to make 376 observations (using the same formula).

You can also check how accurate the number of observations you have made is by reversing the formula to calculate the margin of error (D) as follows:

$$D = \pm \sqrt{[(1.96)^2 P(100–P)/N]}$$

This formula assumes a 95 per cent confidence level. In table 10.14 there are 90 observations for word processing. Inserting this value for N and a value of 42.9 per cent for P gives a value for the margin of error (D) of ±10.2 per cent. It is always a good idea to check your data in this way to see how accurate your sampling size is.

Capacity Plan Example – ABC Building Society

ABC Building Society has a network of 50 branches spread all over the country employing 500 staff in the branch network. Some branches are in rural towns, while others are located in the larger cities. Some branches are larger than others and the volume of business varies from branch to branch. Therefore it is worth carrying out a Capacity Planning exercise to see if each of the 50 branches is adequately resourced. In this exercise you will look at Capacity Plans for two of the branches.

Figures 10.10 and 10.11 show Capacity Plans for an adequately staffed branch (A), and an inadequately staffed branch (B) respectively for a period of one month. The average number of working days per month is assumed to be 21 days, with each employee required to work 7.25 hours per day. Assume that each unit of work has been worked out using work measurement techniques similar to those described in this chapter. Each activity in each branch is listed – they are broken into variable activities and constant activities. For the variable activities, the average volume multiplied by how many units can be handled per hour, gives the total number of required hours assuming each person is working at 100 per cent capacity. For the constant activities, the amount of time set aside each day for these activities multiplied by the average number of working days per month, gives the hours required for constant activities also assuming each person is working at 100 per cent capacity. The difference between the two Capacity Plans is mainly in the average volume of activities – you can see from Figure 10.10 that branch A is a lot busier than branch B. In both branches, time for training is added with time also allowed for absenteeism (1.6 per cent) and annual leave (9.2 per cent).

The total time required for all the activities, plus time allowances in branch A, works out at 1,490.2 hours. This means that at a rate of 21 working days per month (based on a 7.25 hour per day), branch A will need 9.8 people (1,490.2/21/7.25 = 9.8) to meet the workload requirements of the branch. There are 10 people on the payroll which means that there is a positive variance of 0.2, or 2 per cent – therefore the branch is adequately resourced. In branch B (Figure 10.11), the number of staff needed to meet requirements is 8.5, but there are only 8 employees. This results in a negative variance of -0.5, or -5 per cent – therefore the branch is inadequately resourced.

Branch A Business Activities	Average # Days	Hours/ Day	Hours Required @ 100%
Business Development	21	8.6	180.6
Arrears collection	21	5.2	109.2
Sub-Total A			289.8
Process Activities (variable)	Average Volume	Units/ Hour	
Loan Applications:			
Home Loans	15	0.3	50.0
Commercial Loans	10	0.1	100.0
Car Loans	28	0.5	56.0
Personal Loans	32	1.5	21.3
Customer Inquiries	1,550	12.0	129.2
Account Opening	45	2.0	22.5
Account Closing	17	2.0	8.5
Overdraft Renewals	82	5.0	16.4
Arrears Management	13	4.0	3.3
Counter Transactions	4,250	12.0	354.2
Sub-Total B			761.3

Support Activities (Constant)	Average # Days	Hours/ Day	
Servicing of accounts	21	1.4	29.4
Deposits administration	21	2.2	46.2
Housekeeping	21	1.1	23.1
Office Administration (fixed)	21	4.0	84.0
Office Administration (variable)	21	2.8	58.8
Referrals processing	21	1.8	37.8
Sub-Total C			**279.3**
Total Hours based on activities:			1,330.4
Training:			14.5
Total in-branch hours:			1,344.9
Absenteeism (1.6%):			21.5
Annual leave (9.2%):			123.7
Total paid hours required:			**1,490.2**
Current payroll hours:			**1,522.5**
	Current staff	Required staff	Variance
	10	9.8	0.2

Figure 10.10: Capacity Plan for an Adequately Staffed Branch

If Capacity Plans for all 50 branches of the building society's network are measured in the same way, and the variance values for each branch plotted on a bar chart, the resulting chart will look something like Figure 10.12. Variance values ranging from 0 per cent to 2 per cent indicate that the branches in this area (top half of Figure 10.12) are adequately resourced. Variance values in the 0 per cent to -0.5 per cent ranges are considered to be branches that will experience some difficulty with workload slightly exceeding available capacity. Finally, any branch with a variance value less than -0.5 per cent is considered to be inadequately resourced. With these data you can now examine the distribution of resources across the network and see where changes can be made so that all workload requirements are met and that employees in some branches are not over-stretched.

Branch B Business Activities	Average # Days	Hours/ Day	Hours required @ 100%
Business Development	21	6.5	136.5
Arrears collection	21	1.5	31.5
Sub-Total A			**168.0**
Process Activities (variable)	**Average Volume**	**Units/ Hour**	
Loan Applications:			
Home Loans	17	0.3	56.7
Commercial Loans	8	0.1	80.0
Car Loans	25	0.5	50.0
Personal Loans	26	1.5	17.3
Customer Inquiries	1,405	12.0	117.1
Account Opening	42	2.0	21.0
Account Closing	15	2.0	7.5
Overdraft Renewals	71	5.0	14.2
Arrears Management	11	4.0	2.8
Counter Transactions	3,975	12.0	331.3
Sub-Total B			**697.8**
Support Activities (Constant)	**Average # Days**	**Hours/ Day**	
Servicing of accounts	21	1.3	27.3
Deposits administration	21	3.5	73.5
Housekeeping	21	0.9	18.9
Office Administration (fixed)	21	3.5	73.5
Office Administration (variable)	21	2.9	60.9
Referrals processing	21	1.3	27.3
Sub-Total C			**281.4**

Total Hours based on activities:			1,147.2
Training:			14.5
Total in-branch hours:			1,161.7
Absenteeism (1.6%):			18.6
Annual leave (9.2%):			106.9
Total paid hours required:			**1,287.1**
Current payroll hours:			**1,218.0**
	Current staff	**Required staff**	**Variance**
	8	**8.5**	**-0.5**

Figure 10.11: Capacity Plan for an Inadequately Staffed Branch

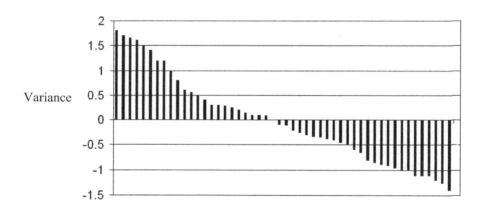

*Figure 10.12: Capacity Plan Variances for a 50 Branch
Building Society Network*

What Do You Do Next?

Once you have determined all your estimates and drawn up your Capacity Plans, it is a good idea to have them reviewed by your team to tease out any issues that might remain. As there are a lot of numbers involved, be sure to check that the correct calculations and formulas have been used. Be careful about staff resistance and suspicion about Capacity Planning – the best way to overcome this is to communicate the benefits of Capacity Planning to all staff, and involve them in your efforts. Pilot studies are also an excellent way to get staff "buy-in".

When dealing with people resources, be careful with figures such as "8.5", which indicates eight and a half people. You may want to have a slight over-capacity to cope with unexpected events such as more than normal customers coming to the building society. 0.5 of a person could be somebody working part time. You may also have a team of people available to be sent out to branches temporarily to cope with under-capacity. With the information elicited from Capacity Planning, you can set standards for timeliness, set realistic production rates, and calculate the number of employees required. Ultimately you will get the best use of resources by having the correct capacity available to meet requirements.

At all times you must build reasonableness into your estimates and calculations – for example by making allowances for holidays, absenteeism, and training when drawing up your capacity plan. When measuring work – always check that what you are measuring is done so in a normal environment. It is a good idea to get an experienced colleague to examine your figures and to discuss them to ensure that they are based on reasonable estimates and calculations. You should also check to see if there are existing data from previous studies in your organisation, or if there are industry standards already in existence that you can use. Be careful with using older data as they may be out of date, e.g. times estimated before a process was automated. Nevertheless – there may be some valuable information that you can use based on older data.

Capacity Planning should be part of a continuous cycle of process improvement. Once you have established an organisation's workload capacity, you can look at ways to increase that capacity. Recruiting extra people resources is one obvious way, but you may also want to look at ways to increase capacity with existing resources. There are several steps you can take to help increase capacity:

- Use work measurement tools, such as those described in this chapter, to get more accurate estimates of volumes and time

- Improve resource usage with training, motivating employees, and making best use of work schedules

- Identify best practices and roll out to other employees and teams

- Do not commit resources to a project without first determining the resources' requirements

- Simplify your organisation's procedures and embark on process improvement initiatives

- Cultivate a culture of Capacity Planning and ensure that the benefits add clearly to business value.

Exercise – Office Cleaning

ABC Cleaning is a company that specialises in all aspects of cleaning small to medium-sized offices. Recently ABC Cleaning has bid for a new contract to clean a suite of executive offices, but is unsure of what resources might be required to fulfil the requirements of this cleaning contract. You have been hired as a Business Analyst to determine the capacity needed to clean the suite of executive offices.

For the purposes of this exercise, assume that the cleaning duties will be as follows:

- Polishing desks

- Dusting shelves

- Vacuum cleaning carpets

- Washing windows

- Emptying bins

- Miscellaneous cleaning duties.

For each office, consider the following:

1. Distinguish between variable activities and constant activities in this exercise

2. Using the Simple Estimation technique, try with a team of people to work out a Whole Estimate, Analytical, and Group Average estimates for cleaning an executive office

3. How would you measure the volume of work required for cleaning an office? Suggest ways to use the Work Volume Measurement technique to work out cleaning times for all offices in the suite

4. Design an experiment to observe an employee cleaning an executive office. Would you use passive or active Observation? Explain why. How many times do you think you should conduct this experiment?

5. Design an Activity Sampling check sheet for this exercise. How would you use this check sheet to determine the volume of work required in cleaning an executive office suite? What sample size would you recommend?

Reflection

At the beginning of this chapter you set out to learn more about resource requirements for your problem-solving initiatives. With Project Network Diagrams, Use Cases, and Capacity Planning you have the tools to help you plan resources more carefully. These tools will be of use in both new process development, and in your process improvement efforts.

In your Learning Journal, answer the following reflective questions:

•   What have you learned in this chapter?

•   Can you identify situations in your organisation where a Project Network Diagram would help you to understand the sequence of activities in a process?

•   Examine some of the systems that you personally use in your organisation. Explore how Use Cases could be used to communicate how you (as the actor) interact with these systems

•   Think about how Capacity Planning techniques might benefit you and your organisation. Are there some areas where there is under-capacity, and other areas of over-capacity? Why is this happening? Can you suggest ways of improving this situation?

•   What other analysis tools will help you to establish resource requirements?

•   What are your next steps after identifying resource requirements?

All your efforts in analysing resource requirements should be part of a continuous improvement cycle. You should think about how you can use the tools described in this chapter to cultivate best practices and a culture where resources are carefully measured and used. Making the best use of available resources is common sense, but many organisations do not deliver products and services in the most efficient and effective way because they do not apply principles such as those discussed in this chapter.

11

ANALYSIS TOOLS FOR
PROCESS IMPROVEMENT

*"Don't dwell on what went wrong. Instead, focus on what to
do next. Spend your energies on moving forward toward
finding the answer."* – Denis Waitley

Introduction

Process improvement is a central part of what a Business Analyst does.
You should always be looking for ways of doing things in order to make
improvements by analysing each situation and its objectives so that you
can create more efficient and effective processes. As with all problem-
solving efforts, you should make use of structured methodologies in your
process improvement efforts. In order to achieve a leadership position,
an organisation must constantly be looking towards improving processes
all the time. It may not always be possible to produce products and provide services at a lower cost, higher quality, and in quicker time than
before – but you should be in a position to look at any process with a
view to improving it in some way.

In this chapter you will look at two analysis tools that will help you
to think about process improvement in a structured way. The first tool,
SREDIM Process Improvement, describes a systematic approach to the
design and improvement in the ways in which processes are carried out.
The second tool, Radar Charts, will help you to look at ways of measuring performance before you embark on process improvement initiatives.

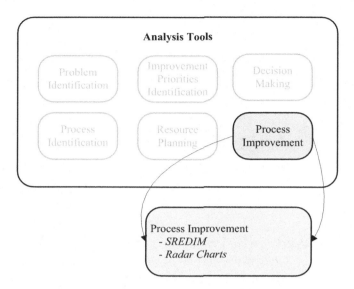

SREDIM Process Improvement

SREDIM is an acronym that stands for **S**elect, **R**ecord, **E**valuate, **D**etermine, **I**mplement, and **M**aintain. It is sometimes referred to as a Methods Study, which is an analysis for the different ways of doing work. Russell M. Currie first published the six step SREDIM process improvement methodology, while working as Head of ICI Central Work Study Department, in his 1960 book entitled "Work Study". SREDIM is an analytical approach of methods study by which the Business Analyst can plan carefully the best sequence of analysis to show where improvement is likely to be most effective. By using a formal method such as SREDIM, combined with your own knowledge and that of others, you stand a better chance of success in your process improvement efforts. Table 11.1 summarises each SREDIM component.

Select	– the problem to be solved
Record	– relevant data on the problem
Evaluate	– the data collected
Determine	– and develop the solution of the problem selected
Implement	– the solution
Maintain	– the solution in practice

Table 11.1: Summary of SREDIM Process Improvement Components

When to Use SREDIM

SREDIM is a common-sense general problem-solving strategy that can be applied in many situations. It is an analytical approach that will be especially useful because it makes use of a carefully planned sequence of analysis. This will help to show you where change is likely to be most effective by pointing out unnecessary and redundant activities and showing where improvement is possible. By using an analytical approach, you and your team will stand the best chance of success in your improvement efforts. It will also prevent you from falling into the trap of taking unnecessary short-cuts.

When you are looking to control and reduce costs and defects, SREDIM is a valuable methodology that can potentially provide significant benefits. Keep in mind that tackling the most obvious costs and defects may not necessarily produce the most valuable improvement. However, the following list shows some examples where you can get the most benefit from using SREDIM:

- Inconsistent quality in products and services

- Poor operation planning

- Health and safety regulations being ignored or not understood

- Build up of queues and bottlenecks

- High rate of product returns

- High levels of employee stress and fatigue.

How to Use SREDIM

SREDIM process improvement is best carried out on a step-by-step basis following the six components in sequence. It is an iterative process that should be part of continuous improvement efforts. While each of the six components of SREDIM follows each other in sequence, keep in mind that within each component there can be several iterative steps taken before you move on to the next stage. As an analysis tool SREDIM makes use of many of the other tools that are described in this book. Let's examine in more detail each of the six SREDIM components and how you use them in process improvement efforts.

Select. The first thing to do is to select the problem to be solved. The most important thing to remember here is that you and your team select only one problem. Other problems should be dealt with by a separate SREDIM process, or by another team. Identifying a problem is a difficult thing to do – be careful not to look only at the symptoms of the problem, but to concentrate on stating what the problem is. You should select the problem on the basis of issues such as delays, capacity problems, costs, poor quality, and breakdowns. Brainstorming will be useful here as well as other problem identification tools such as Cause and Effect Diagrams, Pareto Analysis, Value Analysis, Flow Charts, and SIPOC Diagrams. At the end of this stage you should have a clearly defined problem statement – once you have this you are well on the way to solving the problem.

Record. Record means that you must focus on facts and collect data about the selected problem. Use the requirements elicitation techniques such as Brainstorming, Interviewing, Surveying, Requirements Workshop and 5W2H to help. It is important to distinguish between what facts are relevant to the selected problem and those that are not – judgement and experience are vital here. The question "Why?" the problem is occurring is not asked in this stage – concentrate on eliciting facts.

Part of the Record stage is to ensure that you understand all appropriate and relevant data about the problem you are facing. Flow Charts and SIPOC diagrams will be particularly helpful here. You can also make great use of Check Sheets and work measurement techniques such as Observation and Activity Sampling. Whatever methods and tools that you use, be sure to share the data with your analysis team. Review all data and facts, and critique each other's work until you are happy that all relevant data are recorded.

Evaluate. In the Evaluate stage you and your team will analyse the problem stated in the Select stage using the facts and data gathered in the Record stage. The purpose of the Evaluate stage is to examine the true reasons underlying the problem to be solved. The question "Why?" is central now – you should critique all information gathered and be rigorous in your analysis. Attention to detail is important here – accept nothing at face-value. This stage usually involves asking a lot of questions about the data – brainstorming and the 5W2H method are often used here. Typical of the types of questions you should ask are shown in Table 11.2. These generic questions can be asked in evaluating almost any problem and may yield vital information.

Issue	5W2H	Question
Purpose	Why?	– is this process needed?
		– is this process being done?
		– is this process being done in this way?
Activity	What?	– are all the activities involved?
		– are the essential and relevant activities?
		– else could be done?
		– should be done?
Place	Where?	– is the process taking place?
		– are the employees' offices?
		– is this process being done?
		– should this process be done?
Staff	Who?	– is involved in this delivering this process?
		– else could do this process?
		– should be doing this process?
Time	When	– does this process start?
		– is this process finished?
		– is this process being done?
		– could this process be done?
		– should this process be done?
Method	How?	– do we do this process?
		– else can this process be done?
		– should this process be done?
Cost	How much?	– does this process cost?
		– should this process cost?
		– can the cost be reduced?

Table 11.2: 5W2H Questions to Ask During SREDIM Evaluate Stage

In addition to 5W2H, Cause and Effect diagrams are particularly effective in helping you to get to the root cause of a problem and should be a vital tool here. Be careful not to try and prove that any possible solution to the problem will work at this time – wait until later to do this. Concentrate on evaluating the recorded facts and data. The Evaluate stage is often referred to as the Examine stage.

Determine. If carried out successfully, the Select, Record, and Evaluate stages should lead directly to one or more potential solutions. In this stage, you and your team judge the potential solutions to determine if they are feasible and that they will lead to the desired improvement. Once each potential solution has been thoroughly examined, for example using tools such as Value Analysis, SWOT Analysis and Cost-Benefit Analysis, you should determine which solution is the best to work with. The Determine stage is often referred to as the Develop stage.

While the Determine stage may be primarily the responsibility of you and your process improvement team, you should also encourage other employees in your organisation to put forward solutions to any problem encountered. Even a simple suggestion box might yield valuable possibilities in your problem-solving efforts. Many successful organisations value the contributions and participations of their employees at all levels, and promote a culture of involving them in continuous improvement efforts. The Japanese term "Kaizen" is often used to describe continuous improvement.

Implement. As a result of following the SREDIM process improvement methodology, the point is eventually reached when the agreed solution is ready to be implemented. In the Implement stage, the solution chosen in the Determine stage is implemented. Business Analysts may not be directly involved in the Implement or Maintain stages of SREDIM – however, it is a good idea to be aware of what goes on in these final stages. Implementation will require the active support of everyone involved which can be difficult to achieve. Informing and consulting employees is needed to ensure that the new or improved process is implemented successfully.

The Implementation stage will require a detailed project plan and a budget – usually the overall project manager will be responsible for this. Here risk management is vital to ensure that the implementation does not fail. A full training programme should be considered for the new process, but bear in mind that this will be difficult to create as the new process is not yet fully implemented until the Implement stage is complete. The Implement stage is often referred to as the Install stage.

Maintain. The final stage of SREDIM is the Maintain stage. This is where the implemented solution is maintained in the real world. Maintenance is necessary to deal with the inevitable problems that arise which were not anticipated during earlier stages. Breakdowns nearly always occur, and unforeseen circumstances nearly always arise – it is best to have a plan in place to deal with such events. New processes inevitably will have "teething" problems and it is best to have adequate resources available during the early stages of running the new process. As a Business Analyst you should learn from these problems and review all failures when they occur. This should help you to improve your own skills by learning from mistakes and lead to improved performance in the future.

Formal reviews should be held at regular intervals to check how the new process is working. Radar Charts can be useful here to monitor and compare performance over time. You can also use Benchmarking to compare performance of the current process against the previous process to see if there has been an improvement or not. The Maintain stage is often referred to as the Maintenance or Monitor stage.

SREDIM Example – Job Safety Analysis

To illustrate how SREDIM can be used to improve processes, let's take a look at the example of Job Safety Analysis. This is a procedure which helps to integrate approved health and safety procedures into a particular process or job operation. Most jobs can be broken down into smaller components. In Job Safety Analysis, each basic step is to identify potential risks and hazards for each component, and to recommend the safest way to do the job. SREDIM is often used to improve Job Safety Analysis by measuring the risk in each of the component parts of a job that is being reviewed for improvement. Using a structured approach with

SREDIM helps to develop a safe method for carrying out each stage of a job. The basic procedure for a Job Safety Analysis using SREDIM is as follows:

Select	Select the job to be analysed
Record	Break the job down into its components and record the sequence of steps to complete the job
Evaluate	Evaluate each component part of the job to determine the risk of an accident
Determine	Determine and develop control measures for each component to reduce or eliminate the risk of an accident occurring
Implement	Implement formal written safety procedures and safety instructions for the job being reviewed
Maintain	Review the procedures at regular intervals to ensure they are being used

Now let's use this methodology for a simple electrical task – changing a light bulb. The first part of SREDIM in this example is the simplest – the task to be selected is "Change a defective light bulb". Next, the task is broken down into its components parts and steps (Record). For each step a risk is identified (Evaluate) and then a safety precaution is recommended for each risk identified (Determine). Table 11.3 summarises the steps, risks, and precautions for the Record, Evaluate, and Determine stages. The Safety precautions column can now form the basis of providing written safety guidelines for completing the task (Implement). A formal safety manual or Job Safety Analysis record sheet spells out step-by-step a safe system of work for completing this task. Figure 11.1 shows an example of a typical Job Safety Analysis record sheet. The detail and contents of a record sheet such as this will vary depending on the jobs to be completed, your organisation's standards for written safety procedures, and can be adapted to suit any situation. The ultimate aim could be to carry out this procedure for all jobs in your organisation – especially those relating to health and safety procedures. Job Safety Analysis record sheets can now be used to review the procedures at regular intervals to ensure they are being used (Maintain).

Job Step	Risks Identified	Safety Precautions
Turn off light switch	• Electric shock • Turn off wrong switch	Ensure light switch is in OFF position. Disconnect appropriate fuse.
Get step-ladder	• Strain to back	Carry step-ladder according to load-bearing guidelines. Get help if needed.
Place step-ladder under light bulb	• Step-ladder placed in unsafe position	Ensure step-ladder is placed in a stable position under bulb. Adjust until safest position achieved.
Climb ladder	• Slipping on steps • Falling off step-ladder	Slowly climb step-ladder one step at a time. Hold onto sides of step-ladder.
Remove defective bulb	• Breaking glass • Electric shock • Drop bulb	Check if bulb is a bayonet or screw type. Remove slowly, taking care not to hold the bulb too tight.
Descend ladder	• Slipping on steps • Falling off step-ladder	Slowly climb step-ladder one step at a time. Hold onto sides of step-ladder.
Dispose of defective bulb	• Cuts from broken glass • Recycled incorrectly	If glass is broken, handle with care. Use protective gloves. Ensure that bulb is disposed of correctly in the appropriate recycling location.
Get new bulb	• Damage bulb when removed from packaging	Open packaging with care. Read instructions on packaging.
Climb ladder	• Slipping on steps • Falling off step-ladder	Slowly climb step-ladder one step at a time. Hold onto sides of step-ladder.
Insert new bulb	• Insert incorrectly • Drop bulb • Break glass	Insert bulb according to instructions on packaging. Handle with care.
Descend ladder	• Slipping on steps • Falling off step-ladder	Slowly climb step-ladder one step at a time. Hold onto sides of step-ladder.
Switch on light	• Electric shock • Blowing a fuse	Ensure light switch is in ON position. Reconnect appropriate fuse.

Table 11.3: The Steps (Record), Risks (Evaluate), and Precautions Identified (Determine) for the "Change a Defective Light Bulb" Task

Job Safety Analysis Record Sheet		
Job title:	Department:	Reviewed by:
Date:	Time:	
Job description:		
Job Step	**Risks identified**	**Safety precautions**
Suggested safe system of work:		
Training programmes associated with this job:		
Date for next review:		
Approved by:		

Figure 11.1: A Sample Job Safety Analysis Record Sheet

What Do You Do Next?

Once you have completed a process such as a Job Safety Analysis using the SREDIM analysis tool, it is important to keep reviewing your methodology and to constantly look at ways of using it to improve your processes. Reviews such as this will be more effective if they are structured, and of course if those affected by the reviews are included in the review team. For example, if new employees are taught safety precautions in the beginning, it is less likely they will develop bad habits and be at risk over time.

Whatever you use SREDIM process improvement for, be sure to communicate the benefits of this structured methodology to those affected by it. SREDIM is a common-sense methodology and should be easily understood by all in your organisation. It is a very useful tool that can be applied to almost any task. By using this approach you and your team will have a better chance of making successful improvements to processes in your organisation.

Exercise – Car Maintenance

In this exercise you will use the SREDIM process improvement methodology to create a Job Safety Analysis record sheet for a car maintenance task. To get you started, the job that is to be selected for review is "Changing a car wheel". Using the SREDIM method, complete the following tasks:

- Identify and record all the steps involved in changing a car wheel

- Evaluate all the possible health and safety risks associated with each step

- Determine what safety precautions you would recommend for all the risks that you have evaluated

- Design an appropriate Job Safety Analysis record sheet so that you can implement the safety precautions that you have recommended

- Identify the procedures that you would put in place in order to ensure that your safety precautions are followed and maintained.

Radar Charts

Many analysis tools can be used for process improvement initiatives, but sometimes it is useful to have a tool when you want to look at several different factors at the same time in one view. Radar Charts can be used to illustrate graphically the size of the gaps among several organisational performance areas and are an ideal easy to use tool to help you get started by highlighting areas where improvement is needed most. A Radar Chart can show in a single graphic not only what the gaps are, but the size of the gaps as well. This illustrates the important categories of performance and makes visible concentrations of strengths and weaknesses.

Radar Charts are often referred to as Polar or Spider Diagrams because of their appearance, they are also known as Kiviat Charts. The first use of Radar Charts was by the statistician and mathematician Professor Georg von Mayr who based his diagrams on star plots for data visualisation in 1877. As a data visualisation tool, these charts can be useful to clearly define full performance in each category and captures the different perceptions of all the team members about an organisation's performance.

When to use Radar Chart

Radar Charts are most useful when you want identify gaps among a number of both current organisational performance areas and ideal performance areas. For example, if you wanted to get a "big picture" of a comparison of actual performance data with projected performance data in different areas, a Radar Chart will show you where the performance gaps are. It will provide an overall realistic and useful picture of performance. Radar Charts can be used as an evaluation tool that can include varied perspectives from a team of analysts that has evaluated a number of organisational performance areas.

Before a process can be improved it is important to establish what the existing situation is. Radar Charts can show you gaps in performance for almost any situation. You can use them in business to compare a variety of performance data such as sales figures, rate of returns, delays, breakdowns, capacity problems, queues, costs, and customer complaints. They can be used to compare the performance of individuals, teams, and whole organisations. Finally, they are also useful to compare performance over a period of time – for example, you could compare monthly or annual performance data to see if there is an improvement over a period of time.

How to Draw a Radar Chart

The first thing to do before you start to draw a radar chart is to identify the categories of performance that you want to compare. It is important to get varied perspectives in order to ensure that you identify the most important categories. In all your process improvement efforts you should get as wide a variety of opinions as possible – a good idea here is for you and your team to brainstorm all possible categories and refine them down to about five to seven categories. Anymore than seven categories will result in a cluttered diagram – if you need more than this consider using more than one chart. Once the categories are selected you will need to refine them and set minimum and maximum values. 0 per cent-100 per cent is a common measure for a category, but many other scales can be used – for example, 0-10 where 0 is the lowest performance value and 10 the highest.

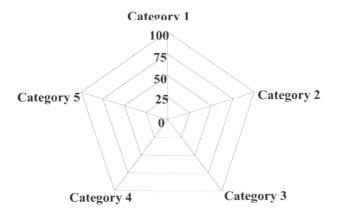

Figure 11.2: Basic Radar Chart

Once you have established the categories of performance that you want to use, it is time to draw the Radar Chart. While you can use charting software to create professional looking Radar Charts, you can also use a flipchart, a whiteboard, or a simple pencil and paper. To begin, draw a large circle with spokes from the centre to the edge representing each category you are comparing. Next, label the categories. Figure 11.2 shows in a pentagon shape a scale of 0 to 100 for each of five categories being examined.

You now have a framework diagram on which you and your team can rate each category. Performance in each category can be measured either objectively or subjectively. You can use actual figures, e.g. sales data, or estimates – whatever values you choose plot them for each category along a separate axis that starts in the centre of the chart (value 0) and ends on the outer ring (value 100). In the example here we will use ratings as a performance measurement. When working in a team, get each individual to rate from 0 to 100 the performance in each category. Each team member then marks the point on the chart where they rate each value for each category as in Figure 11.3.

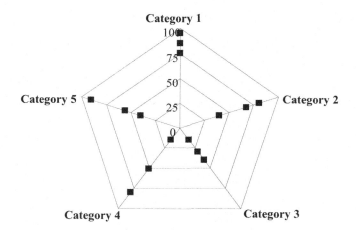

Figure 11.3: Radar Chart with Individual Ratings of Performance

To get a single figure for each category you can discuss the individual ratings within your group and reach a consensus, or you can calculate the average value. When you have a single value for each category, plot these on your Radar Chart as shown in Figure 11.4. You now have several options to simplify your chart. You can remove the individual ratings and leave just the team ratings to reduce clutter. To make the diagram more useful, you can join the remaining dots with a line, or fill in the area on the chart represented by the team ratings.

Tip:
Make the team's ratings clearly visible on the chart. Use different shapes and colours to differentiate the team ratings from individual ratings.

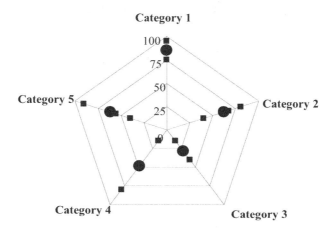

***Figure 11.4: Radar Chart with Individual (small squares) and
Group (large circles) Ratings of Performance***

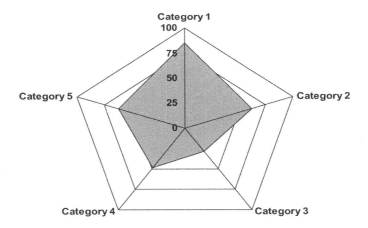

Figure 11.5: Radar Chart with "Big Picture" View of Performance

Figure 11.5 shows the final version of the Radar Chart, which gives a "big picture" view of overall performance in the five categories. From Figure 11.5 you can see that the best performance is in Category 1, while the poorest performance is in category 3. A Radar Chart such as this shown in presentations or reports will illustrate graphically the major strengths and weaknesses so that you can target areas that will benefit most from process improvement efforts. It is also useful in showing overall performance of an organisation in the selected categories.

Radar Chart – Example

To show how Radar Charts can be useful in showing a "big picture" view of performance, let's look at some sample advertising and revenue data for an organisation that is divided into four regions – North, South, East, and West. Table 11.4 shows the amount spent on advertising in each region using five different advertising media – Internet, television, radio, newspaper, and magazine advertising. The totals show the amounts spent for each medium across all regions, and the total revenue for each region.

	North	South	East	West	Total
Internet	€20,000	€52,000	€9,000	€17,000	€98,000
Television	€70,000	€36,000	€47,000	€45,000	€198,000
Radio	€45,000	€59,000	€7,000	€39,000	€150,000
Newspaper	€10,000	€38,000	€15,000	€20,000	€83,000
Magazine	€22,000	€34,000	€20,000	€40,000	€116,000
Revenue	€3,350,000	€3,700,000	€2,600,000	€2,900,000	

Table 11.4: Advertising and Sales Data

There are a lot of options to create Radar Charts using these data – to put all data onto one chart would make for a chart that is too cluttered and would provide little in the way of useful information. Let's say you wanted to look at the advertising spend for each of the five different advertising media, and compare this for each of the four regions. The categories to measure are the five media types. For each region, plot the five values on the charts – this will result in four separate Radar Charts as shown in Figure 11.6. At a glance you can see that the Radar Charts are quite different, showing that there is an uneven spend on advertising in each region and on each type of advertising media. For example, you can see that in the North region that there is a concentration of television and radio advertising. In the South region there is much more even spending on advertising across all five media. In the East region, advertising is concentrated on television, while in the West region spending is lowest on Internet and Newspaper advertising. Placing all four Radar Charts together, as in Figure 11.6, allows you to easily compare the four regions. With this information you can possibly review advertising spending policy with a view to getting better value for money, or to question why there is such a disparity from region to region.

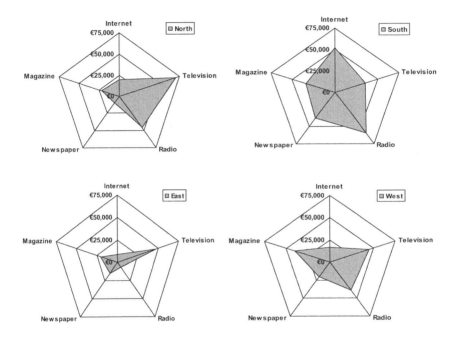

Figure 11.6: Advertising Spending per Region

Table 11.4 also shows some figures for total advertising spending and for total revenue per region. This presents opportunities for further analysis using Radar Charts. You can create a chart for total spending for each advertising medium as shown in Figure 11.7 – this shows that television advertising dominates spending, with radio advertising the next highest. You can also see at a glance that newspaper advertising has the lowest value.

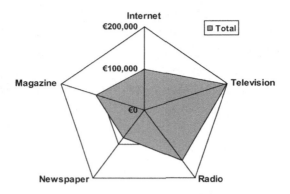

Figure 11.7: Total Advertising Spending

In Figure 11.6 you get a picture of the advertising spending for different types of media by region, but you do not see the effect on sales revenue. From Table 11.4 you can see that the region with the highest revenue is South with €3,700.000 – Figure 11.6 shows that the South region has a relatively even spread of spending across all types of advertising media. The region with the lowest revenue is East with €2,600.000 – Figure 11.6 shows that the East region has a high value for spend on television advertising, but comparatively low values for all other types of media. With this information you can investigate if advertising money is being spent in the best way to yield the highest return. You can also look at improving the balance of spending in each medium if necessary.

What Do You Do Next?

When you are interpreting your Radar Chart, check each axis as well as the overall shape to see how well it fits your business goals. Check that everything is visible and easy to understand. Whenever you prepare a Radar Chart you should always keep a copy so that you can compare it to newer charts after a period of time has elapsed. The Radar Charts shown in this chapter show only actual values for advertising spending. You could also draw up a set of charts for actual versus budgeted spending to get even more value out of your analysis. Radar Charts are also commonly used to identify the gap between actual and desired performance.

Be careful when using Radar Charts, especially when using data like ratings. Whether you are using ratings or hard data remember that your

Radar Chart will help to identify gaps within each category, but not the relative importance of the categories themselves. Establish what the most critical category is and concentrate your improvement efforts on this by working to close the gap in this category.

Exercise – Hospital Appointment Waiting Times

In this exercise you will examine some data recorded for the length of time it is taking patients to get an appointment at a range of five hospitals. In Table 11.5 the figures represent the number of patients recorded as having to wait less than one month, more than one and less than two months, more than two and less than three months, more than three and less than four months, and more than four months for an appointment in each hospital.

	0 < 1 month	1 < 2 months	2 < 3 months	3 < 4 months	> 4 months
Royal Hospital	148	133	87	48	35
Memorial Hospital	312	293	162	63	45
St John's Hospital	114	176	215	201	134
University Hospital	231	196	175	123	54
Central Hospital	165	124	65	23	5

Table 11.5: Hospital Appointment Waiting Times

Assume that the Government Health Department has set a target of lowering the appointment waiting times for 90 per cent of patients to less than three months for all hospitals. Using Radar Charts, compare the performances of each hospital and answer the following questions:

1. Which is the best performing hospital?

2. Which is the poorest performing hospital?

3. Where are the concentrations of strengths and weaknesses for each hospital?

4. What is the overall performance for the combined hospital appointment waiting times?

5. How is each hospital performing compared to the Health Department target?

6. Where would you recommend that priority efforts be made to improve the process of lowering appointment waiting times?

Reflection

At the beginning of this chapter you set out to develop the skills you need to think about process improvement in a structured way. SREDIM process improvement allows you to examine a process, task, or job, in order to concentrate solely on that process – in other words it forces you to look at one process at a time. With Radar Charts, you were introduced to the importance of measuring performance before you embark on process improvement initiatives. You can now look at performance from several different criteria and concentrate on those that are in need of improvement. In Chapter 12, you will look at improving performance in more detail.

In your Learning Journal, answer the following reflective questions:

*   What have you learned in this chapter?

*   Can you identify processes in your organisation that would benefit from a review with a structured methodology such as SREDIM?

*   What measures of performance are you aware of that are used in your organisation?

*   Try to find some data such as sales figures, customer complaints, or number of defects. Use radar charts to plot performance in each area. What can you learn from your charts?

*   What other analysis tools will help you to understand and improve processes?

*   What are your next steps after using tools such as SREDIM and Radar Charts to help you in your process improvement efforts?

Any effort to improve processes should be part of a continuous improvement cycle. The important part of process improvement is identifying the actual process that is most in need of improvement. Once this is done, SREDIM comes into its own as it helps you to adhere to a structured methodology every time – nothing gets left out or forgotten. Ensure that you continue to cultivate best practices and a culture where structured methodology becomes part of all problem-solving efforts and especially in process improvement.

CONTROLLING AND IMPROVING PROCESSES

"Excellent firms don't believe in excellence – only in constant improvement and constant change." – Tom Peters

Introduction

Before a process can be improved a Business Analyst will need to know how well it is performing already. Most businesses will strive to improve their performance over a period of time – for example, to increase sales on a yearly basis, or to decrease the number of defects in a manufacturing process. Not all processes in a business will be performing as well as they can, while other processes will be performing better than what is expected. One thing is certain – almost any process can be improved, and part of your job as a Business Analyst is to look at processes to see how they can be improved. Even something that is performing very well may have potential to perform even better, while it is obviously vital that under-performing processes must be improved. However, most of the time you may be working with limited resources, so it may not be possible or practical to attempt to improve every process. You will have to prioritise which processes are to be targeted for improvement. To do this you will have to be able to measure the performance of a process prior to any improvement effort. For example, how can you go about decreasing the number of defects in a manufacturing process if you don't know what the current and historic rate of defects is? Gathering data and information on current and historic performance is critical to the success of your improvement efforts.

Throughout this book you have looked at analysis tools to help you understand how processes work, gather information about processes, and to identify priorities for process improvement. In this chapter you will concentrate on performance. First, you will look at performance measurement and what the key measures of performance are. Secondly, you will look at benchmarking performance so that you can compare performance of a process with that of another. Finally, you will examine performance from the viewpoint of its importance to customers. Keep in mind throughout that all measures of performance should be based on solid data and information, and that any improvement effort should be aligned with the overall business goals of your organisation.

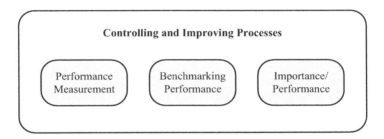

Performance Measurement

Performance measurement will vary from organisation to organisation. For some, overall performance can be measured by the performance of measures such as stock price, market capital, market leadership, market share, sales figures, profitability, and production rates. Each organisation will have a variety of measures to determine how it is performing overall, and how different processes within the organisation are performing. However, you can use general measures to assess performance based on a different evaluation criteria.

Identifying what to measure begins with an understanding of your organisation's mission, goals, and objectives. Some organisations may have hundreds of different criteria for measuring performance, while others may concentrate on a few key performance indicators (KPIs). These indicators represent those few high-level measures that link directly to the goals, objectives, and ultimately to organisation's mission. A KPI is a measure that you can use to measure and track the performance of your organisation to a high level strategic goal. It should provide you with a balanced view of the overall performance of the organisation.

Why is it important to measure performance? At all levels of an organisation you need evaluative information to help you make decisions about the processes that you want to control and improve. At its simplest, this information should tell you if, and in what important ways, a process is working well or poorly, and why. The ability to make good decisions is often hampered by the lack of good and accurate information on the results of improvement efforts. Without measuring performance it will be very difficult to manage or control processes, and make decisions about improving processes. In order to improve management and the increased efficiency and effectiveness of your organisation's processes it is important to set goals and report regularly by measuring performance. By doing this you will have an effective method of determining whether or not your organisation is meeting its goals and objectives, and achieving its mission.

In this chapter you will look at performance measurement using six key performance indicators: time, cost, quality, resources, efficiency, and reliability. All six KPIs are very closely related. The first three KPIs (time, cost, quality/scope) are based on the same three standard constraints used in project management. These are often represented by the project management triangle (Figure 12.1). If any of the three sides changes in size, the other sides must adjust to accommodate. For example, adding new features to a product will add more time, or greater costs, or both. In an ideal world, each project will be completed ahead of

Figure 12.1: The Project Management Triangle of Constraints

schedule, under budget, and have loads of high quality features. In reality, you will be working with a finite set of resources, have to set priorities, and manage time. The second three KPIs (resources, efficiency, and reliability) are important measures to tell you about the resources that an organisation needs to produce its goods and services, and how efficient and reliable these are. Combining the six KPIs (Figure 12.2) gives you an ideal framework to determine performance in each of the six categories of measurement.

Figure 12.2: The Key Performance Indicators (KPI) Framework

Using radar charts you can easily compare performance over a period of time. In the left side of Figure 12.3 you can see that the time and cost KPIs are performing well, the reliability, efficiency, and resources KPIs have some room for improvement, but that the quality KPI is underperforming badly and should be prioritised for improvement. Following improvement efforts over a period of time, you can see on the right side of Figure 12.3 that the quality KPI shows a marked improvement, but at the expense of cost.

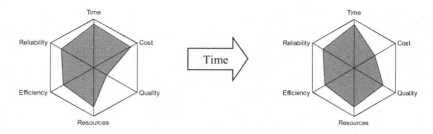

Figure 12.3: Comparison of KPIs Over a Period of Time

Each KPI may be made up of several components and will in turn be a combination of many measurements. Accurate data to give you the information you need is therefore vital to the success of any improvement effort. Where accurate data are not available, be sure to engage expert opinion where estimates are calculated, or assumptions are made. Let's now look at some measures for each of the six KPIs in more detail.

Time

The time KPI is a relatively simple measure of performance. Time will be measured in many different scales from nanoseconds, to hours, and to years. Whatever measure of time you use to determine performance, you will need to know what the performance objective is in the first place. You will need to know what the historical, current, and target performance standards are in order to determine whether you should attempt to improve time-related performance. If your business is delivering its products and services at a slower rate than your competitors, this is not an acceptable performance. However, it is not just a simple comparison with your competitors at a snap-shot in time that will determine overall performance. For example, let's take a look at two key measures of time in a call centre: the time it takes to answer calls, and the duration of each call. Assume that the call centre's primary measure for the time it takes to answer calls is the percentage of calls answered within one minute, and that calls should be completed in less than five minutes. Table 12.1 outlines some performance statistics expressed as percentages and compares current performance with historical and target performance standards. You can see from this table that the current performance of 88 per cent of calls answered within one minute compares well with the historical figure of 85 per cent, and could be regarded as an acceptable performance. However, the target performance is that 90 per cent of calls should be answered within one minute, therefore while the current performance is better than previous performance, it still has some way to go before it achieves the 90 per cent target. While 88 per cent of calls answered within one minute are close to the target of 90 per cent, it may be regarded as an unacceptable performance. The second performance measure shows a current performance rate of 30 per cent of calls having duration of less than five minutes – just below the historical performance of 33 per cent, but well below the target performance of 60 per cent. Clearly this is not acceptable and a lot of improvement needs to be made in order to achieve an acceptable level of performance. Of course it is possible that 100 per cent of calls are answered within one minute and that all calls have duration of less than five minutes – this may not be practical and could be enormously expensive to achieve. However, it does show what is theoretically possible, even though it may never be reached.

	Calls Answered Within One Minute	**Call Duration Less than Five Minutes**
Historical performance	85%	33%
Current performance	88%	30%
Target performance	90%	60%

Table 12.1: Performance Data for a Call Centre

Several measures can be used to determine time-related performance. In addition to measures such as those used in a call centre above, you could also have additional similar measures such as percentage of calls answered within 30 seconds or two minutes, or percentage of call durations less than four minutes. Other measures can be used to show time-related performance. Table 12.2 shows examples of time-related measures for a web site's availability, with a brief description of each measure. For most organisations it is crucial that their web site be available on-line at all times and that downtime be minimised as much as possible. This is especially true in the case of on-line sellers such as Am-

azon, Ryanair, eBay, and Ticketmaster – as even a few minutes downtime could have a serious impact on revenue. Usually a business will
have a Service Level Agreement (SLA) with their web site provider
where an agreed level of availability is signed into a contract.

Website Time Performance Measure	Description
Mean Time Between Failure (MTBF)	The average time between web server failures over a given period of time. In other words, the average time a server will work before failing.
Mean Time to Repair (MTTR)	The average time it takes to repair a web server failure. This is the time measured from the occurrence of the failure to its resolution.
Availability	Availability takes into account the mean time between failure (MTBF), and the mean time to repair (MTTR). A general formula for the availability of a web server is: $\text{Availability} = \left\{ \dfrac{MTBF}{(MTBF + MTBR)} \right\} * 100$
Uptime	Time since last reboot.
Timeouts	The number of occurrences of timeouts reported on the server, possibly due to pages failing to load or broken links.
Downtime	Total time server is not available. Includes planned downtime and unplanned downtime.
Planned downtime	The time planned for scheduled maintenance. This is also known as Service Outage Duration.

Table 12.2: Time-related Performance Measures for a Website

Whatever measures you use, make sure that they fit into an overall
performance measurement framework as part of the KPI framework
(Figure 12.2) so that you have a plan with time measures and designated
responsibilities. Once this plan is implemented and data collected, comparisons can be made and new time-related performance targets can be
set.

Cost

The cost KPI will give you a good understanding of how performance is measured from a financial point of view. At its simplest, you will need to know how the actual financial performance of a business compares to the budgeted performance. This type of analysis will compare a process's outputs or outcomes with the costs to produce them. Simple financial measures used as a KPI include Net Present Value (NPV), Return on Investment (ROI), and Payback (see Chapter 8). As in the case of the time KPI, you will need to know what the historical, current, and target performance standards are in order to determine whether you should attempt to improve cost-related performance. If your business is delivering its products and services at a higher cost than you have budgeted for, this is not an acceptable performance. Table 12.3 outlines a simple example where cost performance is compared for current, historical, and target performance using an example of actual versus budgeted annual expense claims for a small business over a three year period.

	Actual Expenses Claim	**Budgeted Expense Claims**	**Deviation from Budget**
Year 1	€ 12,343	€ 11,897	–€ 446
Year 2	€ 13,891	€ 12,582	–€ 1,309
Year 3	€ 14,283	€ 14,465	€ 182

Table 12.3: Performance Data for Budget Expense Claims

The data in Table 12.3 show that in year 1 there was an over spend on expenses of €446, and in year 2 performance got a lot worse as the over spend increased to €1,309. In year 3, performance has improved so that there is a slight under spend – performance is now at an acceptable level.

Several other measures can be used to determine cost-related performance. In addition to measures such as those used in the expense claim example above, you could also have additional similar measures such as a breakdown of each expense by type, length of time for expense claims to be made, and the length of time for expense claims to be processed. Other measures can be used to show cost-related performance.

Table 12.4 shows some examples of cost-related measures for maintenance of a web site.

Whatever cost performance measures you use, make sure that they fit into the overall performance measurement framework as part of the six KPIs. This can also provide vital information for any Cost-Benefit Analysis efforts as part of process evaluation.

Website Cost Performance Measure	Description
Unit costs of IT services	This cost covers the routine maintenance costs of the website during the measurement period.
Deviation of planned cost for Service Level Agreement	The deviation of the planned cost is the difference in costs between the planned baseline versus the actual budget of the SLA.
Downtime	Direct costs of downtime such as loss of income due to website unavailability.
Waste	Any unnecessary work that has to be done as a result of errors, poor organisation, or communication.
Rework/correction	Costs associated with updating and making corrections to information on the website.
Salaries	All salaries and their associated costs such as tax and insurance, for full-time and part-time employees. Should also include contract employees.

Table 12.4: Cost-related Performance Measures for Website Maintenance

Quality/Scope

All organisations should strive to produce as high a quality of products and services at all times. Quality means different things in different situations – one person may regard a product as having high quality, while another person may regard the same product as having low quality. There is no simple measure to determine if quality is high or low – many factors must be taken into account. The most important of these is scope – the quality/scope KPI is used here as an indicator of quality in a product or service and is made up of several components. Scope forms the basis for an agreement between your organisation and your customers by identifying both the process objectives and major deliverables – in other words what the process will do, and what the process will not do. A clear scope definition is crucial to the success of any process, and it defines a baseline for performance measurement and process control. Many organisations place a great deal of emphasis on quality and have quality assurance procedures in place such as Six Sigma and International Standards Organization (ISO) as an indicator that the quality of the organisation's products and services will meet (and often exceed) customers' expectations. The Business Analysis Body of Knowledge (BABOK®) describes quality as "the degree to which a set of inherent characteristics fulfils requirements", and it describes scope as "the features and functions that characterise a product, service or result".

The quality/scope KPI can be measured in many ways. In the software development process it is often measured by the number of errors (bugs) that occur throughout the software development life cycle and in the post-production phase. Software companies strive to produce bug-free software, but often have to release updates and new versions of their software to fix bugs found. Table 12.5 shows a simple example representing quality/scope KPIs for software development of a new product being prepared for its first release. The table shows an extract from a bug tracking database for each build of the software.

	Build			
	#45	#46	#47	#48
Number of bugs carried over from previous builds	34	35	30	25
New bugs logged for this build	6	3	4	4
Bugs fixed since last build	5	8	9	10
Number of bugs carried forward to next build	35	30	25	19

Table 12.5: Extract from a Software Development Bug Tracking Database

In Table 12.5 you can see that the number of bugs that are being fixed for each build is increasing and that the overall number of bugs logged is reducing with each build. This process is repeated until there are no new bugs and all old bugs have been fixed. Therefore, the software product will meet the quality requirement of no known bugs when released, and that the scope of the product will fulfil requirements.

Several other measures can be used to determine the quality/scope KPI. In addition to measures such as those used in the software development example above, you could also have additional similar measures such as different categories of bugs (e.g. major and minor), and time taken to fix a bug. Other measures can be used to show quality/scope-related performance. Table 12.6 shows some examples of quality/scope-related measures for a manufacturing process, with a short description of each measure.

Manufacturing Process Performance Measure	Description
Number of defects per unit	During a product testing cycle and post release maintenance and support, the number of defects per unit recorded over a period of time is a good indicator of how product quality was changing over the product lifecycle.
Percentage of service requests resolved	Percentage of service requests resolved within a defined and acceptable period of time.
Shipment duration	For a delivery process, compare the order date with the delivery date, and monitor whether the average shipment duration meets requirements.
Service delivery penalties	Total service delivery penalties paid within time period being measured.
Time-to-market	The time it takes from the time a product or service is initiated until it is available in the market place.
Satisfaction scores	Satisfaction scores from customer surveys.
Actions outstanding	Actions outstanding – for example since last Service Level Agreement (SLA) review.
Warranty claims	The number (or rate) of warranty claims over a period of time per product.

Table 12.6: Quality/Scope Performance Measures for a Manufacturing Process

The quality/scope KPI is one of the most important measures of performance. No effort should be spared in controlling and improving quality and keeping projects within scope. In project management, great emphasis is placed on quality. The Project Management Body of Knowledge (PMBOK®) emphasises three important areas within quality management to ensure that a project will satisfy its requirements: quality planning, quality assurance, and quality control. In quality planning, you should determine which quality standards apply and how they should be satisfied. In quality assurance, you should evaluate performance on a regular basis so that you can be confident that quality standards will be met. Finally, in quality control you should monitor quality standards and look at ways of avoiding unsatisfactory performance.

Whatever measure of quality/scope you use make sure that they both fit into the overall performance measurement framework as part of the six KPIs. It is tempting to measure overall performance using a quality KPI on its own – but this would not take into account other key KPIs and should be avoided.

Resources

Resources are the inputs that a business uses to generate its products and services. They include human, financial, facility, equipment, and material resources. In addition to identifying what resources are needed for any process, you will also need to establish what quantities of each should be used to deliver the process activities. Most of a business's resources will be focused directly on the generation of products and services, therefore it is crucial that you measure what the resources are and what they are used for. Quite often you will be working with limited resources, which will make it difficult to control and improve processes, and consequently performance will be affected. The resources KPI is closely related to the cost KPI and very often will be measured together.

At its simplest, the resource KPI determines if an organisation has appropriate people, equipment, and materials available for performing the work needed to produce products and services to a high quality, within budget, and on time. In order to improve the performance of a process, you will need to establish if there are adequate existing resources available to do so. If not, you will need to determine what type of extra re-

sources are required and in what quantity. Mismanaging people resources is often a potential cause of conflict and needs to be monitored
carefully to ensure that there is adequate capacity to meet the requirements of a process, and conversely that there is full use being made of
existing resources. Resource loading refers to the amount of people resources an existing process requires during specific time periods. Over or
under allocation of resources must be avoided in order to reach acceptable performance levels. Figure 12.4 shows in a Gantt chart how three
individuals have been allocated as resources to a process that has duration of two weeks. You can see that John has been over-allocated in the
first week as he has been assigned to tasks A (five days) and D (2 days).
Mary has been allocated correctly to task B (five days), while Peter is
under allocated – he has been allocated to task C (four days) and has not
been allocated to any task on the fifth day. In the second week, resources
are allocated more evenly with both John and Mary being allocated as
resources to tasks E and F respectively for five days each. However,
John may still be in difficulty due to being over allocated in the previous
week. Peter is still under allocated to task G for only three days in this
week and has not been allocated to other tasks. One solution to the uneven allocation of resources here would be to reallocate task D to Peter –
this will reduce the workload for John and make better use of Peter as a
resource. Appropriate allocation of people to tasks is one of the most
important resource KPIs.

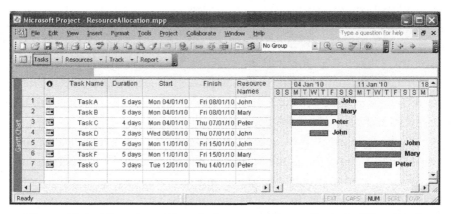

Figure 12.4: Allocation of People Resources Over a Period of Two Weeks

Several other measures can be used to determine the resources KPI. In addition to human resources, you will also need to be able to measure the performance of other resources such as financial, facility, equipment, and material. Table 12.7 show some examples, with short descriptions, of KPIs for a production maintenance process in a manufacturing environment. Measures such as these KPIs will help you to decide if your organisation will need to acquire more resources to accomplish the work needed. If more resources are required you might need to outsource some of the work – without measures of what resources are needed you will not be able to know what amount of extra resource is required, and when it is needed.

Whatever measure of resources that you use, make sure that they fit into the overall performance measurement framework as part of the six KPIs. Many project management techniques, such as resource planning and resource levelling, will be of great assistance in getting the best out of the available resources.

Maintenance Process Performance Measure	Description
Output	Level at which output rate falls below a KPI value (e.g. 90%). This is often monitored on an hourly basis.
Planned maintenance backlog	The amount of maintenance backlog planned for – an acceptable KPI here might be 50 hours of backlog. If the backlog exceeds this KPI value, then action needs to be taken to reduce the backlog and improve performance. Overtime may be necessary to reduce the backlog.
Overtime	The amount of extra work time compared to plan.
Mean Time Between Failure (MTBF)	The average time between process failures over a given period of time.
Mean Time to Repair (MTTR)	The average time it takes to repair a failed process. This is the time measured from the occurrence of the failure to its resolution.
Number of breakdowns	The number of times a piece of equipment breaks down over a period of time. A high rate may lead to a lot of unplanned maintenance.

Equipment availability	A measure of how long a piece of equipment is available in good working order.
Downtime	It is important here to measure both scheduled and un-scheduled maintenance related down-time.
Cost	Maintenance cost per unit of output.
Flexibility	A measure of how easy it is to switch resources around and how quickly they can be re-allocated to another task.
Scalability	A measure of what resources are required in order to increase production and maintenance.

Table 12.7: Examples of KPIs for a Production Maintenance Process

Efficiency

The efficiency with which an organisation converts its resources into products and services is an important process KPI to measure. Very few organisations can operate at maximum efficiency at all times, and make 100 per cent use of all resources. However, all organisations will want to make the most effective use of their resources, and will have a desired efficiency level, e.g. a production rate of between 90 per cent and 95 per cent of maximum efficiency. The actual level of efficiency may be different from both the maximum and desired levels of efficiency. Any type of resource that is not in use, or is not working efficiently, may be costing your organisation money or at best be making very little money. The difference between maximum, desired, and actual levels of efficiency will provide you with an effective KPI to help you in your improvement efforts.

Making the most of any resource is a desirable target for any business. Let's take a look at a simple example of fuel consumption in a transport company. Table 12.8 shows details of diesel fuel consumption figures for four types of vehicle. Each vehicle manufacturer provides official average fuel consumption figures in kilometres per litre (km/L) – this is regarded here as the maximum efficiency for each vehicle. The desired rate of fuel consumption for each vehicle is targeted to be not less than 85 per cent of the official figure.

Vehicle Type	Manufacturer's Official Rate	Desired Rate of Consumption	Actual Rate of Consumption
18 wheeled trucks	2.6	2.2	1.9
6 wheeled trucks	4.9	4.2	4.3
Large vans	10.6	9.0	10.2
Small vans	17.7	15.0	11.2

Table 12.8: Fuel Consumption Rates (km/L) for Vehicle Types

The data in Table 12.8 show that both the 6 wheeled trucks and the large vans are performing well. While the actual fuel consumption rates in both cases are less than the manufacturer's official rates, they are still performing better than the targeted minimum rate of 85 per cent. The 18 wheeled trucks' fuel consumption rate of 1.9 km/L is only slightly below the targeted rate of 2.2 km/L, but this could turn out to be a significant figure if the transport company has a large fleet of trucks covering thousands of kilometres. Finally, Table 12.8 shows that the fuel consumption rates for small vans is considerably below both the manufacturer's and target rates – clearly there is a lot of room for improvement in performance in this case. For a transport company, fuel is a major item of expenditure, and it is imperative that it be used efficiently. Improvement efforts such as making sure that each vehicle is checked regularly, has its engine tuned correctly, and perhaps changing driver behaviour, may all contribute to improved fuel efficiency.

Several KPIs can be used to measure efficiency so that you can continually look for opportunities to improve processes. Table 12.9 shows some examples of KPIs, with short descriptions, for performance of a typical local area network (LAN). The IT department in your organisation will carry out many audits of LAN performance and will monitor each of the KPIs in Table 12.9 regularly – many on an hourly or daily basis.

Whatever measures of efficiency that you use, once again make sure that they fit into the overall performance measurement framework as part of the six KPIs. Many organisations set targets for improving efficiency on an annual basis, and constantly seek to improve performance by becoming more efficient. This can range from reducing waste (such as having a "turn off the lights" policy in offices) by 5 per cent per year, to increasing efficient practices (such as recycling paper) by 10 per cent per year. Finally, remember to use efficiency KPIs that make sense, and be consistent in the measures that you use so that comparisons can be made over time to determine if improvement has taken place in a process.

Local Area Network (LAN) Performance Measure	Description
Data transmission	Data transmission is measured by data actually transmitted or received during a period of time, and is usually measured in bps (bits per second). The higher the data transmission rate, the better the performance.
Data loss	The percentage of data (in the form of packets) that is lost during transmission over the network.
Bandwidth	The percentage of available network bandwidth used.
Network delay (latency)	The time it takes for a packet of data to get from one designated point on a network to another.
Disk space	The percentage of available disk space used.
Disk quota	The percentage of assigned disk space quota per network user used compared to the total assigned disk space quota.
Memory utilisation	The percentage utilisation of available system memory.
CPU utilisation	The percentage utilisation of the CPU (Central Processing Unit) in a system.

Table 12.9: Examples of KPIs for a LAN Performance

Reliability

The final KPI to examine in detail is the reliability KPI. All businesses depend on reliability in various formats – for example, customers you can depend upon, suppliers who deliver on time, and a reliable source of raw materials. In other words you depend on a reliable supply chain to provide your business with the resources it needs to create its own products and services. In addition to these KPIs, you also want your business to be a reliable partner in the supply chains of other businesses – failing to do so may lose you customers. How your customers view how reliable your business is can be just as important a KPI to measure as how reliable your suppliers are.

There are many KPI measures that you can use for determining reliability – many of the other KPIs discussed above can also be used as reliability KPI measures. Let's look at an example of a comparison of three different parcel delivery services – each of which has a performance objective of delivering all parcels to customers within 48 hours of receiving them. Table 12.10 shows the percentage of parcels delivered within 48 hours by quarter for each of the three companies. While the data in Table 12.10 show high rates of delivery within 48 hours, the performance varies between each company. The Quick Parcel company has erratic performance figures from as low as 75 per cent in Q2 to as high as 95 per cent in Q3. The Swift Parcel company shows a significant decline in performance over the year. The Rapid Parcel company shows a consistently high rate of performance that is improving steadily throughout the year. Over the period of a year the Rapid Parcel company can be considered to be the most reliable.

Company	Q1	Q2	Q3	Q4
Quick Parcel	83%	75%	95%	87%
Swift Parcel	94%	87%	83%	79%
Rapid Parcel	86%	87%	90%	92%

Table 12.10: Parcel Delivery Rates by Quarter

Lots of other measures can be used to measure reliability in different business areas. Table 12.11 shows some examples, with short descriptions, of reliability KPIs for a mobile phone service provider. Mobile phone service providers are notoriously difficult to compare performances as they will each use different measures to promote their own levels of service.

Mobile Phone Service Performance Measure	Description
Coverage	Percentage of an area covered by service provider.
Voice quality	A measure of the quality of voice on the cell phone network. Often measured using levels of clarity and background noise.
Congestion	A measure of how congested a network is. This is a measure of the number of users and the available bandwidth.
Signal strength	A measure of how strong a signal is for each mobile phone user.
Dropped calls	The number of calls that are dropped due to lost signal.
Connection time	The amount of time it takes to connect a new customer to the network.
Customer complaints	The number of complaints made by customers relating to quality of service.
Customer "churn"	The rate at which customers switch network providers.
Price plans	Each price plan provides a level of service (e.g. free text messages) that must be delivered. Plans may need to be altered to maximise performance.
Security	The number of security breaches and threats to the network.

Table 12.11: Examples of KPIs for a Mobile Phone Service Provider

Whatever measures of reliability that you use make sure that they fit into the overall performance measurement framework as part of the six KPIs. Be careful not to measure too much and that you are measuring the right things. As we will see later in this chapter, the importance of performance to customers varies considerably so you must be in a position to recognise the most appropriate KPIs to measure. In the end, customer satisfaction will decide if you are delivering reliable products and services. It is also important to continue to improve reliability, or at the very least maintain a high level of reliability.

Benefits of Performance Measurement

Being able to measure performance in all six KPIs shown in the KPI framework (Figure 12.2) gives an organisation the ability to identify performance issues and to investigate them further in order to design solutions. KPIs are therefore a vital steering mechanism for your process improvement efforts – without performance measurement this becomes a very difficult task. Accurate use of KPIs leads to best practices in performance measurement and will enhance your organisation's reputation for excellent performance.

There are many other benefits of performance measurement. At a high level, it can benefit an organisation by enhancing decision making, improving accountability, and support strategic planning and the setting of goals. Performance measurement can also provide improvement in an organisation's ability to motivate its employees. It will also improve both internal and external communication skills as they will be based on accurate information.

KPIs used with other business analysis tools such as Value Analysis and Capacity Planning will give you an excellent overall set of tools that you as a Business Analyst can use when you are looking to control and improve processes. Once you understand your organisation's mission, goals, and objectives, you will find it easier to know what KPIs to measure. Some organisations have hundreds, if not thousands, of KPIs – so it is important that the Business Analyst knows what these are, and how they are measured.

Benchmarking

In performance measurement you set out to use the KPI framework to give you a comprehensive measure of how your organisation is performing in the most important (key) areas. Measuring current performance of your processes is a vital exercise to carry out prior to any improvement effort. However, unless your processes are unique, you will at some stage need to compare your organisation's performance with that of others. Other organisations may be your competitors, or they could be different sections within your own organisation. Your KPIs may be indicating that your processes are performing well, but how do they compare with similar processes in other organisations? Somebody else may have a better way of doing things that you can learn from. Any difficulties that you are experiencing have almost certainly been experienced by others. An organisation that wants to promote a culture of continuous improvement should be encouraged to learn from others, become open to new methods and ideas, and develop tools to improve their processes. Adopting the best practices of other organisations is a very effective way of controlling and improving processes. In this section you will examine benchmarking as an analysis tool that you can use to learn from others.

Benchmarking is the search for industry-wide best practices that lead to improved and even superior performance. The purpose of a benchmarking study is to compare your organisation's practices against the best-in-class practices that exist in your peers and competitors. Benchmarking usually consists of a study of similar organisations to understand how their processes work in order to (if possible) adapt their methods to your own processes. As a Business Analyst you will need to establish how other organisations achieve superior performance levels, and to be able to use this information to design projects to improve similar processes in your own organisation. Benchmarking studies can also be used within organisations to compare performances of individuals, departments, and regions. Where ever there is an individual or a group doing something better than what you are doing – you can learn something from them to improve your own performance.

To begin your benchmarking studies you should look around within your own organisation. Almost every organisation has people who perform better than others. Who is the top sales person? Which of your programmers has a reputation for writing bug-free code? Which trainer gets the best evaluations upon course completion? Which call centre representative solves the most problems over the phone? Who are the winners at your organisation's annual awards ceremony? One thing these people have in common is they are the best performers in their own area – others can learn from them. Ask yourself – how do they do it? Encourage your best performers to share their experiences, provide tips on how they do things, and most important of all to document how they perform. If your organisation's top sales person shares their experiences with new sales recruits, they will gain huge benefit from learning from the best. You can always learn from past success. It is important that where there is success that it should be publicised and shared, so that others may emulate successful practices.

Finding out how other organisations achieve excellent performance in a particular process can be a difficult thing to do. Naturally, other organisations may not freely give away their secrets and will almost certainly not do so to their competitors. However, you can learn a lot from other organisations and use their ideas. Within the public domain you can carry out research, make observations, and draw inferences to generate ideas about how other organisations are performing better. This could be something very simple to do. For example, suppose you own a three star hotel and have ambitions to achieve a four star rating – arrange to stay at several other four star hotels and observe how they do things. In this case you can learn a lot from simple observation.

You can also learn a lot from other material in the public domain. Some very successful people write books about their experiences and methods, or publish articles in trade magazines to share tips about how to be successful. Many organisations publish white papers on their web sites about the latest developments within their organisation and in their industry. Press releases, such as an announcement of a major contract after stiff competition, are also a good source of information, though be sure to take these at face value. Consultancy firms sometimes publish case studies on their websites – for example about the successful implementation of a new application to solve a client's problem. The World Wide Web is a massive source of information that you can research – the key skill is to filter out the most important and useful information from the mass of available information. As social networking gains in popularity you may also find users' reviews and comments on a competitor's products and services that you might find insightful and useful. However, once again be careful to take these views at face value as the source of reviews and comments may not be reliable.

To benchmark accurately against competitor organisations, a Business Analyst will need to first of all identify the most appropriate benchmarking partners that represent the best-in-class products and services that you want to benchmark against. You can collect benchmarking data using interviews, surveys, site visits, archive research, and even attending conferences. Many organisations such as the Gartner Group and

J.D. Power publish results of major studies comparing organisations that you will find useful. Be careful to manage any ethical issues that may arise, particularly when you get insider information about another organisation. It is important then to analyse the data gathered so that you finish up with the information that will give you practical and relevant results that will help you in your process improvement efforts.

The main advantage of benchmarking is that it provides you with information about new methods, ideas, and analysis tools to improve performance. However, it can be time consuming and requires a level of expertise that many organisations may not have. Since benchmarking requires expertise to be able to conduct an analysis and interpret the results – Business Analysts often find themselves playing a central role in benchmarking studies. It is also important to keep in mind that while benchmarking involves comparing your processes with those that have been shown to work somewhere else, with the goal of reproducing them, it does not in itself produce innovative solutions that provide for a sustainable competitive advantage.

Spendolini's Five Stage Benchmarking Model

In 2001, Dr Michael J. Spendolini, in his book *The Benchmarking Book*, illustrates a generic five stage benchmarking model based on the benchmarking process models of twenty-four successful North American organisations. This model illustrates the core activities of the benchmarking process and is shown in Figure 12.5. The model provides a clear structure and a common language for successful benchmarking efforts. The circles and arrows on Figure 12.5 show that in benchmarking you are aiming for continuous improvement. However, the structure can be flexible depending on your organisation's needs. The first three stages emphasise the planning stages for your benchmarking study. Stage four represents the methodology for gathering and analysing the required data. Stage five deals with taking action to initiate the improved process. Let's take a look at each of the Spendolini model's five stages in more detail.

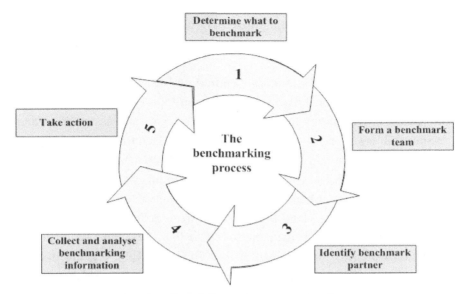

Figure 12.5: Spendolini's Benchmarking Process

Stage 1: Determine What to Benchmark. The first thing to do when you are determining what it is that you want to benchmark is to identify who the customers are for the information and to establish what exactly it is that they want to know. You can then define the specific areas and processes that you want to benchmark based on these needs. This is not an easy exercise and much care should be taken to ensure that you are measuring the right processes – use your established KPIs to help you here. Focus precisely on what it is that you want to measure. For example, suppose that you are a manager in a small transport company, you may want to compare your transport and distribution processes with those of a specialist logistics organisation.

Often your customers will be an excellent source of information on what you should be benchmarking. If a customer tells you that they are moving to one of your competitors because they can get products and services at a lower price and higher quality, it is time to establish how your competitor can do this before you lose any more customers. Find out from your existing and past customers what exactly they want. Finally, be careful with the scope of your benchmarking investigations – once you have determined what it is that you want to benchmark, stay focused on this and do not fall into the trap of going outside the scope of your investigation. Any matters that arise may be the focus of a new benchmarking effort.

Stage 2: Form a Benchmarking Team. As a Business Analyst it is possible to conduct a benchmarking study as an individual. However, most successful organisations form benchmarking teams and assign roles and responsibilities to each of the team members. Determine what type of team that you want and who you want to be on the team. You may want to draw upon expertise from different areas within your organisation as well as using external benchmarking experts such as other business analysts and consultants. Many organisations have dedicated benchmarking teams with experienced team members so that they can participate in continuous process improvement efforts throughout the organisation. A typical team will consist of a project manager, a business analyst, a good facilitator, data collectors, and the benchmarking customer. This team should be supported with adequate resources such as training, library services, clerical assistance, and legal advice.

Stage 3: Identify Benchmark Partners. Once formed, the benchmarking team should next identify any partners that they can use in each benchmarking study. The team should identify benchmarking partners from both inside and outside its organisation – i.e. anybody who can provide the team with information needed for the investigation. In time the team will establish a benchmarking network whose expertise can be drawn upon when needed. The team will gather information from people in this network such as internal and external employees, subject matter experts, analysts, researchers, and consultants. Other organisations such as the government, universities and colleges, trade and professional associations are also very useful benchmarking partners. Whatever information you gather, look for any best practices in your benchmark partners for the area under investigation.

Stage 4: Collect and Analyse Benchmarking Information. In stage four you will use a variety of tools for gathering data – your team members should be experienced in using these tools. The requirements gathering methods and analysis tools described in this book will be of use in these efforts. Whatever methods and tools you use, be consistent in the standards that you use and make sure that all teams members understand how the tools are used and what they are used for. You should only analyse the data that you have gathered in this stage and stay within the scope of your study that was determined in stage one. Analyse the data gathered in order to give you the information you need to create recommended process improvement actions that are based on your customer's original needs.

Stage 5: Take Action. In the final fifth stage it is time to act upon the recommendations made in stage four. In this stage the improved process is initiated and implemented. If the benchmarking exercise is done correctly in the previous four stages, any change to a process to improve it will be based on information you have gathered in response to your customer's needs.

Benchmarking information should be regularly reviewed by the benchmarking team, this will help to develop and improve your skills. You should always be on the look out for new ways to improve the benchmarking process in addition to identifying new additional items for benchmarking. A detailed report and presentation should be prepared to communicate the team's findings to the benchmarking customers.

The Xerox Benchmarking Process

Many organisations have benchmarking methodologies of their own, or have modified models from other organisations. One of the best known and much used benchmarking methods is a model developed by the Xerox Corporation in the late 1970s. At that time Xerox discovered that a USA-based competitor, supported by its overseas manufacturer, was selling equivalent quality copiers for about the same price as Xerox's manufacturing cost. Xerox decided that they needed to take urgent action and decided to try benchmarking in an effort to close the gap with their competitor.

As a large corporation, Xerox decided that a formalised structure was necessary to guide their benchmarking efforts. The process that Xerox uses is outlined in Figure 12.6. This 10-stage model has more detail than the Spendolini 5-stage model described above, but does incorporate all the steps that Spendolini outlines in his model. In the Xerox model, the first three steps are the most important: step 1 – identifying what is to be benchmarked, step 2 – identify comparative companies, and step 3 – determine data collection method and collect data. These steps are all part of the planning phase. Xerox were surprised that the initial findings showed the following gaps in performance:

- Xerox had nine times more suppliers that their competitor

- Xerox had ten times the rejection rate

- It took twice as long for Xerox to get their products to market

- Productivity needed to increase by at least 18 per cent per year for five years just to catch up with their competitor.

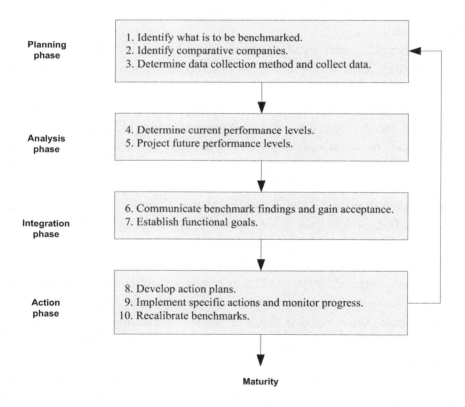

Figure 12.6: The Xerox Benchmarking Process

Using the new benchmarking process in Figure 12.6, Xerox decided to first try to improve customer satisfaction as they regarded this as their number one priority for improvement. The initial results were highly encouraging: satisfied customers for its copiers increased by 38 per cent, complaints decreased by more than 60 per cent, while overall customer satisfaction rose to 90 per cent. Other benefits also gained included:

- The number of defects was reduced by 78 per 100 machines

- Service response times were reduced by 27 per cent

- Inventory costs were reduced by 66 per cent

- Marketing productivity improved by 33 per cent

- Billing errors were reduced from 8.3 per cent to 3.5 per cent.

When Xerox adopted benchmarking they studied the best practices from a wide variety of companies regardless of which industry they belonged to. For example, Xerox initiated benchmarking with the study of the warehousing and inventory management system best practices of a mail-order supplier of sporting goods and outdoor clothing company – L.L. Bean. Other organisations that Xerox benchmarked against included: American Express for billing and collection, Honda for supplier development, Toyota for quality management, Hewlett-Packard for research and new product development, and DuPont for manufacturing health and safety.

The basic principles of the Xerox benchmarking process are now incorporated into the benchmarking processes of many organisations. Planning was crucial to success of the whole benchmarking process at Xerox. Equally important was an understanding of Xerox's own processes – analysis tools like SIPOC diagrams and Flow Charts will help you to improve your understanding of your own organisations processes so that you will be better prepared for any benchmarking study.

Benchmarking Example – Radio Station Survey

In order to see how comparing an organisation's performance against others yields valuable information, let's take a look at an example of a study of how radio stations compare with one another. The Broadcasting

Commission of Ireland (BCI) conducts surveys of radio station listenership in Ireland. Each quarter the BCI publishes a Joint National Listenership Research (JNLR) report to provide reliable estimates of audience to national, regional and local radio stations, as a basis for the planning of advertising schedules. It is an excellent way for radio stations to compare their performance against their competitors over a period of time. Three key performance indicators (KPIs) are used to measure performance: weekday reach (listenership), weekly reach, and weekday market share. Table 12.12 shows some quarterly data for national radio stations extracted from the JNLR survey results for the year ending in March 2009. Using these figures, each radio station can compare its own performance over the year to March 2009. For example, the data show that RTÉ 2FM has declined in performance in all three KPIs over the year. RTÉ Radio 1 on the other hand has shown an increase in each of the KPIs over the same period. These alone are important figures for each radio station to study.

When each set of figures for a radio station is benchmarked against its competitor, further useful information can be used to analyse performance. Based on the figures in Table 12.12, RTÉ Radio 1 has increased its lead over its nearest competitor for weekday reach figures from 6 per cent to 9 per cent over the year. It has also increased its lead over the nearest competitor for weekday share figures from 8.9 per cent to 11.1 per cent, and for weekly reach figures from 5 per cent to 7 per cent. These figures show that not only has RTÉ Radio 1 improved its own performance, but that it has also increased the gap between its own performance and that of other radio stations. Surveys such as this allow each radio station to benchmark its performance against its competitors. Each station can now look at ways to maintain or increase its own share of the market, but it also opens up the opportunity to investigate how other stations have increased their share. In a highly competitive market like broadcasting, even a one percent increase or decrease can have major consequences for advertising revenue. It is therefore vitally important that radio stations benchmark their performance against competitors on a regular basis.

	Weekday Reach Figures			
	Jun 08	*Sep 08*	*Dec 08*	*Mar 09*
RTÉ Radio 1	23%	23%	23%	25%
RTÉ 2FM	17%	17%	17%	16%
Today FM	16%	16%	16%	15%
Newstalk	6%	6%	6%	7%
RTÉ Lyric FM	3%	4%	4%	4%

	Weekday Share Figures (7.00 a.m.-7.00 p.m)			
	Jun 08	*Sep 08*	*Dec 08*	*Mar 09*
RTÉ Radio 1	21.3%	21.5%	21.9%	22.7%
RTÉ 2FM	12.4%	12.3%	11.8%	11.6%
Today FM	11.7%	11.0%	10.9%	10.6%
Newstalk	3.7%	3.6%	3.5%	3.6%
RTÉ Lyric FM	1.6%	1.7%	1.7%	1.7%

	JNLR Weekly Reach Figures			
	Jun 08	*Sep 08*	*Dec 08*	*Mar 09*
RTÉ Radio 1	37%	37%	37%	38%
RTÉ 2FM	32%	32%	31%	31%
Today FM	29%	29%	29%	29%
Newstalk	14%	14%	14%	15%
RTÉ Lyric FM	8%	8%	8%	8%

Table 12.12: JNLR Survey Results for National Radio Stations

Source: All data sourced from www.bci.ie.

Improvement Priorities

So far in this chapter we have looked at how organisations can measure their performance, and compare (benchmark) their performance against other organisations. In the final part of this chapter we will now use our knowledge of performance measurement to help us identify the most important improvement opportunities. These opportunities will be identified using the performance measurement and benchmarking techniques already discussed. However, it may not be enough for an organisation to improve performance in a particular area, or even to perform better in this area that its competitors. You must take your customers into account. If something is important for a customer it should be important for you – therefore if an improvement opportunity is identified in an area of importance to a customer, then this should have priority for improvement efforts over other areas that are not as important to customers. The relative importance of a process to a customer is now a factor that must be taken into consideration.

In 1977, J.A. Martilla and J.C. James introduced the Importance-Performance Analysis (IPA) framework in marketing research in order to assist in the understanding of customer satisfaction as a function of significant attributes and judgments about their performance. In 1994 this framework was further developed by Professor Nigel Slack of the Warwick Business School to study operations strategy in a way that reflects managers' judgement of relationships between importance, performance, and priority of improvement. Actual measures can also be used. This has resulted in an Importance-Performance Matrix which is based on nine-point scales for importance to customers, and performance against competitors.

Importance to Customers

To judge if a product or service is important to customers, we first start out with three high level performance objectives: order-winning, qualifying, and less important. An order-winner is an objective that directly wins business for the organisation. A qualifier is an objective that may not win extra business unless performance improves, but may also lose business if performance deteriorates. A less important objective is relatively unimportant when compared to the other objectives. To judge importance to customers in more detail, each of these three objectives is divided into a nine point scale based on whether each performance objective is strong, medium, or weak. This is then used to determine if a product or service meets its objectives according to relative importance to customers. Figure 12.7 shows each of the nine levels of judging importance to customers. In order to use this scale, as a business analyst you will need to determine first of all if a product or service is an order-winner, a qualifier, or is less important. Once this is done, you should then judge whether each objective is strong, medium, or weak (based on the criteria in Figure 12.7), and then assign a value of 1 to 9 for each objective. Requirements elicitation techniques such as surveying or interviewing customers are ideal for determining the relative importance of a product or service to a customer. You can even break the product or service down into processes and sub-processes (as done in Value Analysis – see chapter 7) and determine the relative importance of each component to a customer.

Order Winner	1	Strong	Provides crucial advantage
	2	Medium	Provides an important advantage
	3	Weak	Provides a useful advantage
Qualifier	4	Strong	Needs to be up to a good industry standard
	5	Medium	Needs to be up to a median industry standard
	6	Weak	Needs to be within close range of the rest of the industry
Less Important	7	Strong	Not usually of importance but could become more so
	8	Medium	Very rarely considered by customers
	9	Weak	Never considered by customers

Figure 12.7: A Nine point Scale of Importance to Customers

Source: Based on "The Importance-Performance Matrix as a Determinant of Improvement Priority" by Nigel Slack (1994), *International Journal of Operations & Production Management*. Vol. 14, No. 5, pp 59-75.

Performance against Competitors

An organisation's overall performance standard can be divided into three parts by judging simply if the performance achieved is better, the same, or worse than that of its competitors. These simple criteria were used earlier in Value Analysis and will give you a high level overview of the relative performance of a product, service, or process against your competitors. A nine-point scale for performance objective against competitors similar to the importance to customers is shown in Figure 12.8. In order to use this scale, as a Business Analyst you will need to determine first of all if a product or service is better, the same, or worse than your competitors. Once this is done, you should then judge whether each objective is strong, medium, or weak (based on the criteria in figure 12.8), and then assign a value of 1 to 9 for each objective. Use the KPIs described earlier in this chapter as a measure of performance, and benchmarking studies to compare this performance with competitors.

Better	1	Strong	Considerably better than competitors
	2	Medium	Clearly better than competitors
	3	Weak	Marginally better than competitors
Same	4	Strong	Sometimes marginally better than competitors
	5	Medium	About the same as most competitors
	6	Weak	Slightly lower than the average of most competitors
Worse	7	Strong	Usually marginally worse than most competitors
	8	Medium	Usually worse than competitors
	9	Weak	Consistently worse than competitors

Figure 12.8: A Nine Point Scale of Performance Against Competitors

Source: Based on "The Importance-Performance Matrix as a Determinant of Improvement Priority" by Nigel Slack (1994), *International Journal of Operations & Production Management.* Vol. 14, No. 5, pp. 59-75.

The Importance-Performance Matrix

Once you have judged the importance of a product, service, or process to a customer, and then judged the performance against your competitors, you should have series of values from 1 to 9 for each objective that you have measured or judged. The priority for improvement each objective can be given is now determined based on comparing the values for importance and performance. This is done using the Importance-Performance Matrix as shown in Figure 12.9. The matrix plots the three high level objectives and the nine-point scale for importance for customers on the X-axis. Similarly, the scales for performance against competitors are plotted on the Y-axis. The matrix is divided into four areas which indicate the improvement priority for each objective plotted on the matrix. The lower bound of acceptability (line AB on figure 12.9) marks the line which indicates acceptable performance above the line, and unacceptable performance below the line. The line CD distinguishes between the improvement area and an urgent action area. For example, an objective with a value of 3 for importance and 7 for performance will fall into the urgent action area and will therefore be a high priority for improvement. This is an important objective that is performing poorly. An objective with a value of 8 for importance and 7 for performance will fall into the improvement area and will therefore be a lower priority for improvement. This is a value for a low performing objective that is of low importance to customers – nevertheless, it should be considered for improvement as it is below the bound of acceptability.

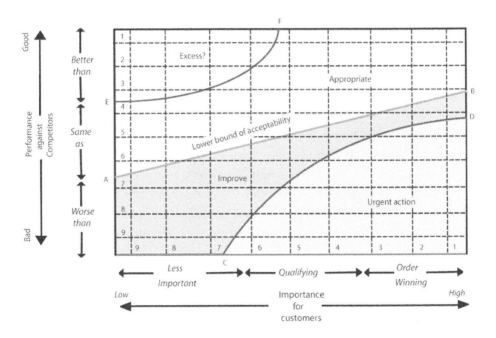

Figure 12.9: Priority Areas in the Importance-Performance Matrix

Source: Reproduced with permission from *Operations Management* by Slack, Chambers and Johnson, 5th edition, 2008, Financial Times/Prentice Hall.

The EF line separates the appropriate and excess areas on the matrix. An objective with a value of 7 for importance and 2 for performance will fall into the excess area. This means that the objective is performing very well, but is not very important to customers. At this time, resources should not be allocated to improving this objective as they will be more valuable elsewhere. An objective with a value of 6 for importance and 3 for performance will fall into the appropriate area and is considered as satisfactory.

The Importance-Performance Matrix is a useful tool to help you to decide what the most important performance objectives to prioritise for improvement are. It is also useful to compare importance and performance over a period of time. It will be useful to see any changes in the position of an objective due to improvement efforts. You should also pay attention to objectives that are close to boundaries. A change in value of 1 or 2 points on any of the scales could move a point on the matrix from one area to another. For example, a rating of 3 for performance and 2 for importance falls into the appropriate area. Should performance fall in rating by just 2 points, it now falls into the urgent action area.

Finally, be careful when rating importance and performance. Use accurate figures whenever you can from reliable sources. Where you have to judge or estimate values, make sure you have the best information available to you and that you have expertise in your team that can help with the ratings. If there is disagreement within a team as to the rating for any particular objective – first, see where the values are plotted on the matrix (they might all fall within the same area), and then come to an agreed value. You can also use values up to one decimal place if needed, e.g. assign a value of 6.5 as a compromise between ratings of 6 and 7.

Importance-Performance Matrix – Example

To illustrate how an Importance-Performance Matrix can be used to identify improvement priorities, let's take a look at an example of a mobile phone company operating in a competitive environment. The performance objectives used here are the KPI performance measures for mobile phone service taken from Table 12.11. Assume that a customer survey has been carried out to determine the ratings for importance to customers, and that a benchmarking exercise has been used to generate the ratings for performance against competitors. Table 12.13 shows the resulting ratings for both importance and performance for each performance objective. These values are now plotted onto the Importance-Performance Matrix as shown in Figure 12.10.

Mobile Phone Service Performance Measure		Importance to Customers (1-9)	Performance Against Competitors (1-9)
A.	Coverage	5	4
B.	Voice quality	5	6
C.	Congestion	6	3
D.	Signal strength	3	2
E.	Dropped calls	4	8
F.	Connection time	8	2
G.	Customer complaints	3	5
H.	Customer "churn"	8	1
I.	Price plans	2	8
J.	Security	5	5

Table 12.13: Importance-Performance Ratings for Mobile Phone Service

Figure 12.10 shows that the coverage (A), congestion (C), and signal strength (D) objectives are above the lower bound of acceptability and are deemed to be satisfactory. The voice quality (B), customer complaints (G), and security (J) objectives are below the lower bound of acceptability and are worthy of improvement efforts. Note that in each of the latter three objectives, a one or two point improvement in performance against competitors will move each objective into the acceptable area.

The dropped calls (E) and price plans (I) fall into the urgent action area. These are both relatively important performance objectives for customers, but in both cases a significant improvement in performance against competitors is required in order to reach an acceptable level. Urgent action is required to improve these two objectives. The connection time (F) and customer "churn" (H) fall into the excess area. Both objectives are performing well against competitors, but are relatively unimportant to customers. These objectives are therefore the lowest priority for improvement. In fact, a significant fall in the performance against competitors rating of up to three points will still leave each of these objectives above the lower bound of acceptability.

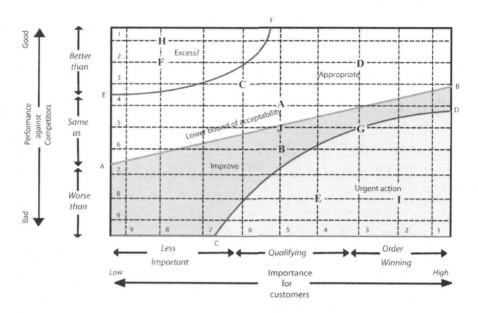

Figure 12.10: Importance-Performance Matrix for Mobile Phone Service

Exercise – Executive Training Evaluation

In this exercise you will develop an Importance-Performance Matrix based on an evaluation of an executive training course which will be compared to similar courses offered by other Training providers. Emerald Training provides business courses aimed at the executive training market. It has recently noticed that there has been a slight fall off in the number of managers enrolling as students on their courses, and has decided to investigate why this is happening and how the situation can be improved.

As is common in most training providers, students complete an evaluation survey upon completion of the course. Table 12.14 is a summary of all evaluation surveys for the past year completed for Emerald Training courses. Emerald Training uses a six-point Likert scale where students rate performance for each objective with a value of 1 for the lowest rating and a value of 6 for the highest rating.

Performance Objective	Likert Scale Ratings (1=low, 6=high)					
	1	**2**	**3**	**4**	**5**	**6**
Good course notes provided	9%	14%	31%	33%	8%	5%
Online course resources available	27%	30%	23%	18%	2%	0%
Trainer has good presentation style	0%	5%	15%	32%	34%	14%
Trainer varied presentation style	4%	14%	28%	28%	19%	7%
Audio-visual media worked well	23%	27%	31%	15%	4%	0%
Seats and desks were comfortable	0%	2%	8%	27%	46%	17%
Course objectives clearly stated	4%	18%	34%	23%	16%	5%
Course met it objectives	8%	17%	29%	26%	13%	7%
Tea and coffee provided at breaks	0%	2%	3%	12%	47%	36%
Pastries provided at breaks	0%	4%	7%	18%	41%	30%

Table 12.14: Student Survey Ratings for Course Evaluation

A recent independent training industry survey, in which Emerald Training took part, showed mixed results against its main competitors. Table 12.15 shows a summary of these results for Emerald Training and for two other training companies – Ruby Training, and Diamond Training. In this survey, the ratings used were simply: Very good, Good, Average, Poor, and Very poor. The performance objectives compared are similar those used above for Emerald Training's own evaluation.

Use both Tables 12.14 and 12.15 to judge values for each performance objective on the nine-point Importance-Importance Matrix scale, to give values for importance against competitors. To judge how important each of the performance objectives are to customers, use your own experience as a student to give a rating for each objective. Remember to first decide if an objective is order-winning, qualifying, or less important – and then to decide if the objective is strong, medium, or weak. Preferably you should judge this rating with fellow students or colleagues to get agreed ratings. Once you have both sets of ratings, you are now in a position to draw an Importance-Performance Matrix. When you have completed the matrix, answer the following questions?

- Which performance objectives would you recommend that Emerald Training target as priorities for improvement?

- What recommendations would you make to improve performance in the target objectives?

- What other performance objectives would you suggest be used?

Industry Performance Objectives	Emerald Training	Ruby Training	Diamond Training
Quality of course notes	Average	Good	Good
Use of on-line course resources	Very poor	Good	Very good
Presentation styles	Good	Very good	Very good
Variety in presentation style	Average	Good	Very good
Quality of audio-visual media used	Poor	Average	Good
Quality of facilities	Very good	Average	Good
Course objectives clearly stated	Average	Poor	Average
Course met it objectives	Average	Poor	Good
Standard of catering (basic)	Very good	Good	Average
Standard of catering (advanced)	Very good	Poor	Average

Table 12.15: Training Industry Survey Results for Three Companies

Reflection

At the beginning of this chapter you set out to use performance measurement as an aid to controlling and improving processes. With performance measurement, benchmarking, and the Importance-Performance Matrix, you now have a good understanding of the importance of measuring performance using Key Performance Indicators (KPIs), how performance is compared to that of others so that you can learn from their experiences, and how improvements are prioritised based on comparing performance with importance to customers. In your Learning Journal, answer the following reflective questions:

- What have you learned in this chapter?

- Can you identify any KPIs used in your organisation?

- Can you identify processes in your organisation that are not measured? In what ways can they be measured?

- What other analysis tools will help you to understand performance measurement better?

- How is the importance of products, services, and processes to customers measured in your organisation?

- What recommendations would you make to improve performance in your organisation?

Performance improvement should be a continuous process – you should never take for granted that making an improvement will keep you ahead of your competitors. Bear in mind that many processes will take a lot of time and resources to improve – it is therefore vital that you understand what is involved in process improvement, and how performance can be used to drive your improvement efforts. Be sensible when using performance data. For example, in an Importance-Performance Matrix you may find out that a performance object falls into the appropriate or excess areas – it can be tempting to ignore these objectives in favour of others that fall into the improvement or urgent action areas. You must monitor constantly all your performance measurements and your customer's attitudes to your products and services – otherwise if you ignore or fail to maintain high or appropriate levels of performance, you may have problems at a later time. Keep in mind throughout that all measures of performance should be based on reliable data and information, and that any improvement effort should be aligned with the overall business goals of your organisation.

Finally, it is of course possible to improve performance so that your organisation achieves a market leadership position and that other organisations benchmark themselves against you. Attaining and maintaining such a position takes a lot of hard work and dedication within your organisation. Many successful organisations never make it to the top, but by using best practices in performance measurement they can become a best in class or a world class organisation.

SELECTED FURTHER READING

Below are the titles, authors and publishers of some books recommended for further reading that learners will find useful, and should consider adding to your personal or organisation's library.

A Guide to the Business Analysis Body of Knowledge® (BABOK® Guide). Version 2.0 (2009). International Institute of Business Analysis.

A Guide to the Project Management Body of Knowledge. 4th Edition (2008). Project Management Institute.

Operations Management. 5th Edition (2008). Nigel Slack, Stuart Chambers and Robert Johnston. Financial Times/Prentice Hall.

Essentials of Management Information Systems. 8th Edition (2008). Jane Laudon and Kenneth Laudon. Pearson Education.

Business Information Systems: Technology, Development and Management for the E-Business. 4th Edition (2008). Paul Bocij, Andrew Greasley and Simon Hickie. Financial Times/Prentice Hall.

Seven Steps to Nirvana: Strategic Insights into e-Business Transformation (2001). M. Sawhney and J. Zabin. McGraw-Hill.

Six Sigma Tool Navigator: The Master Guide for Teams (Tool Navigator) (2003). Walter J. Michalski. Productivity Press.

Effective Requirements Practices (Information Technology) (2001). Ralph R. Young. Addison Wesley.

The Road to the Unified Software Development Process (2000). Ivar Jacobson and Stefan Bylund. Cambridge University Press.

101 Creative Problem Solving Techniques: The Handbook of New Ideas for Business (2005). James M. Higgins. The New Management Publishing Company.

The Memory Jogger II: A Pocket Guide of Tools for Continuous Improvement and Effective Planning (1994). Michael Brassard and Diane Ritter. Goal/QPC.

Index

Made in the USA
Monee, IL
18 February 2022

91411890R00175